Building State Capability

Building State Capability

Evidence, Analysis, Action

Matt Andrews, Lant Pritchett, and
Michael Woolcock

OXFORD
UNIVERSITY PRESS

OXFORD
UNIVERSITY PRESS

Great Clarendon Street, Oxford, OX2 6DP,
United Kingdom

Oxford University Press is a department of the University of Oxford.
It furthers the University's objective of excellence in research, scholarship,
and education by publishing worldwide. Oxford is a registered trade mark of
Oxford University Press in the UK and in certain other countries

First published 2017
First published in paperback 2019

Published in the United States of America by Oxford University Press
198 Madison Avenue, New York, NY 10016, United States of America

British Library Cataloguing in Publication Data
Data available

Library of Congress Cataloging in Publication Data
Data available

ISBN 978–0–19–874748–2 (Hbk.)
ISBN 978–0–19–885303–9 (Pbk.)

This book is dedicated to those who do—those who wake up every day and try to make the world a better place, strive to make the systems that are supposed to work actually work, and who overcome to do their jobs. Our modest contribution, we hope, is to help the people who do by providing a language and a framework that articulates what the more successful already know intuitively, explaining why doing is often so very hard, and helping them build a larger community of doers able to take tangible steps forward.

Foreword

Building a public sector capable of implementing both basic and (increasingly) complex tasks, at scale, for everyone, is a defining characteristic of what it means for a country to be 'developed' and provide high levels of well-being for its citizens. Even a cursory comparison of the Millennium Development Goals (2000) and Sustainable Development Goals (2015), however, reveals how vastly more expansive, ambitious, and complex the development agenda has been acknowledged to be. The challenges will only grow in the coming decades. Progress on the SDGs by 2030 and the vision of improved well-being they embody will require not just 'more money', 'better policies' and 'stronger political will' but a wholesale revolution in how we think about and respond to implementation challenges. The historical reality is that the development process, even when it succeeds, just keeps getting harder, not easier. *Building State Capability* is our modest contribution to this challenge.

We are delighted with the positive response to *Building State Capability*, from both researchers and (especially) practitioners, thereby warranting the production of a paperback edition. The key ideas laid out in our work on implementation dynamics in development—initially published in 2013 then consolidated and expanded in the book—stress the importance of building implementation capability in public organizations as the foundation for realizing key policy objectives. 'Good policies' are of course better than bad ones, but if any policy is really only as good as its implementation then it became increasingly apparent to us that the importance of this had been vastly underappreciated: hundreds of books have been written on development policy, but one struggles to name even a handful explicitly addressing implementation issues. When such issues were acknowledged, they were typically defined as a "capacity building" problem best addressed by some combination of technical experts, training programs, technology upgrades, and the transfer of 'best practices'. That so many "capacity building" initiatives had yielded so little for so long seemed to us a situation requiring empirical documentation, analytical explanation, and—most importantly—a pragmatic alternative. We offered Problem-Driven Iterative Adaptation, or PDIA, as one such alternative. (Consistent with its principles, 'PDIA' was initially called something else; only after considering several options did we cast our lot with it!)

Well before the book's release in early 2017 we committed ourselves to practicing what we preach: using the principles of PDIA to refine and extend

PDIA itself. These efforts led to a number of initiatives through the Building State Capability (BSC) program at Harvard University's Center for International Development. Work at BSC has involved action learning policy engagements in various countries that have included blended learning models integrating online and in-person training. These engagements have informed our practical approach to doing PDIA, and the production of an accessible PDIA Toolkit[1] (available in English and Spanish) for practitioners to use. Applications of this Toolkit have led to numerous positive PDIA applications (described in detailed case studies from different countries and sectors, documenting the experience of dedicated teams as they have embarked upon PDIA's 'long voyage of discovery'). We have also produced various research papers assessing the size and nature of the gaps between institutional appearance and performance, and blog posts from those on the front lines of public sector reform in difficult places.[2] A number of different on-line courses have also been created, to draw on the materials in the book and help practitioners translate these into concrete changes in how they and their organizations define problems, frame alternatives, act, reflect on their action, and improve. These courses have been completed by over 1,500 people from around the world who are now part of a growing and active PDIA Community of Practice. This course has both helped us see concrete progress by participants and also refined and extended our own understanding of PDIA.

In the long run, the fruits of this labor will likely take us in several new and different directions: extending the 'frontier' of research and practice on PDIA, translating materials into many more languages (replete with local examples), and finding ways to contribute to an expanding global social movement committed to 'doing development differently'. Presenting that work will require a subsequent volume; for now, the more groups in more countries engaging these challenges with PDIA, the better!

A special thanks again to Salimah Samji, the Director of the Building State Capability program, who has worked tirelessly over many years to not only bring the PDIA agenda to life, on numerous fronts, including the PDIA course and toolkit, but doing so by infusing it so constructively with her unique blend of professional and life experience. We can do what we do because she does what she does so well.

Matt Andrews
Lant Pritchett
Michael Woolcock

August 2019

---

[1] The toolkit is available as a free downloadable pdf at https://bsc.cid.harvard.edu/PDIAtoolkit
[2] This material, including a free downloadable copy of the book itself, is available at https://bsc.cid.harvard.edu/

Acknowledgments

Implementing a book on implementation has required the collective capabilities of an extraordinarily diverse group of individuals and organizations. We especially thank the World Institute for Development Economics Research, part of the United Nations University, who provided the funding for the foundation on which we have built. Finn Tarp and Tony Addison showed a willingness to support our ideas long before they came to the broader attention of the development community (and beyond).

We have PDIA-ed our way to PDIA and hence wish to thank the thousands of participants who have attended the dozens of seminars, lectures, and workshops to which we have contributed in countries all around the world; they, and especially our students at Harvard Kennedy School, have provided us with all manner of feedback, careful critique, and helpful suggestions.

Particular thanks go to Salimah Samji, the intrepid manager of the Building State Capability program at Harvard University's Center for International Development. Salimah somehow deftly channels our collective quirks and musings into a coherent whole, and has been the key person pioneering our passage into the world of Massive Open Online Courses (MOOCs), wherein we have offered condensed versions of this book to hundreds of practitioners around the world (for free). This book is both the scholarly-yet-accessible complement to this venture while also remaining, we hope, a stand-alone volume for students of international development and those seeking a comprehensive integration of critique and action. We originally thought that this book would naturally precede a course, but the astute advice of Bruce Ross-Larson—for many decades the editorial maestro behind all manner of high-profile development reports—that "books are dead" convinced us that a better book and more readers would result if the book followed a course.

Several others have contributed directly to the book itself. The papers we wrote warming up for the book have many co-authors, including Greg Larson, Peter Ajak Biar, and Frauke de Wiejer. Greg Larson helped us draft the first version of this book, and even though the content has since been greatly refined and the sequence of chapters completely altered, we are most grateful for his efforts. Emily Pritchett transformed our key concepts into the delightful cartoons that open each chapter and her great pictures say at least a thousand words each. Our editor at Oxford University Press, Adam Swallow, has been a continuous source of support, and indulged all our pleas for "more time." We hope the finished product is better for the additional months (and there have been many of them) we've taken.

A special final thanks to those who, in their own professional setting, have taken the initiative to adopt the PDIA approach (whether its spirit or letter) as part of a broader strategy for responding to their prevailing development challenges, and provided us with vital feedback on its virtues and limits. Some amazing people are showing that existing instruments can actually have more flexibility than it sometimes appears, and that PDIA-type approaches can be implemented even in very difficult places (such as Afghanistan, Sierra Leone, and Tajikistan). But having long railed against seeking "silver bullet" solutions to development's many challenges, we are acutely aware that PDIA is not one of them.

Lant, on the occasion of his fifth book, thanks his wife Diane of thirty-five years for never having any of it.

Matt dedicates this book to his late brother Steve, whose example of commitment and grit will never be forgotten. Thanks to Jeannie, Samuel, Joshua, and Daniel for support beyond reason.

Michael extends enduring gratitude to Connie, Jenn, and Nathan for tolerating his numerous absences, all done in the name of supporting his seemingly esoteric way of trying to make the world a better place. He is able to offer what he has, and to do what he does, because they (and many others) do what they do; any positive outcomes are a team accomplishment. The lost time cannot be regained, but he has to believe it has not been in vain.

Contents

List of Figures

List of Figures

List of Tables

List of Boxes

Then all the elders of Israel gathered together and came to Samuel at Ramah, and said to him, "Look, you are old, and your sons do not walk in your ways. Now appoint us a king to judge us [and rule over us] like all the other nations." But their demand displeased Samuel when they said, "Give us a king to judge *and* rule over us." .... Samuel reported all the words of the Lord to the people who were asking him for a king ... But the people refused to listen to Samuel. "No!" they said. "We want a king over us. Then we will be like all the other nations ... "

Samuel 1:8 (c. 600 BCE)

We must not make a scarecrow of the law,
Setting it up to fear the birds of prey,
And let it keep one shape, till custom make it
Their perch and not their terror.

William Shakespeare, *Measure for Measure* Act 2, Scene 1

Theory is when you know everything and nothing works. Practice is when everything works and nobody knows why. We have put together theory and practice: nothing is working ... and nobody knows why!

Attributed to Albert Einstein

We have added much new cultural material, the value of which cannot be discounted; however, it often fits so ill with our own style or is so far removed from it that we can use it at best as a decoration and not as material to build with. It is quite understandable why we have been so mistaken in our choice. In the first place, much has to be chosen, and there has been so little to choose from.

Ki Hajar Dewantara, Indonesian educator (1935)

[W]e tend to meet any new situation by reorganizing, and a wonderful method it is for creating the illusion of progress at a mere cost of confusion, inefficiency and demoralization.

Charlton Ogburn Jr., *The Marauders* (1959: 72)

The term "implementation" understates the complexity of the task of carrying out projects that are affected by a high degree of initial ignorance and uncertainty. Here "project implementation" may often mean in fact a long voyage of discovery in the most varied domains, from technology to politics.

Albert Hirschman, *Development Projects Observed* (1967: 35)

If you can't imitate him, don't copy him.

Baseball great Yogi Berra, advising a young player who was mimicking the batting stance of famed slugger Frank Robinson

Introduction

The "long voyage of discovery"

Seeking to look like something you're not because you're envious, desperate or afraid. "Reforms" that yield only cynicism and illusions of progress. Being given ill-fitting material that at best can be used as decoration, and that routinely fails to deter those forces arrayed against it. The disjuncture of theory and practice. The importance of eschewing short-term expedience to embark instead on long voyages of discovery to resolve deeply complex problems—those defined by high degrees of initial ignorance and uncertainty.

These themes, encapsulated in the opening epigraphs, convey the essence of the challenges this book addresses and to which it seeks to respond. Whether two and a half thousand years ago or today, those striving to envision and then instantiate a better way of doing things have lamented with disarming regularity that too often the prevailing solutions are actually part of the problem. In recent decades, a long line of venerable thinkers—Charles Lindblom in the 1950s, Albert Hirschmann in the 1960s and 1970s, David Korten in the 1980s, Dennis Rondinelli in the 1980s and 1990s, "complexity" theorists in recent years (among others)[1]—have argued for taking a more adaptive or experimental approach to engaging with vexing development challenges. These calls bear repeating, but their failure to gain lasting traction could mean either that the underlying diagnosis is in fact inadequate or that the challenges it seeks to overcome are just too daunting. But we suggest that the ingredient missing from previous efforts has been the failure to mobilize a

---

[1] See, among many others, Lindblom (1959), Hirschmann (1967), Korten (1980), Rondinelli (1993), and Ramalingam (2013). See also Uphoff (1992). The more recent interest in "delivery units" (Barber 2015) within governments (e.g. Malaysia, Tanzania) to focus specifically on implementation issues has a broadly similar but narrowly quite different intellectual pedigree and modus operandi from the approach outlined here.

vibrant social movement of citizens, researchers, and development practitioners in support of the necessary change.

While hardly a "manifesto" for such change, this book seeks to bring the analysis of policy implementation dynamics in development into direct dialogue with the latest scholarly literature and hard-won experiences of practitioners. We ourselves sit at precisely this precarious juncture of thinking and doing. If there is a key lesson from our collective engagements so far it is that teams of committed people change things, indeed that—echoing Margaret Mead—"it is the only thing that ever has." We bring to this quest the combined skills and sensibilities of an economist (Lant) who works on education and health, a public administration specialist (Matt) who specializes in public financial management and budget reform, and a sociologist (Michael) who works on local justice and governance. All three of us have worked at Harvard Kennedy School and the World Bank, and have a combined seventy-five years of experience working on and living in countries seeking to engage with the problems we spell out.

The work on which this volume is based stems from an initial realization that across our respective disciplines, sectors, and countries a common and repeated problem is apparent: articulating a reasonable policy is one thing; actually implementing it successfully is another. Development discourse is replete with discussions of the "policy implications" of particular findings from research and experience—hire contract teachers, use biometrics to improve attendance, introduce new procurement systems to reduce corruption—but rarely is there a follow-up discussion on who, exactly, will implement these "implications," or whether the administrative systems charged with implementing *any* policy can actually do so, or whether a given policy success or failure actually stems less from the quality of its "design" and more from the willingness and ability of the prevailing apparatus to implement it. All manner of key questions pertaining to the replication and "scaling-up" of policies and programs deemed to be "successful" turn on whether adequate implementation capability is (actually or potentially) present, but explanations of weak implementation seem too often to be attributed to "low capacity" (of individuals), "perverse incentives," or "lack of political will." Elements of these explanations are true, but a more comprehensive and detailed approach is needed to guide action.

One of the great paradoxes of contemporary development is that this wondrous project—to bring a measure of prosperity and peace to the whole world—has both succeeded spectacularly and failed miserably. It has succeeded spectacularly because, by many measures, the world has never been in better shape. Despite what one might infer from the daily headlines, on average we live longer, have higher incomes, are better educated, enjoy more political freedoms, and are physically safer than at any point in human history.[2] Most developing countries have met most of the Millennium Development Goals—the eight targets set by the community of nations in 2000—on schedule (i.e. by 2015), a good many even earlier. Large-scale famines, pestilence, and plagues, long the scourge of human existence, have mostly been consigned to history books. Even wars are smaller scale, resulting in vastly fewer deaths than those of the first half of the twentieth century (and before). But we have also failed miserably, because we have done the easy part, and because the key to taking the next vital steps—building institutions able to implement increasingly complex and contentious tasks, under pressure and at scale—is not only *not* improving but in most developing countries steadily declining. The "easy" part of development entailed stopping doing awful things (genocide, *gulags*, apartheid, exclusion)[3] and then going from nothing to something in the provision of positive things: from essentially no public services of any kind to the provision of a building called a school, occupied by a person called a teacher deploying some resources called textbooks. Such provisions constituted, mathematically speaking, an infinite improvement and together they generated correspondingly real advancements in human welfare.[4]

As important as these achievements have been, however, they are the beginning, not the end, of "development." To complete the development journey, we now need to do the hard part, namely ensure that buildings, teachers, and textbooks routinely *combine* to produce actual learning, generating the knowledge and problem-solving skills that enable students to become functioning members of the twenty-first-century global economy, and to become informed citizens meaningfully participating in domestic political debates.[5] Having defined education as enrollment, and gender equality as enrollment equality, it has been possible to declare victory. These "inputs," however, are necessary but very insufficient for taking the next steps toward establishing a high capability education *system*, one able to assure the reliable provision of high-quality public services for all.[6] Moreover,

---

[2] See Kenny (2010), Pinker (2011), Deaton (2013), and Radelet (2015) for ample supporting evidence of these broad claims.

[3] Seeking to end violence and discrimination, of course, is a dangerous and noble task, and in many respects a constituent feature of development; our point here is that stopping destruction, suppression, and division is a great start, but that it is something else to initiate the long process of constructing a modern society, economy, polity, and public administrative system that reliably works for all.

[4] Needless to say, we are categorically *not* arguing that the absence of a formal state apparatus for delivering public services implies that no services at all are being provided (or as a colleague aptly put it, that in such circumstances there is a "blank slate" on which development actors then "write"). Babies are born, children learn, and justice is dispensed in all communities everywhere, often via mechanisms that are accessible and locally legitimate; the *development* challenge is ensuring that high quality neonatal care, education, and justice are provided equitably to all.

[5] See Pritchett (2013) for details on this dynamic in the specific case of education.

[6] See World Bank (2004).

beyond services that enjoy broad support, development also entails the crafting of a state able to legitimately and equitably impose difficult obligations—taxation, regulation, criminal justice—that everyday citizens (let alone powerful interest groups) may have occasion to actively resist. Delivering on such tasks requires a mutually binding and broadly legitimate "social contract" between citizen, state and provider, and a state that itself has the organizational capability to implement such tasks. On *these* development tasks, unfortunately, the empirical record in recent years is much more sanguine; indeed, in most developing countries, the quality of institutions presiding over such tasks is flatlining or actively declining. As we shall see, even delivering the mail—a non-controversial and almost entirely logistical task—seems to be beyond the capability of many countries (and not just the poorest ones).[7] Too often countries are being asked to run before they can walk—to implement "green growth," to build an effective justice system, to introduce a progressive tax code and pension systems before they have the resources or capability to fix potholes in the roads.

In the face of such challenges, the prevailing development literature and policy discourse is conspicuously silent or at best confused. Our reports, papers, and memoranda are of course replete with strident calls for enhancing "development effectiveness" and "good governance," for promoting "the rule of law," "social accountability," "transparency," "participation," and "inclusion" as a basis for building "sound institutions," but relatively little attention is paid to the mechanisms and logics by which such activities are justified, enacted, and assessed. Even if seasoned practitioners readily concede that bona fide "tool kits" for responding to these challenges remain elusive, our collective response seems to have been to double down on orthodoxy—on measuring success by inputs provided, resources transferred, "best practices" replicated, rules faithfully upheld—rather than seeking to forge strategies that respond to the specific *types* of development problems that "building effective institutions" necessarily requires.

The provocative claim of this book is that the dominant strategies deployed in response to such challenges—by international organizations and domestic agencies alike—are too often part of the problem rather than part of the solution. We contend that such strategies produce administrative systems in developing countries that *look like* those of modern states but that do not (indeed, cannot) perform like them; reforms yield metrics that satisfy narrow bureaucratic scorecards in donor capitals (and thus enable funds to continue to flow and legitimacy to be sustained), but that mask a clear inability to actually implement incrementally more complex and contentious tasks.

---

[7] Chong et al. (2014).

Anti-corruption laws are only one case in point: in 2012, Uganda received a score of 99 out of 100 from Global Integrity (a watchdog NGO) for the quality of its anti-corruption laws; on the day we happened to arrive in Kampala for a workshop, however, the headline story in the newspapers announced that the British government was suspending a large project because of . . . a massive corruption scandal. What systems look like (their form) and what they can actually do (their function) are often conflated; the claim or hope, in effect, is that good form will get you good function. We argue, on the contrary, that success (effective functioning) stems less from "good institutions" (form) but that success *builds* good institutions. The challenge is thus how to enhance the frequency, quality, and robustness of this success.

Beyond mere critique of orthodoxy, we seek to outline a strategy and collection of tactics that we believe—on the basis of the historical record, contemporary evidence, and our own hard-won experience—offers a coherent and supportable strategy for nurturing this success. Rather than "selling solutions" (or a "tool kit" of universal "best practices" as verified by "rigorous evidence") we propose strategies that begin with generating locally nominated and prioritized problems, and that work iteratively to identify customized "best fit" responses (sometimes by exploiting the existing variation in implementation outcomes), in the process working with an expanding community of practice to share and learn at scale. We call this approach problem-driven iterative adaptation (PDIA). We are very conscious that others before us and around us today have articulated similar diagnoses and prescriptions, but we like to think the PDIA approach is unique in providing a detailed explanation of the problem, a pragmatic and supportable response to it, and a commitment to building an expanding social movement that can adopt and adapt it in practice. As such, it's the second word—not the first or final word—on a long journey of discovery.

Part I

The Problem—The Creation and Consolidation of Capability Traps

1

The big stuck in state capability

Lant once visited a rather desultory game park. He and a few other visitors were driven into the park seated on benches built onto the back of a flatbed truck. A guard carrying a vintage rifle was also in the back to protect them from any beasts they might encounter. As they drove along increasingly bumpy and rutted roads, Lant became concerned that the driver often had his wheels directly in the ruts. He mentioned to the guard that perhaps the driver should stay out of the ruts. "Don't worry," the guard replied, "the driver knows what he is doing. Just look for animals." Another fifteen minutes later, there being no animals to observe, Lant mentioned again to the guard that driving in the ruts was a risk. "We do this every day," said the guard. "We know what we are doing, just let us do our job." Not ten minutes later—whump!—everyone was thrown forward as the truck, with wheels in the ruts, ground to a halt, completely high centered. The truck was stuck, with the rear wheels spinning uselessly in the air. As the visitors jumped down from the truck, the guard said: "Damn, same thing happened yesterday."

Like the truck in this game park, many developing countries and organizations within them are mired in a "big stuck," or what we will call a "capability trap": they cannot perform the tasks asked of them, and doing the same thing day after day is not improving the situation; indeed, it is usually only making things worse. Even if everyone can agree in broad terms about the truck's desired destination and the route needed to get there, an inability to actually implement the strategy for doing so means that there is often little to show for it—despite all the time, money, and effort expended, the truck never arrives. This book seeks to document the nature and extent of the capability for policy implementation in developing countries, to explain how low capability exists and persists, and—most importantly—to offer an approach for building a state's capability to implement its core functions (i.e. for getting "unstuck"). Put more forcefully, we argue that countries are as "developed"—as economically prosperous, socially inclusive, and politically well governed—as their capability for implementation allows. Steadily acquiring this capability is a defining characteristic of what it means for a country to become and remain "developed," but alas the track record of an array of strategies purporting to achieve this capability over the last sixty years is at best thin. What might be done? Where to begin?

An initial sense of the scale of the challenge can be gleaned from an examination of three different data sources that measure a country's current level and growth of state capability for policy implementation. Based on their current (2012) level of capability on these measures we can divide the 102 historically developing countries[1] into those with very weak, weak, middle,

---

[1] We take the UN's World Economic Situation and Prospects classification as "developed" (not "high income") which includes thirty-five countries; this is basically the old OECD (prior to accessions to historically developing countries like Mexico and Korea) plus a few of the more

and strong state capability. Analyzing the levels and recent growth rates of the countries reveals the pervasiveness of the "big stuck" in state capability:

- Only eight of the historically developing countries have attained strong capability. Moreover, as these eight are mostly quite small (e.g. Singapore, Bahamas, United Arab Emirates), fewer than 100 million (or 1.7 percent) of the roughly 5.8 billion people in historically developing countries currently live in high capability states.

- Almost half (49 of 102) of the historically developing countries have very weak or weak capability, and, as we show, these low levels of current capability themselves show that, for these countries, the long-run pace of acquiring capability is very slow.

- What is more worrisome, three-quarters of these countries (36 of 49) have experienced *negative* growth in state capability in recent decades. More than one-third of all countries (36 of 102) have low and (in the medium run at least) *deteriorating* state capability.

- If we calculate the "business as usual" *time to high capability*—i.e. how long it would take to achieve high state capability at current rates of progress— then of the forty-nine currently weak capability states, the time frame for the thirty-six with negative growth for attaining high capability is obviously "forever." But even for the thirteen with positive growth, only three would reach strong capability in fewer than ninety years at their current medium-run growth.

- The problem of the "big stuck" or capability trap is not limited to the weak capability (or "fragile" or "failing" states) but also applies to those in the middle. Of the forty-five countries with middle levels of capability, thirty-one (more than two-thirds) have experienced *negative* growth in capability since 1996.

- The *time to high capability* calculations for these forty-five middle capability countries suggest that only eight will reach strong capability before the end of this century (and of those, four will take more than fifty years at current trends).

Once one is stuck, doing the same thing one did yesterday (and the year before and the decade before), simply attempting to put more power into spinning the wheels, is not a wise course of action. Something different is needed.

The Implementation Imperative

Many engaged in development—elected and appointed politicians, government officials, non-governmental organizations (NGOs), professionals of the

advanced countries in Eastern Europe (e.g. Hungary, Poland, Slovenia, Slovakia). Obviously if we are saying there are few "historically developing country" successes then reclassifications of successful countries like Korea or Singapore or Chile as "developed" would create bias.

United Nations, OECD, development banks and bilateral aid agencies, researchers, academics, and advocates—spend vast amounts of time and effort debating and acting on three Ps: policies, programs, and projects. But what if they don't really matter? What if the policy as officially adopted, the program as approved and budgeted, or the project design as agreed upon are actually of secondary importance? If whether a policy, program, or project produces the desired outcomes hinges on how well it is implemented, then the real determinant of performance is not the three Ps but capability for implementation. We contend that today many states have skewed capabilities—the capability to routinely and repeatedly propose the three Ps, but not the capability to implement them.

A recent study illustrates that even when governments have adopted *the exact same policy*, outcomes across countries range from complete failure to perfection. In a recent experimental study,[2] researchers examined differences in how well countries handle international mail. For our purposes the results are interesting not because the post office is intrinsically fascinating or international mail a hugely important governmental function, but because all countries have exactly the same policy. The Universal Postal Union convention, to which 159 countries in the world are signatories (i.e. nearly all), specifies a common and detailed policy for the treatment of undeliverable international letters, including that they are to be returned to the sending country within thirty days. None of the observed differences in performance across countries in handling international mail can be attributed to differences in the *de jure* policy.

To examine governmental effectiveness, the researchers mailed 10 deliberately misaddressed letters to each of the 159 countries and then just waited and counted how long, if at all, each letter took to return. If measured by the number of letters which were returned within ninety days (already more than the official policy of thirty days), the performance ranged from zero to 100. In countries like Finland, Norway, and Uruguay, 100 percent of the letters came back within 90 days. In 25 of 157 countries *no* letters came back within 90 days (in 16 countries none of the letters came back ever). These zero performance countries included unsurprising places like Somalia, Myanmar, and Liberia but also included Egypt, Fiji, Ghana, and Honduras that are considered "middle-income" countries. In the lowest quartile of countries by income, less than 1 in 10 letters was returned (0.92) and in the bottom half by schooling only 2.2 of 10 were returned (Figure 1.1). This range of outcomes is not because some countries had "good policies" and others did not—all had exactly the same policy—but because some countries have post offices that implement the adopted policy while others do not.

[2] See Chong et al. (2014).

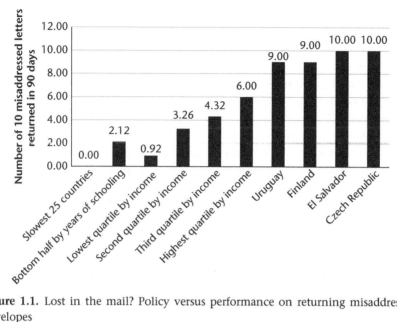

Figure 1.1. Lost in the mail? Policy versus performance on returning misaddressed envelopes

Source: Based on Chong et al (2014: table 2)

In our own professional experience in fields as diverse as public finance, basic education, legal enforcement, and others we have encountered similar outcomes that convince us that many states have poor outcomes not because they lack "good policies" but because they lack implementation capability. For instance, governments across the developing world have now adopted similar "best practice" budgeting rules but many still fail miserably to execute their spending plans. Other governments have adopted common policies to increase the number of trained teachers in schools. They succeed in passing these teachers through training colleges but cannot ensure their active and effective presence in classrooms. Similarly, governments across the world have made great progress introducing policies aimed at increasing the procurement of vital medicines in their countries but struggle to get the medicines to health posts or to assure the medicines are being properly dispensed and used. Over twenty-five years after signing the global convention on the rights of the child, and committing to register all children at birth, countries such as Bangladesh, India, Mozambique, Nigeria, Pakistan, and Uganda still register less than 40 percent of children. They have the policy ideas and commitments in place that other countries found sufficient for success, but just cannot implement these in a consistently effective manner.

We argue that building an organizational or governmental capability to implement is of primary importance for realizing development objectives.

As noted above, building robust capability for implementation is itself a defining characteristic of being "developed"; moreover, it is a challenge that only intensifies as the tasks to be completed by the state in increasingly prosperous and open societies—taxing citizens, regulating business, providing healthcare and pensions—themselves become more complex and contentious. We believe that implementation failures hold many countries back from realizing their own stated development goals, and that, even worse, many governments lack the capability to overcome repeated implementation failures even after years of reforms designed to strengthen state capability.

This problem has a long history. Since the beginning of the development era in the aftermath of World War II and the accelerating creation of newly independent nation-states, there has been massive intellectual and ideological debate about *what* governments *should* do. However, there was less debate about *how* governments *could* do what they chose to do—that is, about how to build the capability of the state. The result is that more than half a century into the development era there are many states that lack the capability to carry out even simple functions, like delivering the mail, about which there is essentially no debate at all. How is it that countries like Ghana and Egypt and Honduras and Fiji (and most other developing countries) do not have a post office that implements simple policies that they have adopted? In seeking to identify answers to these questions, we begin by returning to the available cross-national data on state capability, the better to establish a broad empirical foundation regarding global trends. In subsequent chapters we will explain these trends, explore their manifestations within particular countries and sectors, and outline a practical strategy for responding to them.

Cross-National Data on State Capability

A number of different organizations have created cross-national measures of "governance," albeit with various objectives in mind. For our purposes, however, the concept of "governance" is too broad and includes many conceptual elements that are distinct from state capability. In particular we are *not* trying to measure four things often lumped together with "governance." All of these are important, but nonetheless remain conceptually and empirically distinct.

First, we are not trying to measure politics, how the citizens choose (or not) who will exercise sovereign power, nor how that is procedurally constrained. So we do not rely on measures of "democracy" or "autocracy" (as in the Polity measures) or on indicators like "constraints on the executive." A country can be a democracy with low state capability or an autocracy with high capability. Second, we are also not trying to measure the protection of political rights or human rights or freedom (as in the Freedom House indicators), or direct citizen voice or participation in the operation of government. Countries with either high or low capability can engage in the suppression of human rights. Third, we are not trying to directly measure economic (e.g. GDP per capita, poverty) or human development (e.g. education, health, HDI—i.e. Human Development Index) outcomes directly. That is, while we feel that state capability is an important determinant of these outcomes, we do not want to conflate state capabilities and outcomes. For instance, with technological progress or increases in incomes human development outcomes could be improving even with stagnant levels of state capability. Fourth, we are not measuring whether a country has "good" or "bad" policies (on any criteria) but rather how well they implement what policies they have. A country could have a counterproductive policy but implement it very effectively, or have a terrific adopted policy but just not be able to implement it.

We use three different sources as reassurance that our broad characterizations of the current levels of state capability and its evolution are not artefacts of one measure or the biases of any one organization. The Quality of Government (QOG) Institute provides a measure derived from the International Country Risk Guide (ICRG) data that is the simple average of the three ICRG indicators: "Corruption" (range 0–6), "Law and Order" (range 0–6) and "Bureaucratic Quality" (range 0–4), then rescaled 0–1. This state capability measure has the advantage of being available from 1984 to 2012 for many countries and of being comparable over time. The Failed State Index (FSI) rates countries by eleven different indicators related to the likelihood of conflict (e.g. "group grievance," "fractionalized elites," "external intervention") but we just use as the FSI state capability measure their indicator of "Public Services" which rates countries on carrying out core state functions like policing and criminality, infrastructure, roads, water and sanitation, education and health. Finally, the World Governance Indicators (WGI) have six components, each of which is an index built up from underlying data sources in a statistically sophisticated manner (e.g. Kaufmann et al. 2009). For our state capability index we use from the WGI the simple average of "government effectiveness," "control of corruption," and "rule of law."[3] This data is available from 1996 to 2013 and is comparable across countries from year to year but is rescaled in each year so it is, strictly speaking, only comparable over time for a given country relative to all other countries.

In order to compare these three separate data sources (QOG, FSI, WGI) we rescale each of them to a zero to 10 range by assigning the lowest recorded country/year observation as zero (this was typically Somalia) and the highest recorded country/year observation as 10 (this was typically Singapore).

---

[3] We do not use "voice and accountability" (which we take as a measure of polity and politics), "political stability/violence" (which we regard as an outcome measure), or "regulatory quality" (as this measures the quality of the policies).

This assumes each of the underlying variables are cardinal and linear. As this linear scale is arbitrary (it could be 0–1 or 0–100) the intuitive way to understand the results is that they are on a "Somalia to Singapore" scale—a movement of 1 point, say from 3 to 4, is a move of 1/10th the Somalia-to-Singapore difference in state capability.

Before presenting any analysis using these indicators there are three important empirical questions one should ask about this data on state capability. First, are they measuring roughly the same thing? The pairwise correlations of the three variables are all above 0.83. A slightly more sophisticated analysis, which accounts for the attenuation bias due to pure measurement, suggests that all of the variables have roughly a one-to-one linear relationship, as would be expected in rescaled data.[4] Even on the more demanding question of the correlation of growth, the medium-run (1996 to latest) growth rates of WGI and QOG have a correlation of 0.55.

Second, are these measures measuring something specific to a country's state capability or merely capturing broad cross-national differences in general governance and socioeconomic conditions? That is, perhaps there are just generally "good" places like Denmark with high prosperity, good policies, high human development, human rights, democracy, and state capability, and "bad" places like Somalia or Democratic Republic of Congo that lack all of those. Drumm (2015) addresses this question directly by taking all of the forty-five measures from four sources—WGI (six variables), ICRG (twelve variables), FSI (twelve variables), and Bertelsmann Transformation Index (fifteen variables)—and asking the technical question of whether all of them load on a single factor or whether the data suggest the various indicators are measuring identifiably different phenomena. His analysis of all forty-five governance indicators identifies four underlying factors (not just one or two) that he calls "effectiveness," "political gumption," "absence of internal tensions," and "political support and absence of external pressures." As such, he argues that the governance indicators clearly distinguish between something like state capability (his "effectiveness") and something like "democracy" (his "political gumption"). The mapping of the variables to the factors looks a lot like our choices made before we saw his analysis. So, the WGI's "government effectiveness," "rule of law," and "control of corruption" indicators load onto "effectiveness" while the "voice and accountability" indicator loads onto "political gumption." The three ICRG indicators used in the QOG measure ("bureaucratic quality," "corruption," and "law and order") are among those

---

[4] Using either "reverse regressions" to bound the coefficient or instrumental variables regressions (using a third indicator as instrument for the "x" variable) to correct for measurement error (not as an attempt establish causality) shows the linear relationship of each of the four on each other to have a relationship not statistically different from one.

that load onto the factor "effectiveness," while "democratic accountability" from the ICRG ratings loads onto "political gumption." The correlations between his estimated "effectiveness" factor and our variables are WGI .95, QOG .87, FSI .92.

Third, are we asserting that country-level indicators of state capability are sufficient and capture all of the relevant information? No. As we show in Chapter 4, there can be tremendous differences in capability across public sector organizations in the same country, and as we show in Chapter 5, different tasks require very different types of capability. India illustrates these points. In 2014 India put a spaceship into orbit around Mars—a task requiring very high technical capability. India's institutes of technology are world renowned. The Indian Election Commission carries out free and fair elections in the world's largest democracy. At the same time, India's capability for implementation-intensive activities of either service delivery (health, education, water) or imposition of obligations (taxation, regulation) is "flailing" (Pritchett 2009), at best. The gaps in capability between organizations in the same country is central to our book's overall line of argument, as we maintain that strategies at the organization and sector level can produce progress in building capability even when country conditions are not propitious.

The indicator of state capability we use in the analysis in this chapter is the simple average of the scaled WGI, QOG, and FSI indices of state capability. We report here only these results for simplicity and as illustrative, but we have done similar analysis of the levels and rates of growth of state capability for each of the indicators separately (see Pritchett et al. 2010), other indicators such as the BTI, the Drumm (2015) government effectiveness factor, the World Bank's internal indicators, and other indicators of state fragility (see de Weijer and Pritchett 2010). We also stress that the basic findings we report are robust using all these different indicators of state capability. We are not focused on the results for individual countries and their relative rankings or estimates of growth but on the big picture. With different indicators countries might move up or down somewhat but the broad patterns across countries we report remain the same.

The Big Stuck: Level and Growth in State Capability

Our results use two key estimates for each country's level of state capability in 2012 on our state capability index (the average of the three WGI, QOG, and FSI) from 0 to 10, and the medium-run growth of state capability as the average of the growth rates of the QOG and the WGI from 1996 to 2012 (QOG) or 2013 (WGI).[5] Table 1.1 presents the results of this analysis for the

[5] The growth rates are calculated as the least squares growth rate over the entire period, not end-point to end-point, which smooths out underlying variability.

102 historically developing countries for which all three indicators were available. The table has two dimensions: the classification of countries on the current (2012) level of capability, and the growth of capability since 1996.

We divide countries into four levels of capability based on the value of the 0 to 10 state capability (SC) scale: *very weak* (less than 2.5), *weak* (2.5 to 4), *middle* (4 to 6.5), and *strong* (above 6.5). These levels and categories are simply a convention we adopt for simplicity of discussion and do not imply that we think there are somehow important differences between a country at SC 2.4 versus 2.6 or at SC of 3.9 versus 4.1. Given the ranges of uncertainty of these indicators,[6] there are surely countries that could easily be in the category just above or just below but we doubt there are many countries misclassified by two or more categories (e.g. the strongest "very weak" country is Niger and the weakest "middle" country is Ghana, and it is implausible that the ordering of those two by capability is wrong).

We chose 6.5 as the threshold for "strong" state capability. This is not a high standard, as there are at least some countries at 10 (by construction) and the typical level of a developed country is 8. The countries just below the threshold are Uruguay and Croatia and just above is Bahrain. When we calculate "time to strong capability" we are not thinking of reaching OECD standards or "getting to Denmark" (at 9.5) (Pritchett and Woolcock 2004) but achieving 6.5, just above Uruguay.

The first striking point of Table 1.1 is that there are only 8 of the 102 countries that have "strong" state capability. Moreover, as noted above, these eight include four small population oil-rich states (United Arab Emirates, Bahrain, Brunei, Qatar), one city-state (Singapore), one tiny island (Bahamas), and only two large countries (Chile and South Korea). The total population of these countries is around 85 million—smaller than Ethiopia or Vietnam.

The lower threshold, below which state capability is "very weak," we chose as 2.5. (Keep in mind that zero was the lowest of any country in any year.) In the WGI, for instance, Somalia was only 0 in 2008 and in 2013 its ranking was 0.58—even though it effectively lacked a state. In the QOG data the only zero is Liberia in 1993 in the midst of a horrific civil war and on that scale Somalia, even in quasi-anarchy in 2003, was rated a 1.3. States at 2.5 or below are "fragile" or "failing" in that they are at significant risk of not being able to maintain even the Weberian definition of "stateness," namely a "human community that (successfully) claims the monopoly of the legitimate use of physical force within a given territory."[7] For instance, in the WGI in 2013 Yemen was rated as a 2.5 and has since collapsed as a state, while Iraq in 2013 was rated by WGI as 2.3 and yet could not hold territory against the

---

[6] See the confidence ranges in Kaufmann et al. (2010) for instance.
[7] Weber (1919 [1965: 77]).

incursion of a non-state actor in 2014. Tragically, there are twice as many (17 of 102) countries in this "fragile" or essentially failed state category than successes and, since these have much larger populations there are half a billion people living in these "very weak" states. But we separate this lower category to emphasize that while there are "fragile" states the problems of state capability are *not* limited to those places—very low state capability is in fact pervasive. Hence we don't really focus on these countries in the discussion below of positive and negative growth in capability of the weak and middle countries.[8]

The dividing line between "weak" and "middle" at an SC score of 4 is perhaps the most arbitrary, but we thought it worth separating out the serious and pressing challenges of improving state capability in the "middle": large, mostly functional states at no immediate risk of collapse and which are often thriving economically like China, India, Brazil, and the Philippines from those of "weak"—but not (currently) failing—states like Uganda, Honduras, and Papua New Guinea. Referring to countries below 4 as "weak" makes sense because, as we show in Chapter 4, India has many concrete and well-documented examples of weak capability for implementation in education, health, policing, and regulatory enforcement (e.g. licensing, environment, banking) yet India has an SC 4.61 rating; hence countries with an SC rating under 4 are plausibly called "weak." Moreover, SC 4.0 separates the strongest of the "weak" (the Gambia, El Salvador, and Belarus) from the weakest of the "middle" (Ghana, Peru, Russia): while some might have qualms saying Ghana, Peru, and Russia are not themselves weak capability states, few would dispute that Belarus, Gambia, and El Salvador are. These thresholds produce forty-five "middle" and thirty-two "weak" capability countries.

The second dimension of Table 1.1 is how rapidly the medium-run growth of state capability has been. For this we use the QOG and WGI data (the FSI dates only to 2006) from 1996 (when the WGI begins) to the most recent data (2012 for QOG, 2013 for WGI).[9] We divide the pace of growth into very

---

[8] There are three countries (Niger, Guinea-Bissau, and Liberia) whose very strong rebounds from very weak capability imply their "time to strong capability at BAU" will be short. It is worth pointing out that in two of the three the average short-run (since 2006) state capability progress has turned negative.

[9] One might object to the use of the WGI growth rates because the procedure for producing the WGI renormalizes the measures from year to year such that the cross country average is zero and hence the growth rate of the average is zero by construction. Hence tracking growth of a given country is only tracking their relative growth year to year relative to all other countries. However, we could renormalize the WGI growth rates by adding in a trend rate of growth of the average country and then the WGI estimates would capture cross-national variation and have an externally imposed trend. But the average trend in the "short run" (since 2006) is: QOG .0058 and FSI .011 and WGI −.0029. Hence the trend is so close to zero in the QOG data (in fact the median is zero) that little is lost in just using the raw WGI data. In fact, for the 1996–2012/2013 data the average growth of the QOG data is −0.046 whereas for WGI is −0.0023. Hence using the unadjusted WGI data to compute the average growth for each country gives a much more optimistic picture than if we use the QOG data alone.

Table 1.1 The "big stuck" in state capability: low levels, stagnant growth

The "big stuck" in state capability of low levels and stagnant growth of state capability. Only the thirteen "historically developing countries" in bold are on a plausible "business as usual" path to have strong capability by the end of the twenty-first century.

	Rapid negative	Slow		Rapid positive
	(g<−0.05)	Negative (−0.05<g<0)	Positive (0<g<05)	(g>0.05)
Strong (SC>6.5)		BHR, BHS, BRN	CHL(0), SGP(0), KOR(0), QAT(0)	ARE(0)
8	0	3	4	1
Middle (4<SC<6.5)	MDA, GUY, IRN, PHL, LKA, MNG, ZAF, MAR, THA, NAM, TTO, ARG, CRI	PER, EGY, CHN, MEX, LBN, VNM, BRA, IND, JAM, SUR, PAN, CUB, TUN, JOR, OMN, MYS, KWT, ISR	KAZ(10,820), GHA (4,632), UKR(1,216), ARM(1,062), RUS (231), BWA(102), **IDN (68), COL(56), TUR (55), DZA(55), ALB (42), SAU(28), URY (10), HRV(1)**	
45	13	18	14	0
Weak (2.5<SC<4)	GIN, VEN, MDG, LBY, PNG, KEN, NIC, GTM, SYR, DOM, PRY, SEN, GMB, BLR	MLI, CMR, MOZ, BFA, HND, ECU, BOL, PAK, MWI, GAB, AZE, SLV	UGA(6,001), AGO (2,738), TZA(371), BGD(244), ETH(103), ZMB(96)	
32	14	12	6	0
Very weak (SC<2.5)	YEM, ZWE, CIV	SOM, HTI, PRK, NGA, COG, TGO, MMR	SDN(7,270), SLE (333), ZAR(230), IRQ(92)	NER(66), GNB(61), LBR(33)
17	3	7	4	3
102	30	40	28	4

Source: Authors' calculations using the average of the rescaled indicators of state capability from *Quality of Government, Failed State Index* and *World Governance* indicators (Data Appendix 1.1).

negative, slow negative, slow positive, and rapid positive. The dividing line for "slow" is 0.05 points per year; at this pace it would take 200 years to move from zero state capability to the strongest (e.g. $10/200 = 0.05$).[10]

Using the 2012 level and the medium-run growth rate we calculate for each country the *time to strong capability*; this is not a prediction or a forecast but just an arithmetic calculation of the hypothetical question, "if a country were to maintain its recent medium-run pace of growth into the future, how long would it take to reach 6.5?" Obviously for the seventy countries with negative recent growth the answer is "forever" as they are headed backwards. But even

---

[10] The crude analogy would be a growth of GDP per capita of about 2 percent per annum at a pace that, if sustained to 200 years, would take a country from roughly Niger's GDP per capita to that of the USA.

for those with positive growth this extrapolation suggests very long time frames. As an illustration, Bangladesh's current state capability is 3.26 and its annual growth is 0.013, so it will take 244 years[11] to reach strong capability.

The Big Stuck: Weak Capability States

Explaining why so many states have stagnant or declining levels of capability for policy implementation requires a more detailed examination of the factors shaping the dynamics within both the states themselves and the broader ecosystem of development assistance in which they are embedded. To conduct such an examination we begin not with the very weak (or "F-states") but rather the states between the very weak and middle—the weak capability states. There are three things we can learn.

First, the fact that there are a lot of weak capability states today, even after most nation-states have been politically sovereign for over fifty years (and some, like the nine Latin American countries, for centuries), tells us that long-run progress in state capability has been very slow. Don't we need measures of state capability over time in order to measure the rate of progress? Yes, of course, and yet in an important way, no. Imagine walking into a forest and encountering trees of very different heights. One might think you cannot say anything about how fast or slow the trees grow. But actually with three pieces of information the long-run rate of growth of each tree can be calculated. If we know the tree's current height, its starting height, and its age then we know the average growth rate of the tree from seed to today exactly. This of course does not reveal anything about dynamics: if the tree grew fast when young and then slowed, or grew faster in wet years than dry years, or anything about its future growth, but we actually do know long-run growth from current height and age because we know it started from zero.

Using the analogy of inferring long-run growth in state capability from the height of trees in a forest, we know that if countries still have weak capability today and if we assume a lower bound of "stateness" of 2.5 then the overall trajectory of growth of state capability from that lower bound has to have been low. Take Guatemala, for instance. Its current state capability rating is 3.43. It has been politically sovereign since 1839. Hence the long-run rate of growth of state capability in Guatemala can have been at most 0.0054.[12] Even countries with less time since independence who are weak cannot have been improving too rapidly. Pakistan gained independence in 1947 and its upper bound growth rate is 0.017.[13] Again, this is not suggesting constant growth at this rate, just that the overall trajectory has to be consistent with very slow

---

[11] That is $(6.5-3.26)/0.013 = 244$.

[12] Since $(3.43-2.5)/(2012-1839) = 0.0054$.   [13] Since $(3.62-2.5)/(2012-1947) = 0.017$.

growth. Even without data on growth we can infer a "big stuck" (or at least very slow progress) just from the current low levels of capability.

Second, we do have some data on growth of state capability from 1996 to 2012, a period of sixteen years which we call "medium-run" progress. Strikingly, of the thirty-two weak capability states twenty-six have negative medium-run growth in capability. This is partly mechanical, as countries with negative growth will have lower current levels, but this does mean that if we calculated a "business as usual" extrapolation of "time to strong capability" the answer for most weak capability countries is "forever." In the short-run growth (average of growth since 2006 of all three indicators) only thirteen countries have positive recent growth and only five with "rapid" progress. Even for those six weak capability states with positive capability progress the pace is slow. The range of "time to strong capability" ranges from 96 years in Zambia to 6,000 in Uganda. These are obviously not meant as "forecasts" as no one knows what the world might look like in a 100, much less 6,000, years but this does illustrate that weak capability countries are not on a promising path.

Third, even the most rapidly progressing countries in the medium run do not show very rapid progress. The 90th percentile of state capability growth is only 0.032 points per year. At that pace even the strongest weak capability country at a level of 4 would take another seventy-eight years (almost to the next century) to reach strong capability.[14] We return to this point in Chapter 3, where we show that attempts to tackle state capability that presume that a three- or five-year plan can build state capability are not "plans" but just wishful thinking—and wishful thinking that can be damaging.

All three points about capability can be illustrated in a single figure that calculates the time to strong capability under various scenarios. Take Guatemala, illustrated in Figure 1.2.[15] Its medium-run growth has been $-.051$. Obviously if this pace were maintained Guatemala never achieves strong capability. To calculate the upper bound of long-run growth we start with the fact that Guatemala has been politically independent since 1839. Its 2012 average SCPI was 3.43. Assuming 2.5 as a lower-bound of state capability, then if it was 2.5 in 1839 and arrived at only 3.43 in 2012 this implies the overall historical growth rate (again which could be periods of advance and decline or long periods of absolute stagnation) was only 0.005 points per year.[16] At that pace it would take one hundred years to add just 0.5 units of capability. At the very long-run pace Guatemala would only reach strong capability in the year 2584. We repeat that this is obviously not meant as a forecast but rather as a

---

[14] Since $(6.5-4)/0.032 = 78$.

[15] This same graph is available for all countries with weak capability on the book's website.

[16] Since $(3.43-2.5)/(2012-1839) = 0.005$.

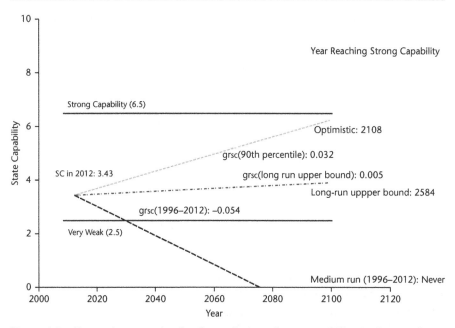

Figure 1.2. Alternative scenarios for the evolution of state capability in Guatemala

simple way of pointing out that the very low level today implies very slow long-run growth. Finally, even if Guatemala were to attain and sustain the optimistic scenario of the 90th percentile of growth of 0.032 points per year, it would still take until 2108 to reach high capability.

The Big Stuck and the Muddle in the Middle

There are forty-five countries that are in the middle range of state capability—neither weak nor strong. One might argue that the existence of this middle shows that all is well with state capability, at least in many countries, and hence suggest that "development" problems are mostly behind us. Such suggestions are the result of a particularly confused but nevertheless pernicious logic that reasons that since economic prosperity depends on "institutions," then the existence of rapid growth in countries like India and China proves that state capability is getting better. But all is not well: over two-thirds of countries in the middle also have negative medium-run growth and hence, although they have had sufficient progress in the past are not now on the right track. Even those with positive growth, few are demonstrating growth that puts them on a foreseeable path to strong capability. Let's clarify the muddle in the middle with four categories (or trajectories) of growth.

In the first category are those countries with *rapid deterioration* in state capability. This includes thirteen countries including many middle-income countries like South Africa, Argentina, Morocco, the Philippines, Thailand, and Iran. For instance, Argentina's QOG rating was 6.8 in 2000 and had fallen to 4.8 by 2012. Clearly in these falling capability countries there has been nothing to be complacent about.

A second category includes eighteen countries that had *negative growth* in state capability. This includes both India (with −0.022 per year) and China (with −0.015 per year). Again, while it may seem anomalous that the rapidly economically growing Asian giants had deterioration in state capability, this makes the mistake of inferring state capability from economic growth. Indeed, many observers feel that economic growth, while providing more resources to the state, has also created pressures and expectations that have weakened the state apparatus. This group also includes countries that have had prominent difficulties—e.g. the Arab Spring countries of Egypt and Tunisia where citizen dissatisfaction with the state and arbitrary enforcement (as well as high-level nepotism and crony capitalism) played at least some role in the uprising. The two largest Latin American countries, Brazil and Mexico, are also in this category, both with moderate capability but under pressure as capability stagnates and threats increase from non-state actors (e.g. criminality in Mexico) or corruption (the massive scandals in Brazil in 2015).

The third and fourth categories both had positive growth, but we divide these into those that, if current trends persist, would reach strong capability by 2100 and those that would not. The third group are the six middle countries in 2012 with positive, but very slow, progress since 1996: Kazakhstan, Ghana, Ukraine, Armenia, Russia, and Botswana. The time to strong capability for these countries are all over one hundred years, so while perhaps not retrogressing or in a completely stagnant "big stuck" they are nevertheless vulnerable. (And positive sentiment about medium-run progress in either Ukraine or Russia as of 2012 might be revisited in light of their conflict and of declining oil prices, which created a massive fiscal cushion in Russia).

The final group in the middle are those eight countries for which "business as usual" would produce high capability by the next century. These are (with their "years to strong capability"): Indonesia (68), Colombia (56), Turkey (55), Algeria (55), Albania (42), Saudi Arabia (28), Uruguay (10), and Croatia (1).

Where Does the Evidence on Building State Capability Leave Us?

The "development era" was ushered in by the end of World War II, which effectively began an era in which explicit colonialism ended and countries made their way into political sovereignty (always with the exception that most of Latin America had been politically independent since the early nineteenth century). This "development era" began with high expectations that these new nation-states could experience accelerated modernization. They needn't "reinvent the wheel" but could produce effective state organizations by transplanting success. While many recognized that this component of nation-building would be a long-term undertaking, certainly fifty or sixty years would be enough to realize a vision of a capable state.

On this score, the results in Table 1.1 and discussed in this chapter are sobering. There are few unambiguous successes in building state capability. Examples like South Korea, Chile, and Singapore prove building state capability is not impossible but that there are so few successes (and that so many of the measured successes are oil rich) is worrisome. Moreover, only another eight countries are, if current trends were to persist, on a path to reach strong capability within this century. Put most starkly, *at current rates less than 10 percent of today's developing world population will have descendants who by the end of this century are living in a high capability country.*[17] The "business as usual" scenario would end the twenty-first century with only 13 of 102 historically developing countries having attained strong state capability.

At the other extreme, seventeen countries as of this writing are at such a low level of capability that even "stateness" itself is at constant risk—in Somalia, Yemen, and DRC (and more recently joining them Syria) there is no Weberian state (and it is worth noting the data did not include other F-states like South Sudan and Afghanistan). Among those countries with minimally viable states, fifty-seven of the seventy-seven (three-quarters) of the weak and middle capability countries have experienced a trend deterioration in state capability since 1996. Twelve of the sixteen largest developing countries—including China, India, Pakistan, Brazil, Mexico, Egypt, Vietnam, the Philippines, Thailand, and South Africa—had negative trends in state capability.

What do these broad facts imply about the conceptual models we use to understand, and even to act on, building state capability?

First, if state capability were coming to the party it would be here by now. Many of the early ideas about accelerated modernization suggested a "naturalness" of the process of development. Just as the "natural" course of affairs is for a baby to crawl then walk then run and the "natural" course of affairs is for natural systems to tend towards entropy, the "natural" course of affairs was for nation-states to become "modern" and acquire Weberian organizations capable of ordering, administering, and implementing. On this score, countries or

---

[17] ~0.8 percent = (Population of these 8 countries)/(Total population of today's developing world) = (~470M)/(~5.9B). And this number is only that high largely because of Indonesia, which accounts for over half the total.

sectors or organizations that failed to acquire capability were treated as anomalous pathologies that required explanation. But the pervasiveness of slow and
uneven progress suggests that explanations of slow progress in building state
capability in the development era need to be general, both across countries
and sectors. That is, the appropriate question to ask is: what are the common
features affecting public finance, the post offices, police forces, education
systems, health ministries, and regulatory mechanisms in many countries
that can account for slow progress?

Second, many broad ideas about how to build state capability that are
attractive (either politically, normatively, or pragmatically)—like "democracy
will build capability" or "more schooled populations will build state capability" or "new information technologies will build state capability" or "economic growth/higher incomes will build state capability"—are in fact very
difficult to sustain. The basic correlations or estimated impact, for example,
are not present in the data, or are not even in the "right" direction. While
nearly all good things—like state capability and GDP per capita, or state
capability and education, or state capability and democracy—are associated
across countries in levels (for a variety of causally entangled reasons), the
correlations among these same variables in changes or rates of growth are
much weaker. Economic growth over short-to-medium horizons is almost
completely uncorrelated with improvements in state capability (and some
argue that growth is associated with reductions in state capability).[18] Moreover, establishing causation among aggregate variables is almost impossible—
while Denmark or Finland are rich, democratic, highly educated, and have
high state capability and Nepal or Haiti or Mali are none of those things, it is
hard to parse out which are horses and which are carts.

Similarly, even though more countries are democratic, schooling has
expanded massively, technological progress (particularly in information technology) has been revolutionary, and economic growth (while highly variable)
has been mostly positive, it is hard to conclude that this is a result of or
contributor to enhanced state capability. For instance, the schooling of the
adult population has increased massively (from two years to seven years) quite
uniformly across countries (Pritchett 2013). If more schooling causes better
state capability then this massive expansion in schooling could be part of
explaining why state capability had improved, if it had. But it hasn't. The
puzzle of why state capability did not improve on average is made more, not
less, puzzling by education or democracy or income or technology or global
activism or support for state building—all of which have, on all standard
measures, increased substantially.

---

[18] Kaufmann and Kraay (2002) for instance argue higher incomes lead to lower government
effectiveness.

This slow progress in state capability is not for want of trying (or at least efforts that look like trying). For decades the development enterprise at global, regional, and national levels has endeavored to build state capability. The orthodox strategy stresses "getting institutions right" because it relies on a theory of change that believes institutions and organizations produce success and result in high state capability. The orthodox approach thus aimed to build successful institutions and organizations by transplanting the forms and structures of existing successful institutions (or continuations of colonial/ adopted forms). This is manifest in tactics such as passing laws to create institutions and organizations, creating organizational structures, funding organizations, training management and workers of organizations to imple- ment policies, or policy reform of the formulas the organizations are meant to implement. None of these are particularly bad ideas in and of themselves, but together they represent an orthodox theory of change—"accelerated modern- ization through transplantation of best practice"—that, as we have shown, has seen widespread failure and, at best, tepid progress.

We are hardly the first to point to disappointing outcomes in efforts to build state capability. These are, at least within the development community, well known and widely acknowledged. Twenty years ago a 1996 assessment of national capacities in Africa, conducted on behalf of African governors of the World Bank, concluded: "Almost every African country has witnessed a systematic regression of capacity in the last 30 years; the majority had better capacity at independence than they now possess" (World Bank 1996: 5) and this "has led to institutionalized corruption, laxity and general lack of discip- line in the civil service" (p. 2). African governments seemed to be getting weaker, but not for lack of effort. Between $40 and $50 billion was spent during the 1980s on building government capability.[19] The rise on the devel- opment agenda of issues of governance and corruption is due in large part to the recognition in the 1990s that in many countries state capability was in retrogress, if not collapse.[20]

The Way Forward

There are two common adages: "If at first you don't succeed, try and try again"; and "Insanity is doing the same thing and expecting different results." Given the apparent contradiction, perhaps a more accurate and clearer version

---

[19] Cited in Lancaster (1999: 57).

[20] Quotes from the World Bank report are taken from Klitgaard (1997). One of the World Bank's leading civil service experts, Barbara Nunberg wrote "basic personnel management in many developing and transitional country administrations is in a state of collapse" and that "[m]echanisms of authority and often probity have broken down." (Nunberg 1995).

of the first adage is: "If at first you don't succeed, try something different." This book attempts to show that the orthodox strategy for building state capability in developing countries has failed, and we offer a new hypothesis for how to do things differently. Just as Edison did not invent a commercially feasible light bulb by trying the same filament ten thousand times, perhaps not just the tactics and strategies but the fundamental paradigm of how state capability is built is wrong and it is time to try again—with a different paradigm. In that case, we come to two conceptually distinct questions:[21]

- Is there a persuasive, or even plausible, explanation of why the building of state capability has generically gone so badly?
- Given where we are now today, with the global order and national outcomes as they are, do we have any idea what countries or those in public agencies or their citizens or external agents can do to help build state capability?

The rest of the book grapples with these two questions. Our hypothesis is founded in the belief that in order to build capability, we should focus on solving problems rather than importing solutions. Our theory of capability is, in a sense: "You cannot juggle without the struggle"—capability cannot simply be imported; the contextually workable wheel has to be reinvented by those who will use it. In this sense, building capability to implement is the organizational equivalent of learning a language, a sport or a musical instrument: it is acquired by doing, by persistent practice, not by imitating others.[22] Chapters 2–3 present our "techniques of successful failure" that reconcile the ongoing efforts of the current development paradigm that give the appearances of constant forward motion with the reality of the "big stuck." Chapters 4 and 5 delve more deeply into capability for policy implementation.

Our theory stems from our belief that success builds capability, and not vice versa. Institutions and organizations and state capability are the result of success—they are the consolidation and reification of successful practices. Our approach aims to produce success by solving pressing problems the society faces in ways that can be consolidated into organizations and institutions. This begins with what we call problem-driven iterative adaptation (PDIA): a process of nominating local problems, authorizing and pushing positive deviations and innovation to solve problems, iterating with feedback to identify solutions, and the eventual diffusion of solutions through horizontal and interlinked non-organizational networks. Part II (Chapters 6–10) presents our strategy for responding to failures of state capability.

---

[21] We thank Hunt Allcott for this clarity.

[22] The popular adage that one should "fake it until you make it" may work in the short run for individuals performing certain tasks, but is far from a viable strategy for building long-run capability in organizations undertaking complex and contentious tasks.

2

Looking like a state

The seduction of isomorphic mimicry

Matt, an expert in public financial management (PFM), was recently working in Mozambique. In many respects the country's progress since the end of the civil conflict two decades ago has been impressive, reflected, for example, in multiple peaceful elections and transitions in top leadership. When assessed using the donor-defined criteria of good PFM, the Public Expenditure and Financial Accountability (PEFA) assessment framework,[1] Mozambique's PFM system comes out as stronger than all African countries apart from South Africa and Mauritius. But there are some disconcerting problems. When assessed on the de jure—what is on the books—Mozambique gets a B. But when assessed on de facto—what actually happens—the ranking slips to a C. Perhaps unsurprisingly, there are many questions about the extent and quality of implementation of the new laws and systems, and of what really happens in the day-to-day functionality in the PFM system. Budget processes at the apex are strong and budget documents are exemplary, but execution largely remains a black box. Information about execution risks is poor, with deficiencies in internal controls and internal audit and in-year monitoring systems, and weak or unheard-of reporting from service delivery units and the politically powerful, high-spending state-owned enterprises. Officials in line ministries, departments, and agencies note that the new laws and systems that claim to be the solution are also part of the problem. They *look* impressive but are poorly fitted to user needs, require management capacities they do not have, and attempt to institutionalize scripts that reflect international best practice but not political and organizational realities on the ground. The impressive new PFM system garnered kudos from international actors for the ministers but was a missed opportunity to craft a system that works to solve their specific needs.[2]

Mozambique is not alone is looking good on the surface at PFM. Uganda has had its anti-corruption laws rated 99/100—on paper Uganda is the best anti-corruption country in the world. Yet Uganda is also rated as having the largest gap between law and practice and is regularly beset by corruption scandals. As it happens, the newspaper headlines on the day in 2013 all three of us arrived in Kampala for a PDIA workshop announced that the UK was canceling a large loan because of . . . corruption.

In order to articulate a persuasive alternative approach to building state capability we first need a coherent diagnosis as to why the prevailing approach is flailing. The diagnosis of the status quo must be able to not only document the lack of capability of public sector organizations (Chapters 1 and 4) but also explain how and why they have demonstrated so little improvement in the half a century or more of the development era. Building state capability has

---

[1] See Andrews (2008).   [2] See Andrews et al. (2010).

been a declared goal and yet, despite the lack of improvement, many states have maintained sufficient internal and external legitimacy that they have continued to receive domestic budget and funding from international agencies throughout this period on the pretext that they are capable of implementation and/or that improvement in capability is imminent. We refer to this combination of capability failure while maintaining at least the appearance and often the legitimacy and benefits of capability as "successful failure." This raises three key questions. What are the techniques of successful failure that allow state organizations to fail year after year and yet maintain themselves? Why are these techniques so widespread among state organizations in developing countries? And, how can these techniques that have proven successful and robust in protecting failure be subverted?

In this chapter we argue *isomorphic mimicry* is a key "technique of successful failure" that perpetuates capability traps in development (Pritchett et al. 2013). The concept of isomorphic mimicry is not new, but for present purposes our rendering draws on three existing literatures. Mimicry as a type of camouflage is widespread in the natural world, as in some environments animals can gain survival value by looking like other animals. Some moths, for example, have coloration on their wings that look like eyes; some flies look like bees and have even evolved to buzz like a bee but do not actually have stingers; the scarlet kingsnake has the same yellow, red, and black banded coloration of the deadly poisonous eastern coral snake, but without the bother of actually having venom. The sociologist John Meyer pointed to the "structural isomorphism" of nation-states in a global system (Meyer et al. 1997). Organizational theorists Paul DiMaggio and Woody Powell have emphasized isomorphism as a strategy for both public and private organizations (DiMaggio and Powell 1983).

Isomorphic mimicry conflates *form* and *function*: "looks like" substitutes for "does." Passing a labor law is counted as success even if lack of enforcement means it never changes the everyday experience of workers. A policy of agreeing to return misaddressed mail makes one appear to be a modern post office and is an achievement even if it never happens. Going through the ritualistic motions of "trainings" (Swidler and Watkins 2016) counts as success even if no one's practices actually improve. A child in school counts as success even if they don't learn anything. Appealing budget documents count even if they don't determine spending outcomes.

Isomorphic mimicry is unique to neither developing countries nor the public sector. In many ecosystems, organizations adopt "isomorphism"—looking like successful organizations—to enhance their legitimacy. Indeed, the pioneering work of DiMaggio and Powell (1983) coined the expression on the basis of their studies of aspiring private sector firms in Silicon Valley: if you want to convince venture capitalists your fledgling enterprise *is* the next

Apple, *look* like Apple. As an even partial explanation of the big stuck in state capability we cannot just invoke that organizations in developing countries utilize isomorphic mimicry as a technique; we need to explain why it is particularly virulent, pervasive, and effective in delaying progress in *state* organizations in *developing* countries.

We therefore shift the focus from the organization to the ecosystem in which organizations exist. What is it about the ecosystem in which state organizations in developing countries live that makes isomorphic mimicry so frequently an attractive, perhaps even optimal, organizational strategy to adopt? We argue there are two key features related to how systems cope with novelty. One, public sector systems are often *closed* to novelty—particularly closed to the appearance of novelty via new organizations. Two, developing country public sector systems often evaluated novelty strictly through whether the novelty aligns with agenda conformity rather than enhanced functionality. This evaluation of novelty on *agenda conformity* is particularly rife in developing countries because the global system—often with donor agencies as the vector—promotes the "transplantation of best practice" and other global agendas that distort local changes. This leads to "institutional monocropping" (Evans 2004).

We also argue that ecosystems in which isomorphic mimicry is an attractive organizational strategy can sustain capability traps because once a system is locked into a closed and agenda-conforming ecosystem and organizations, and once leaders and front-line workers have adapted to that ecosystem, the usual strategies for improvement of organizations—training, reform, generating better evidence, forcing compliance—will fail.

An Ecosystem in which Organizational Isomorphic Mimicry Is Optimal

Figure 2.1 is a schematic of an ecosystem for organizations. It has three layers: the *organization* is in the middle and is embedded in an *ecosystem* and *agents* (within which we distinguish "leaders" and "front-line workers") operate within organizations. We represent the choices of the types of agents and organizations along a spectrum.

Front-line workers (policemen, teachers, doctors, nurses, regulators, tax collectors, bureaucrats) can choose to either act entirely with pure *self-interest* (including absenteeism, corruption, abuse of power, laxity, inattention) or act with *performance orientation*. Performance orientation is when the front-line workers take the actions that promote the best purposes of the organization and can often go beyond mere compliance with formal policies and procedures. Organizations are most successful when front-line workers act with

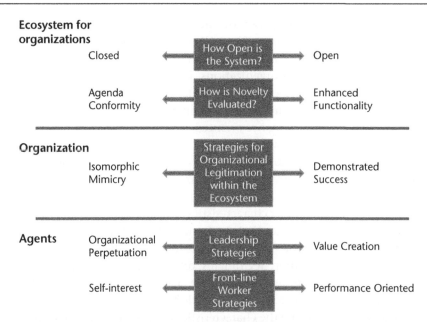

Ecosystem for organizations

Closed ←→ How Open is the System? ←→ Open

Agenda Conformity ←→ How is Novelty Evaluated? ←→ Enhanced Functionality

Organization

Isomorphic Mimicry ←→ Strategies for Organizational Legitimation within the Ecosystem ←→ Demonstrated Success

Agents

Organizational Perpetuation ←→ Leadership Strategies ←→ Value Creation

Self-interest ←→ Front-line Worker Strategies ←→ Performance Oriented

Figure 2.1. The organizational ecosystem: agents, organizations, and system

performance orientation. As we detail in Chapter 4, weak organizations cannot even induce compliance.

Leaders of organizations (and this does not just mean the head but also those in positions of authority and responsibility who constitute the leadership) can choose along a spectrum from pure *organizational perpetuation* to *public value creation*.[3] Managers of front-line workers ("leaders") can use the resources and authority over which they have responsibility to further their own purposes ("elite capture") with organizational perpetuation (which may or may not be based on performance) or to lead the organization toward higher levels of performance.

Organizations also have an array of strategies. We are not treating the organization as either completely under the control of leaders nor as a unitary actor but as an entity with independent ontological status. In an analogy with evolution, the fundamental drive of organizations is survival and we assume that key to organizational survival is *legitimacy*. (Keep in mind we are articulating a framework that encompasses organizations as varied as police forces, religious denominations, central banks, hospitals, universities, charitable NGOs as well as private sector for profit firms.) Legitimacy is integral to attracting both human and financial resources. Organizations have two

---

[3] The expression "creating public value" is the title of Moore (1995).

means of securing legitimacy: isomorphic mimicry and demonstrated success in producing outputs and outcomes. All organizations deploy some mix of these (and other) strategies in different proportion.

Note that the actions of organizations, leadership, and front-line workers work best if they are *coherent*. That is, it is difficult to maintain an organization that is an isomorphic mimic if its fundamental legitimation strategy with front-line workers is performance oriented, in part because their performance cannot be evaluated and rewarded by the organization on criteria related to performance if the organization itself does not have a strategy of achieving and demonstrating success. When organizations are mimics then internal evaluation (of both leaders and front-line) tends to revert to assessing mere compliance or, worse, worker characteristics or connections that are irrelevant (or inimical) to performance. High-performing organizations (in the public, non-profit, or private spheres) tend to be coherent on the right-hand side of Figure 2.1 (the organization legitimates on demonstrated success, leaders strive for value creation, and workers are performance oriented) and low-performing organizations coherent on the left.

The question is, what are the characteristics of ecosystems or environments in which organizations operate such that isomorphic mimicry is an attractive strategy? We discuss just two elements of such ecosystems in the following sections, namely: Is the ecosystem within which the organization exists open or closed to novelty? And, does the system evaluate an organization's novelty on the basis of demonstrated functionality or agenda conformity? We think that these two system characteristics can help explain the prevalence, persistence, and success-at-failure of isomorphic mimicry as a strategy for many state organizations in developing countries.

We use the term "novelty" (Carlile and Lakhani 2011) to avoid the positive connotation of the word "innovation." Novelty just means new and different, not necessarily better. Evolutionary-like systems have sources that generate novelty and then sources which evaluate novelty and, with more or less success, eliminate negative and proliferate positive novelty. We don't start with a presumption that "different is better"—after all, in evolution nearly all genetic mutations are harmful and organisms have ways of constantly eliminating and reducing the impact of harmful mutations.

Are Organizations Open or Closed to Novelty?

The organizational ecosystem can be closed or open to novelty via two channels: first, whether the system itself is closed or open to the entry of new organizations; and, second, whether the organizations in the space are themselves closed or open to novelty.

What often distinguishes public sector organizations is that they have a monopoly, if not on the provision of services and obligations then on the receipt of public resources for funding them. The deployment of state power to impose obligations in particular is by its nature a monopoly: a given jurisdiction can only have one army or one police force or one imposer of taxes or one arbiter of property rights or one regulator of air polluters' emissions or one court of final appeal. Monopoly-like situations arise in service provision as well. Some is due to economies of scale, such that it is only economical to have one distributor of electricity in a locality or one rail line or one set of pipes carrying water; such situations create organizations that, whether they are directly owned and operated by the state, act with the franchise of the state. Another source of closure is that in some services the public sector acts as an arbiter of value and hence is only willing to pay publicly mobilized funds for certain services. For instance, many (though not all) nation states channel public funds for primary schooling exclusively through government owned and operated schools as a means of control of the content of schooling that receives state support (Moore 2015; Pritchett and Viarengo 2015). Hence new organizations can arise providing schooling but they will not receive public funds.

In a subsystem or sector of a market economy that is open and competitive, like restaurants, the "market" provides space for new firms to emerge. The "novelty" of these new organizations is ultimately evaluated entirely functionally—by their ability to attract resources from paying clients. Success in such a sector requires either incumbents to compete successfully against novelty (and incumbents compete—through means both fair and foul—to close off the space and prevent new entrants from gaining sales) or new entrants to generate novelty within a system that is set up to reward organizations and has leaders (entrepreneurs) who can deliver it. These ecosystems create *ecological learning* or, in Schumpeter's evocative phrase, "creative destruction," in which overall productivity increases as more productive firms replace less productive firms. Open systems facilitate novelty while closed systems may be more narrowly efficient in some circumstances but are at risk of being closed to novelty.[4]

One important lesson from these competitive market ecosystems is not that private firms are all wonderfully productive and capable and effective at learning and responding to change, but in some sense the opposite: markets illustrate just how hard it is both to create a new organization that persists and how hard it is for organizations to respond to changed circumstances. In the United States, half of all new firms are gone within five years. What is even

---

[4] See the related discussion in Brafman and Beckstrom (2006) on the distinction between "spider" (centralized, closed) versus "starfish" (decentralized, open) systems.

more striking is that even successful, even dominant, firms often fail to respond to changed circumstances and shrink or go bankrupt. Peters and Waterman's (1982) management classic studied forty-three of the best-managed US private firms to draw management lessons. Many of these large firms singled out as well managed have since disappeared or gone bankrupt. In a system that lack openness to new entrants Wang Labs and Digital Equipment might still be household names and Delta Airlines might not have gone bankrupt. The US retail sector has been transformed not because the dominant firm of the 1980s (Sears) learned and successfully implemented new approaches, but because new firms have arisen from Sears to Kmart to Walmart to Amazon. Building capability without either the ecological learning embedded in entirely new entrants—or the pressure they put on incumbents—makes the dynamics of building capability more difficult.

A strategy for building state capability has to confront the vexing problem of encouraging, recognizing, and rewarding innovation in organizations that have a monopoly in the utilization of state authority and resources (for whatever reason). There should only be one police force (even though there may be many private security firms) so the openness in competitive markets cannot be harnessed, either to facilitate the introduction of novelty or to put performance pressure on the incumbent.

A second element of how open or closed a system is to novelty is whether the organizations themselves are open to novelty, in the sense of whether they have existing mechanisms of generating new ideas. All organizations have to balance "confirmatory" ("Hey, we are doing great") and "disconfirmatory" signals ("Hey, something is not going right here"): too many of the former, and problems are ignored until they become a crisis; too many of the latter, and the organization may lose internal legitimacy. Many organizations actively suppress the emergence of novelty (including new evidence about performance) as it may reveal disconfirmatory signals. When organizations are competing for internal and external legitimacy it is possible that "it pays to be ignorant" (Pritchett 2002)—that is, it can be better to limit availability of evidence by examination of performance in order to more effectively transmit confirmatory signals that all is well.

While all organizations have means to limit novelty, this can be particularly true of state organizations and bureaucracies. When a bureaucracy is understood as implementing a preset policy or program, the "authorizing environment" (Moore 1995)—the political and social context—may signal to leaders and front-line workers that their job is not to reason why. Perhaps in some instances this is indeed "optimal" as for relatively routine logistical activities such as issuing drivers' licenses achieving compliance is all organization requires; no "novelty" is needed or wanted. But this can also mean that even the leadership of state organizations do not perceive that it is their mandate to seek out novelty.

One anecdote illustrates this tendency. A friend of ours had developed and proven that a non-standard classroom technique worked to raise the reading scores of children. He then went to the top-level bureaucrat in charge of education in the jurisdiction and told him about this new approach. The response of the administrative head of the education ministry to this novelty was: "You misunderstand my job. My job is to make sure the ministry runs according to the existing rules and procedures. Implementing ways to improve learning is not my job."

Another anecdote comes with data (making it "anecdatal"?) from an attempt to do a rigorous impact evaluation of ways of improving the functioning of the police force in Rajasthan, India (Banerjee et al. 2012). The researchers were working closely with the Indian Police Service (IPS) officer who had formal authority over the police. They settled on a number of possible innovations with the goal of finding which, if implemented, would lead to improvements in measures of police effectiveness. They did the usual "treatment" and "control" groups. What they found was not the relative effectiveness of the various innovations; what they found instead is that for several innovations (like those that affected the scheduling of policemen) the extent of the "treatment" in the treatment group was exactly the same as the "treatment" in the control group: they just didn't do it. This organization was closed to (certain types of) novelty—even when the leader of their organization was demanding it.

How Is Novelty Evaluated? Agenda Conformity or Functionality

The second characteristic of the ecosystem for organizations is the way in which novelty is evaluated. If an organization proposes doing something different, how will this novelty be evaluated by the internal and external actors that provide the organization with legitimacy? One pole is that novelty is evaluated on the basis of "agenda conformity"—does it reinforce or intensify the existing agenda? The other pole is that novelty is evaluated on "enhanced functionality"—does the new way enhance the organization's ability to carry out functions of producing the outputs and outcomes that are the organization's (formal and at least ideal) purpose? This section explains the contrast of agenda conformity and enhanced functionality.

The standard "logical framework" or "theory of change" or model of any program, policy, or project is intended to be a complete, coherent, and correct causal chain from inputs to activities to outputs to outcomes. That is, if I want safer driving I can provide inputs (both financial and state authorization) to an organization to issue licenses to drive only to those who have demonstrated competence in operating a motor vehicle. These inputs lead to activities by front-line workers like carrying out specific assessments of applicants' driving skills. These activities lead to outputs—some people are legally authorized to drive and others are not. These outputs are intended to lead to an outcome of safer driving. This chain of "inputs–activities–outputs–outcomes" can be produced for any organization's purposeful activity: environmental regulation, promoting financial access, tax collection, assigning titles to land, pre-natal care, promoting the reduction in HIV, etc. The key difference between "agenda conformity" and "enhanced functionality" is whether novelty is evaluated on the near end of the chain (were more inputs spent? Were activities carried out in accordance with specified processes? Were activities "intensified"?) or the far end of the chain (were more outputs actually produced? Did those outputs actually lead to intended outcomes?).

There are several common types of agenda conformity: focus on inputs, process compliance, confusing problems and solutions, and intensification.

Inputs. The easiest thing for an organization to do is ask for more. Asking for more budget (or inputs) is a simple and clear ask that often mobilizes internal and external supporters of the organization. One might propose, for example, that all countries spend 4 percent of GDP on education, even though it cannot possibly be anyone's goal that countries spend whether it impacts students or not.

Process compliance and "control." Another common element of "agenda conformity" is novelty that will claim to increase process compliance or increase management control, like management information systems, irrespective of whether there is any evidence the processes actually are strongly related or "tightly coupled" with outputs and outcomes or not.

Relabeling problems and solutions. Defining the lack of a particular solution as the problem is a popular practice as it makes the adoption of the solution to be the solution—whether it solves any real problem or not. One could start from genuine problems in volatility of budgets over time that lead to real negative consequences for the timeliness of project execution (e.g. roads left half finished). One could then argue that *one possible* solution was a medium-term expenditure framework (MTEF). But this can easily elide into defining the budget problem not as the consequences to outputs and outcomes but as the lack of an MTEF. If that is how the problem is defined, then MTEF adoption means the problem defined as the lack of the solution is solved whether the solution solves the actual problem (an incomplete road) or not.

Intensification (or "best practice"). Another mode of agenda conformity is to adopt new inputs (e.g. computers) or trainings ("capacity building") or "upgrades" that appeal to internal constituencies, independently of their impact on outputs or outcomes. In the Solomon Islands, for example, a consortium of donors help finance the construction of an expensive state-of-the-art courthouse as a response to civil war in the early 2000s, one cause of which was deemed to be a weak criminal justice system (Allen and Dinnen 2010). The courthouse was built with local labor, sourced with local materials, completed with few setbacks, and situated to capture on-shore breezes (thereby eliminating the need for air-conditioning, thus ensuring its compliance with "green" building codes and enabling it to boast that it had a "low carbon footprint"). Such projects are a donor's delight: they comply with (even exceed) all administrative requirements, look impressive, are photogenic, please senior counterparts, and thus readily comport with demands for "clear metrics" of taxpayer money well spent. But the courthouse is used infrequently, and not two blocks from the courthouse a police station remains backlogged with hundreds of cases, most of which do not need a courthouse to reach a satisfactory resolution. The post-conflict justice concerns facing most Solomon Islanders most of the time are not those amenable to resolution via formal systems that are expensive, remote, time-consuming, and alien. As Christiana Tah, former Justice Minister in Liberia, aptly puts it,

> For these kinds of problems in post-conflict countries ... there is no quick fix, no textbook solution, no best practice; rather, there is a need for a diligent inquiry into the deep-rooted causes of specific problems that will guide the development and application of innovative, probably unique, and, hopefully, adequate solutions that are likely to endure.[5]

Ecosystems for state organizations are particularly susceptible to evaluation of novelty by agenda conformity, for several reasons. The most obvious difference is that private firms in competitive markets have a hard bottom line: if they cannot generate revenue, they cannot pay their bills. State organizations are allocated budget through political processes. Another difference is that, by being monopolies, state organizations are tasked by political processes to accomplish many different outputs and outcomes, often far more than they even ideally could (more on this in Chapter 3). As the adage goes, if an organization has more than three goals it has no goals. Also, state organizations, by being universal, must satisfy many constituencies and cannot simply be effective in one segment or niche of a market. This provides even more pressure for diffuse goals. Finally, the causal connection between the organization's actions and the outcomes is often complex and difficult to demonstrate. In these instances nearly all organizations will seek legitimation among internal and external stakeholders by agreeing upon agendas: inputs and activities, rather than promoting accountability to hard targets on outcomes.

In an organizational ecosystem that is closed (both to new entrants and to novelty itself) and/or in which novelty is evaluated on the basis of agenda conformity, often such that there is no agreed-upon, regular, and reliable reporting on outputs and outcomes, then this cascades into the behavior of organizations, leaders, and front-line workers.

Organizations optimally choose isomorphic mimicry—the pursuit of agenda-conforming reforms that reform forms and ignore function—as an

---

[5] Cited in Desai et al. (2012: 54).

organizational strategy. Leaders inside the public sector choose to administer and promote, at best, compliance with existing processes than pursue changes to enhance value. Front-line workers have a difficult time being "performance oriented" when the organization and leaders themselves cannot provide clear and coherent measures of what actions of theirs lead to the organization's vision of "performance."

Isomorphic mimicry is consistent with the observation that organizations and leaders are constantly engaged in "reforms" putatively to improve performance and yet very little performance is achieved.

Global Systems, Agenda Conformity, and Isomorphic Mimicry

The conditions for isomorphic mimicry to be widely used as a technique of successful failure that supports capability traps (ecosystems that are closed and evaluate on agenda conformity) are particularly prevalent for state organizations in developing countries. Organizations around the world are embedded both in national systems but also in a global system in which agendas are set by processes that often do not reflect the factual conditions these countries face. DiMaggio and Powell (1983, 1991) identify three types of pressures for isomorphic mimicry: "coercive" (in which external agents force isomorphism on the organization), "normative" (in which organizations adopt mimicry because it is an acknowledged "best practice"), and "mimetic" (in which organizations simply copy other organizations' practices). All three of these pressures for mimicry operate from a global system to country-level organizations and up to "structural isomorphism" (Meyer et al. 1997) in which organizations in developing countries are encouraged to adopt global agendas, "solutions," and the forms and formal apparatus of policies that are identified as "best practice"—whether they address locally nominated problems or are adapted to the local context or not. While foreign assistance agencies are often singled out as the vectors of this global system isomorphism, the underlying phenomena are deeper and hence affects countries even where donors have little presence or leverage.

Figure 2.2 is a representation of a "domain" or "sector" or "field"[6] or "movements": an area of endeavor in which there is some common purpose. This figure can be related to a type of organization (e.g. university or trade union or museum), academic disciplines (economics or electrical engineering), professions (doctors, lawyers, actuaries, architects), sectors of the economy (electricity,

---

[6] In the sense of Bourdieu (1993).

Direction of global movement setting of "themes"

Global: DFID, World Bank, UN (UNESCO, UNICEF, etc.), International Academics, Think Tanks, Commissions

Direction of national action plans

(National) Cosmopolitan: Ministers, top tier academics and think tanks, top consultants, NGOs, activists

Taking plans into actionable designs: budgets, programs, projects

National: Politicians, policy makers and advisers, academics, think tanks, heads of NGOs, top consultants, activists

Administration of implementation of budget, programs, projects (e.g. approvals, training, monitoring

District/bloc: Government officials, NGO implementers, regional elites

Front-line implementation of routine activities, programs, projects

Intersitial elites (village level): lowest tier government functionaries, grassroots implementers, activists, volunteers

Engagement with implementation (scale of passive to active)

Recipients/participants in action (e.g. citizens, members, program "beneficiaries"), mass movement base

Figure 2.2. A structure of global systems in fields of endeavor

tourism, hotels), social activism or movements (human rights, environment, religion), or domains of government endeavor (basic education, environmental regulation, public financial management). In each there are spheres of discourse, cooperation, and action, each of which can be weaker or stronger in affecting the course of events and each of which plays a typical role.

There is a "global" level, often with an identifiable apex organization or association. The global level often sets "themes"—what is on or off the global agenda in that domain. These themes change in response to changes in the world (e.g. the rise of HIV/AIDS as a disease, climate change) or changes in ideas (e.g. the shift from demographic programs to reproductive health, the shift to "independent central banks"). To be effective these themes have to be translated into action at various levels from national to local. There are national cosmopolitans—those who interact directly with the global level (and may move back and forth)—who are often responsible for translating global themes into national action plans or goals or national agendas, which can either be explicit or implicit, but still in the realm of ideas. To take these into practice national actors need to translate these ideas into policies, programs, and projects that have budgets and tasked actors with roles and responsibilities—the kinds of things that have inputs–activities–outputs–outcomes that can, in principle, be implemented. For some kinds of activities, like central banking, this is as deep as implementation needs to go. However, as we detail in Chapter 5, many activities are "transaction intensive" and require many, many actors to achieve results. This is the level below the national level (and below the state or provincial level in large nations) which can be called the "district"—which could be a city or municipality, or could be an administrative unit like a district or block. This is the level at which people are responsible for the *management* of the implementation of policies, programs, and projects. Then there are the front-line workers who are often, in the terms of Swidler and Watkins (2016), the "interstitial elites"—those with connections both at the village/local level but who have technical capacity to implement. These are policemen, engineers, teachers, nurses, officials, tax collectors, etc. who are the day-to-day implementers ("street-level bureaucrats") and interact directly with citizens in the course of their functions. Most populous of all are the citizens who are, in an ideal sense, the "recipients" or "beneficiaries" of state action.

The global actors in these systems often create themes that are accompanied by various scripts or concrete measures that define not only goals but also the desirable *forms* of action that attract legitimacy. The PEFA indicators focus developing countries on conforming to characteristics ostensibly reflecting "good international practices... critical... to achieve sound public financial management."[7] The Doing Business indicators tell the ways that governments can create a climate conductive to investment. The apex organizations in HIV/AIDs like UNAIDS created themes for addressing HIV that national commissions were expected to translate into national action plans. In domains like basic education global organizations articulate and promote goals, processes, and recommended practices.

These global pressures can be a powerful force for good, bringing into national systems both positive pressures in important areas and potentially bringing in relevant expertise. Ironically, however, global systems can also be among the drivers of capability traps in developing countries because they create and reinforce processes through which global players set agendas and constrain local experimentation. This can facilitate the perpetuation of dysfunction as organizations can gain external legitimation and support with agenda conforming mimicry.[8]

At times these global scripts have essentially closed the space for novelty in the development system, imposing narrow agendas of what constitutes acceptable change. Developing countries and organizations operating within

---

[7] See PEFA (2006: 2).

[8] Our argument at the institutional and organizational level is similar to that made by van de Walle (2001) about "structural adjustment" in Africa. He points out that engagement of governments in the process of reform—even when patently insincere on the part of governments and when reforms were not implemented—brought external legitimacy. This contributed to the puzzle of the region with the worst development outcomes having the most stable governments.

them are regularly evaluated on their compliance with these scripts, and the routine and generalized solutions they offer for establishing "good govern-ance," facilitating private sector growth, managing public finances, and more. Organizations like finance ministries or central banks gain legitimacy by agreeing to adopt such reforms, regardless of whether they offer a path toward demonstrated success in a particular context. Leaders of the organizations can further their own careers by signing off on such interventions. Their agree-ment to adopt externally mandated reforms facilitates the continued flow of external funds, which can further various public and private interests. Front-line workers ostensibly required to implement these changes are seldom part of the conversation about change, however, and thus have no incentive (or opportunity) to contribute ideas about how things could be improved.

The example of procurement reform in countries like Liberia and Afghani-stan is a good instance of this dynamic in action. PEFA indicators and United Nations models of good procurement systems tout competitive bidding as a generic solution to many procurement maladies, including corruption and value for money concerns. Competitive bidding regimes are introduced through laws, as are the creation of independent agencies, the implementa-tion of procedural rules and the introduction of transparency mechanisms. These various "inputs" are readily evaluated as "evidence" that change is in effect. Countries are rewarded for producing these inputs: with new loans, a clear path to debt forgiveness, and higher "good governance" indicator scores (which in turn may attract additional foreign investment). Government entities and vendors subjected to such mechanisms are assumed to simply comply. In these situations, the result is a top-down approach to building procurement capacity (and beyond) through which external role players impose themselves on local contexts and crowd out potential contributions local agents might make to change. These local agents have every incentive to treat reforms as signals, adopting external solutions that are not necessarily politically accepted or practically possible in the local context. Local agents have little incentive to pursue improved functionality in such settings, espe-cially when they are rewarded so handsomely for complying with externally mandated "forms" (appearances).

Global systems inhibit particularly disruptive innovations. How can genu-inely useful innovation be reliably distinguished from innovation for its own sake, or just another "best practice" imitation masquerading as an innov-ation? Personal computers, for example, completely altered the world of computing, replacing mainframes as the dominant way in which everyday computing was conducted. At the time (1980s) it was obvious that PCs were a decidedly inferior technology to the existing mainframes. As Christensen (1997) details, PCs were a *disruptive* innovation in that they were an inferior technology—one that was dismissed by engineers at the "best practice" firms as a mere toy for hobbyists. But as the PC came to meet the actual functional objectives of the vast majority of users better than mainframes, it was the "excellent" firms that were left by the wayside. Had the profession of computer engineering itself been in a position of choosing innovation, the PC could have never emerged—but markets had a space for novelty and a way of evaluating novelty so that consumers could vote with their keyboards (and dollars) for the new. Within development agencies, one hears frequent reference to the quest for "cutting edge thinking" and the importance of taking "innovative approaches," but how can such agencies enhance the likelihood that PCs (rather than just new-and-improved mainframes) will emerge?

Donors as a Vector of Isomorphic Mimicry

Isomorphic mimicry has sustained the current, third, phase in development practice. The first phase, the accumulation or "big push" phase of the 1950s and 1960s, said "Rich countries have more stuff (e.g. bridges, factories, ports) than poor countries, hence building stuff is the key to development."[9] The second phase, the policy reform or "structural adjustment" phase of the 1980s and 1990s, said: "Rich countries have good policies, hence adopting good policies is the key to development." The third, current phase, says: "Rich countries have good institutions, hence promoting good institutions is the key to development." Isomorphic mimicry was not unknown in the first two phases—a poor country could convey the allure of becoming "developed," to its citizens and to donors, by showcasing seemingly impressive new infrastructure (first phase) and notionally committing to policy reforms (second phase)—but is vastly more insidious in today's third phase, since "institutions" are as ephemeral as they are important. The processes by which "effective institutions" are realized reside in an entirely different ontological space than constructing highways, immunizing babies, or adjusting exchange rates. But if the legitimacy of development actors, and their country counterparts, depends on continued narratives of success in building "good institutions" when actually demonstrating success is problematic even in a best-case scenario, isomorphic mimicry becomes the technique by which business as usual continues.

Promoting "good institutions" has, by and large, meant attempts to transplant Weberian-styled bureaucracies (and their associated legal instruments) throughout the developing world. There is a powerful logic driving

---

[9] Romer (1993) describes this initial phase of development thinking as one preoccupied with filling "object gaps," which in turn gave way to a second phase concerned with filling "ideas gaps" (education, policies).

transplantation: If Weberian organizations underpin modern economic, administrative, and political life in high-income countries, isn't the shortest distance between two points a straight line? If we know what effective and capable state organizations look like—if indeed there is a "global best practice"—why not introduce them as soon as possible? Why reinvent the wheel?

Programmatic approaches to "good institutions" routinely conflate form and function. The form of "institutions"—from constitutions to commercial codes to agencies overseeing land administration to procurement to how schools look—is easy to transplant. Countries can adopt the legislation that establishes forms: independent central banks, outcome-based budgeting, procurement practices, public–private partnerships in electricity generation, regulation of infrastructure. Reforms are costly and consequential; if they routinely fail to deliver, then the very legitimacy of the reform process is fatally compromised. Isomorphism through the transplantation of best practice allows governments and ministries to secure their legitimacy through simply imitating those forms—rather than through functionality or proven performance. Their reform efforts enable them to "look like a state" without actually being one.

Organizations in developing countries have been required to accept such interventions for decades now. As Rodrik (2008: 100) notes, "institutional reform promoted by multilateral organizations such as the World Bank, the International Monetary Fund, or the World Trade Organization (WTO) is heavily biased toward a best-practice model. It presumes it is possible to determine a unique set of appropriate institutional arrangements ex ante, and views convergence toward those arrangements as inherently desirable." Such apparent convergence is undertaken to ensure continued legitimacy with, and support from, the international community. A common example is procurement reform: laws requiring competitive bidding are a procedure that many development organizations require their client countries to adopt in order to receive financial support. Such requirements, for instance, were among the first demands international organizations made in postwar Liberia, Afghanistan, and Sudan (Larson et al. 2013). They are intended to constrain corruption, discipline agents, and bring an air of formality and legitimacy to the way governments operate.

The conditions we allude to have characterized the politics and processes of international development since at least the 1980s, a period when government reform became an important dimension of development work. At that time, many external development organizations began tying their funds to such reforms, as well as using conditions in structural adjustment and other budget financing initiatives (e.g. "sector wide" approaches). This has made it increasingly difficult for a developing country to receive external financial assistance without committing to change their government and market structures. The commitments must be made ex ante and promise reform that is open to visible evaluation in relatively short time periods, such that external development partners have something tangible to point to when justifying the disbursement of funds. In this relationship, development partners have to accept proposed reform ideas and sign off on their attainment.

When certain forms are perceived as "best practice," their unwitting trans-plantation prevents new forms from emerging, and displaces existing modes—or, as is often the case, is justified by simply pretending they are not there at all, succumbing to "the illusion of the blank slate," as one of our colleagues aptly puts it. Ostrom (1995) tells of a World Bank financed irriga-tion scheme for which the loan documents claimed the project would bring benefits because there was no irrigation in that valley. However, when the project was delayed and there was time to do additional surveying there were in fact thirty-two existing and fully operational irrigation schemes. But since these were farmer-managed schemes not controlled by the government they were invisible to the "high modernist" reality of the World Bank and the government of Nepal. Importantly, these schemes might not have been "modern" but they were not inherently inferior. Detailed studies of the oper-ation and productivity of the irrigation schemes with modern head-works found that they were actually less productive in delivering water to system tail-enders than were farmer-managed irrigation schemes without modern infrastructure.[10] The supposed trade-off was between the technical benefits of the modern infrastructure versus the erosion (or shift) in social capital needed to underpin the modern infrastructure, but when informal was not replaced with effective formal administration the new schemes could be "lose–lose": i.e. worse at social capital *and* worse at irrigation.

A consequence of believing that form drives function is that it permits—even creates an imperative for—transplanting "best practices" from one con-text to another. Having deemed that a particular development intervention "works," especially if verified by a notionally "rigorous" methodology, too many researchers and policymakers mistakenly take this empirical claim as warrant for advising others that they too should now adopt this intervention and reasonably expect similar outcomes (Pritchett and Sandefur 2013; Woolcock 2013). Among the many difficulties with transplantation is that the organizations charged with implementing the intervention in the novel context are grounded in neither a solid internal nor an external folk culture of performance at a local level (for local services) or even at times at an elite level. It is process—the legitimacy of "the struggle" by which outcomes are attained—that matters for success, even if that success comes to be consolidated into forms

---

[10] Related work by Uphoff (1992) on irrigation schemes in Sri Lanka reached a similar conclusion.

that look very much like others. It may well be, for example, that all successful post offices have many very similar features which are driven by the nature of the task, but success is unlikely if transplantation of that form is undertaken without the struggle that creates the internal folk culture and the external performance pressure.

History versus Transplantation

We are not arguing against the superior functionality of the state organizations in developing countries. What we are arguing is that the process of *transplantation* of the forms is a counterproductive approach to achieving high capability.

The first reason is that it is the *process* of arriving at state capability, not the form, which matters for sustained functional success. Form really does not matter that much one way or the other; the same form could work in lots of contexts and many different forms could work in the same context. This is clear enough by examining so-called "universal" best practices in rich countries. Take education. The public education system in the Netherlands, for example, may appear "Weberian" from a distance, but is in fact quite different to its counterparts elsewhere in Europe and North America: it essentially funds students to attend a school of their choosing. Dutch education is not a large, centralized, service-providing line ministry as it is elsewhere in the OECD, but rather a flat organizational structure that funds a highly decentralized ecology of different educational organizations—and yet produces some of the best educational outcomes in the OECD. This system evolved idiosyncratically under particular circumstances unique to the Netherlands—which is exactly how the education systems formed in *all* the rich countries, whether or not they resulted in large, centralized systems. For present purposes we make no normative judgment as to which system is "better"; our key point is that high standards of education demonstrably can be attained by a system that varies significantly from the canonical Weberian ideal.[11] In short, a variety of institutional and organizational forms can deliver similar performance levels and identical institutional and organizational forms can give rise to diverse performance levels.

Developed countries are much more similar in their functionality than their forms. A close examination of countries with high "governance" scores (Andrews 2008) reveals that, far from having identical Weberian characteristics,

---

[11] How such a system emerged historically is crucial to understanding whether and how it can be adopted elsewhere. As such, even if the Dutch education *system* produced the highest achieving students in the world, it is far from clear that Chad and Uruguay could emulate it by importing its constituent *organizational structures*. We recognize, however, that a given state may have capabilities that are adequate for one challenge but inadequate for another.

the administrative structures that underpin such countries instead exhibit an extraordinary variety of organization forms, some of them classically Weberian but many of them significantly different (e.g. the relationship between banks and states in Japan versus the United Kingdom).[12] Again, we make this point not to attack Weberian structures per se or to celebrate alternatives just because they are different, but rather to stress that the Weberian ideal is not inherently the gold standard to which everyone should aspire and against which alternatives should be assessed. Finally, even in the most celebrated cases of Weberian effectiveness, such as Japan's Ministry of International Trade and Industry (Johnson 1982), it is not clear that its effectiveness was achieved because of, or in spite of, its "Weberian-ness."

State organizations in the developed countries occurred in a period where the global system was not providing agendas or best practice or scripts. State organizations had to struggle their way into legitimacy of control of their domains in a process that was strongly contested, not just by "special interests" but also because they were displacing local and "folk" modes of accomplishing the same objectives.[13] This led to a gradual process in which "modern" systems had to adapt and remain organically grounded in folk roots (see Carpenter 2001). The contribution of Putnam (1993) on the role of social capital in the effectiveness of certain Italian states was so powerful in part because it emphasized that even in modern states which are formally Weberian, and where social ties play no explicit role, the informal nonetheless strongly affects the functionality of the formal. Put differently, the top-down accountability systems work reasonably well largely because the social norms of folk accountability survive in practice. Moreover, while one can complain about the annoying facets of the modern bureaucracy—long queues to get your driver's license, or surly postal workers, or "red tape" of government bureaucracy—historically administrative modernism had to struggle its way into control by proving it was effective.

A Capability Trap Is a Trap

What makes a trap a trap is that one can avoid getting into it, but once in, it is difficult to get out. When the ecosystem for organizations in a given domain is closed and novelty evaluated on agenda-conformity then this creates cascading behavior of organizations, leaders, and front-line workers. Organizations adopt

---

[12] See also the classic work of Hall and Soskice (2001) on the "varieties of capitalism." Similar arguments can be made for "democracy"; there are all manner of institutional designs that constitute any given democratic country.

[13] See Hays (1959) on the progressive conservation movement in the United States.

strategies *looking like* successful organizations. Leaders seek organizational survival, continued budgets (and a peaceful life) by complying with agenda conforming standards of legitimacy. Front-line workers choose routine compliance (at best; at worst, often corruption or malfeasance) over concern for the customers and citizens they serve. Once the trap is sprung it creates self-reinforcing conditions from which it is hard to escape.

If there is no functional evaluation of performance then an organization—a schooling system, a police force, a revenue service, a procurement branch—has no means of securing its legitimacy through demonstrated performance. If it already occupies a monopoly position then it can survive (and perhaps even thrive) simply by projecting an appearance of being a functional organization by adopting "best practice" reforms. Once an ecosystem responsible for the organizational/administrative oversight is "stuck" in such a dynamic the options for an organization on its own to engage in successful reform that affects functionality become extremely limited.

Just because a tire is flat does not mean the hole is on the bottom. The diagnosis of isomorphic mimicry is meant to shift focus from the usual litany of the *proximate* symptoms that are offered to explain poor performance. An organization is like an organism and constantly faces threats to its efficacy. *Shared purpose* is an organization's immune system. Organizations born through transplantation that did not have to struggle their way into existence defending their legitimacy on the basis of functionality are creatures without an immune system. Eventually something will kill its functionality; it will fall prey to one or some of the many diseases that affect governmental organizations.

People who have weak immune systems are at risk of dying of pneumonia. But pneumonia is only the proximate cause, the weak immune system is the real cause. Consider one of the most common "illnesses" affecting the functionality of state organizations: patronage. If politicians can reward their supporters with government jobs, the pressure on organizations is powerful. If the organization's internal and external support is based on a strong performance basis and there is a strong consensus that the performance requires merit-based hiring and promotion, then the damage from a patronage politician can be resisted or minimized by that healthy organizational immune system. On the other hand, if an organization's "merit-based hiring" was based on transplantation and is merely isomorphism, then these will provide little resistance to the ubiquitous pressures for patronage. But the organization's problem wasn't patronage, it was lack of purpose-driven practices. If the organization had not succumbed to patronage, it would have died of something else. Statements that allege a country would progress if only it had less corrupt leaders and more capable and concerned civil servants miss the point. This perspective has yielded efforts to discipline agents, reduce corruption and patronage by organizational interventions such as civil service, judicial, and public finance reform that are themselves transplantations.

Capability traps persist because there is a big difference between reforming a functional organization with problems and bringing a dysfunctional organization back from the brink. An achievable absence level is 5 to 7 percent. If an organization's absences have crept up to 10 or 12 percent then there are a variety of administrative or management reforms that could bring absence down. However, in the health sector of India (remember, a country rated above average in our generic state capability measures in Chapter 1) studies show that absenteeism rates of health workers in Rajasthan and Karnataka range from 40 to 70 percent. Once dysfunction has reached this level standard reform initiatives—like introducing tighter leave policies, enhanced (biometric) monitoring of attendance, threatening to dock pay or leave time—have been shown to have either no impact, or perhaps even perverse impacts. The titles of the papers themselves suggest the degree of success: "Band-aids on a corpse" and "Deal with the Devil."

Some promise hope that new "leaders" or "change agents"—potentially dynamic individuals with skill-sets to be potential innovators and reformers—can build capability or restore functionality even when in an ecosystem where the optimal legitimacy-promoting strategy is isomorphic mimicry. However, these leaders will get pushback from above and below. Those to whom the organization is accountable will worry that, in the absence of a well-defined metric for functionality, the innovations will actually put the organization at risk. If the innovations actually "look" worse and appear to generate less organizational control (perhaps because front-line agents are given more autonomy), they can be blocked by higher authority. Even if the changes would lead to superior results there is no way to prove this without a prior agreement on the standard of functionality or public value creation—which is often precisely what is absent. From below, organizational managers and front-line workers will resist innovation because without a clear metric of functionality their optimal strategy is compliance with internal processes and procedures that frees them of potentially negative accountability. In such circumstances, the prospect and consequences of demonstrated failure for leaders vastly outweigh the gains that might accrue to attaining notional success.

This is not to say there are not pockets of success—it is that these are effervescent—small bubbles that shoot up and disappear. This leads to the phenomena illustrated in India by Kapur (2007) of a life cycle of innovations (he illustrates it with institutional success) such that at any given time there are innovations being born, innovations maturing to scale (at the local or state level) but there are also reforms petering out and ending. If the reform death rate and birth rate are similar, then there will always be a stream of reforms, but no forward progress. As long as the reforms are dependent on a particularly engaged and determined civil servant these will often disappear with the officer (for case studies of reform in India see Chand 2006).

The difficult reality is that once the "capability trap" is sprung there is no incentive—and often no possibility—for any one organization or leader or front-line agent to break out of it. Even if the space for innovation is closed, often no functional evaluation of innovation is possible because organizations systematically eliminate the possibility of their being judged against anything other than their form and their compliance with "accepted" procedures.

Moving out of the system isn't a solution either. Many dynamic leaders move outside the state sector and their own organization. But even if that organization proves locally successful, closed spaces for organizational innovation may lead to a brief localized success but with no scalable impact on the system. This can explain the contradiction between the appearance of dynamism and long-run stagnation. At any given time it may seem as if there are many promising innovations at the "pilot" stage but the systemic functional performance never improves: these "pilots" never scale as there is neither an external space for innovation nor can the externally generated innovations be internally adopted.

Development of state capability is about moving the ecological equilibrium in Figure 2.1 from the left to the right. Put differently, "modernization" is an ongoing process of discovering and encouraging which of the diverse array of context-specific institutional *forms* will lead to higher *functionality*. Characteristically, however, responses to project/policy failure (or explanations of success, for that matter) tend to focus only on individual elements of this ecology (capacity building for front-line staff, concern that rules and "best practices" are not being followed, etc.) that are "legible" to and actionable by external actors; we argue that it is the broader fitness environment of this ecology for its constituent elements that primarily shapes observed outcomes.

Finding and fitting solutions to local problems is a collective capability, acquired only through the process of trial and error. Just as individuals learn skills such as speaking a language, riding a bicycle, or playing a musical instrument by being awful before they become good, so too must organizations charged with responding to "wicked hard" problems learn how to struggle together to implement an optimal solution. Taking lots of training seminars on how to ride a bicycle is no substitute for actually sitting on it at the top of long slope, falling off multiple times on the way down, and bravely persisting until one's brain eventually figures out how to stay upright while in motion on two wheels. Similarly, while much is made of the different playing styles of top tennis professionals, their underlying stroke mechanics of service, forehand, and backhand are nearly identical. The underlying biophysics pretty much demand a very narrow range of ball-striking behavior to generate the velocity and direction desired. One size pretty much does fit all. But nevertheless (and alas) you cannot transplant Roger Federer's forehand onto your tennis game. Without your own personal struggle of training, of hitting the ball under pressure in many competitive situations, you cannot develop a high-performing forehand.

By extension, this is especially true for mediating inherently political contests, where the legitimacy of the process by which an outcome is reached is crucial; protecting the space wherein these contests take place, and ensuring that they are minimally equitable, is itself a collective capability acquired through a "good struggle."[14] Whether learning to juggle or to build an arbitration council, there are two distinct, but not mutually exclusive, reasons why you perhaps cannot "skip the struggle."

---

[14] See Adler et al. (2009).

3

Premature load bearing

Doing too much too soon

Building Paper Bridges

You could build a paper-mache bridge. Done well, this could look a lot like a real bridge, perhaps even a beautiful bridge. But if one became confused and tried to drive heavy traffic across the bridge, the bridge would soon reveal itself as not robust to pressure and will fail—quickly, spectacularly, and tragically. To cross a chasm sometimes one can use an arrow to shoot a thread across the span. With the thread pull a string, with a string pull a small rope, with a rope pull a larger rope, with a large rope pull a steel cable. Once the steel cable is fixed on both sides one can send across very heavy loads. Sending those loads on the string would have thwarted the whole process. These are examples of *premature load bearing*—putting too much weight on a structure before it is able to support it not only does not accomplish the task at hand, it sets progress back.

While perhaps little is known with certainty about how to build state capability, destroying it seems easy. Requiring organizations and institutions to perform tasks before they are actually capable of doing so can create too much pressure on the organization and its agents and lead to collapse even of what small capability might have been built. When such processes are consistently repeated, premature load bearing reinforces capability traps—by asking too much of too little too soon too often (the "four toos"), the very possibility and legitimacy of reform and capability building is compromised.

The often twinned forces of *isomorphic mimicry* and *premature load bearing* can leave countries stuck in capability traps in spite of well-meaning conscious efforts to accelerate modernization by both domestic actors ("reform champions") and external development agencies. Importing "best practices" and placing unrealistic expectations on the presumption that the level of performance and pace of change achieved elsewhere is possible everywhere, including "here," is a temptation. After all, to suggest anything less than perfection would make one seem a pessimist, an apologist for the unacceptable who doesn't want the best for others, or a profligate indulgently wasting time and money "reinventing the wheel" when the best practice solution is already known. This leads to paper-mache bridges to nowhere.

The weakness of premature load bearing becomes apparent when newly formed organizations are asked to implement the functions that similar organizations perform in rich countries—but which put them under enormous pressure immediately. There are many examples from regulation and taxation. Dubash (2008) describes the reforms that introduced an "independent regulator" to set electricity tariffs in India. Even with the transplantation of the exact legislation and organizations of the "independent" regulation of electricity from other countries, this did not produce the hoped-for results of the "independent" (in name) regulator: resisting strong political and social

Organizational capability for enforcing
tax compliance

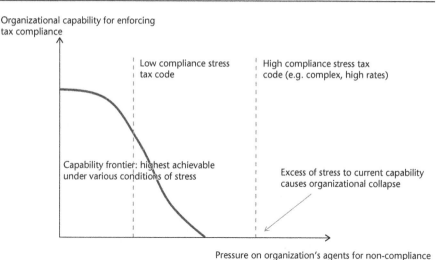

Figure 3.1. If implementation stress exceeds organizational robustness, then "premature load bearing" can lead to collapse of capability

pressures and setting higher, cost-recovering, tariffs. In hindsight, none of the background institutions, professional norms, social conditions, political history and accumulated organizational capability that made this particular package of reform successful in its original environment was present in the Indian states adopting this "global best practice."

Figure 3.1 illustrates a hypothetical case in which the existing tax code—because of its complexity, level of rates, or definition of base—creates pressures for individual tax-collecting agents to deviate from compliance that exceeds not only what the organization is capable of but the *maximum* organizational capability even if those elements under control of leadership (e.g. the "management" elements of accountability) were optimally designed. This leads to a shift from high capability to low capability from which it is hard to recover.

The weak and very weak capability states in Chapter 1—including the various "F" designations (failing, flailing, fragile)—are particularly prone to premature load bearing, as their robustness to stress is lower and they are often interacting with external actors who serve as a vector for transmitting overambition. While any description of the "typical" development effort in a fragile state loses specificity, there are common features to these efforts as they are often premised on three main notions. First, there is an implicit assumption that the country is a "blank slate" with no pre-existing state capability, or such weak capability that it can be easily replaced or subsumed. Second, there is the expectation that function will follow form, quickly. Third, the actions of the international development community are based on the same theory of change that has become familiar thus far in the book: namely, their actions are based on the transplantation of best practices with little regard to the actual capability of the organizations charged with implementing it.[1] The upshot is that aid dollars flow to the fragile state, accompanied by technical expertise from all over the world. All factors seem to be in place for a rapid rise to better living standards, for the emergence of an increasingly effective and reliable state, and for a steady convergence with the rest of the world.

Unfortunately, reality proves more stubborn than wishes. The overly optimistic expectations of the possible rate of change of state capability—coupled with institutional incentives that focus on form rather than function—lead to persistent implementation failure. When the international community and the fragile states interact, stresses get created, which, if not managed well, actually undermine state capability rather than build it. In such situations, the danger is not just that reform or the building of state capability may take longer than expected. Deepening isomorphic mimicry produces a loss of institutional integrity and coherence, which presents itself in a widening gap between the de jure and the de facto. Organizational imperatives on both sides of the equation interfere with one another in a way that deepens isomorphic mimicry, and leads to the existence of two parallel universes that no longer communicate with each other: a universe of reporting requirements declaring success but in fact only building state capability on the surface, and a universe underneath the surface in which the gap widens between form and function. The legitimacy of the system to *external* actors is increasingly derived from isomorphic mimicry but without the internal legitimacy borne of either accommodating pre-existing rules systems or demonstrating superior performance. Once a fragile state is locked in a capability trap, a change in the notional, or de jure, policy universe has little to no effect on the de facto reality, i.e. actual performance on the ground. When these incipient institutions and organizations are then put under the stress of actual implementation they are likely to collapse, leading to a worse situation than before because repeatedly failing in this way delegitimizes the very possibility of improvement. Our goal in this chapter is to elucidate some of the underlying dynamics of these troubling patterns.

---

[1] For a detailed analysis of a specific fragile state (South Sudan) in these terms, see Larson et al. (2013); on the challenges of redefining fragile states in ways that incorporate and promote metrics more readily reflecting a given country's trajectory of building state capability for implementation, see Woolcock (2014).

A Simple Vignette of Premature Load Bearing

There are various sources of premature load bearing; perhaps the most easily illustrated is when an organization is overwhelmed with the complexity of the tasks being demanded of it. Certain tasks require a vast interplay of many moving parts, which are all necessary to carry out a function effectively. Collecting tax is one such example: it requires both a capable state and an acceptance by the population that this is a legitimate role of the state. The now-wealthy countries built this capability slowly, but developing countries are expected to quickly acquire the capability to conduct this task, despite the fact that such tasks are complex and often contentious.

The number, scope, scale, and expected quality of the tasks a government is expected to perform have increased tremendously over time, and post-conflict countries have frequently failed to keep up. Needless to say, to begin implementing all these complex tasks all at once—and in particular in a post-conflict setting suffering from asymmetrical power dynamics and insecurity—is not easy. Beyond the complexity, there is the critical budgetary constraint to consider. Poor country governments are expected to perform this multitude of state tasks despite the fact that they are, well, poor. Almost by definition, these governments have far less government revenue per capita at their disposal than do industrialized countries. This creates obvious limitations for what a poor-country government can realistically be expected to do.

As Thomas (2015) shows, however, the external actors' expectations of the range and magnitude of what governments can do seems to be based on those of a state capable of massive revenue mobilization. But a country like Afghanistan has only about $10 per year to spend on its citizens, as compared to the $17,554 the US has available. Including aid flows this number increases in Afghanistan to $105, but this is obviously not a "sustainable" source of revenue. And even if Afghanistan could manage to obtain $105 from domestic sources, this would still only bring it up to the level of India, which is still a factor of 175 lower than the US—and a factor of 5 lower than the US at the turn of the twentieth century (i.e. well over a century ago, when it was at the level of development of today's middle-income countries)—see Table 3.1.

Thomas (2015) argues that in light of these figures it is impossible to expect Afghanistan to build effective and universal-access institutions across the range of domains that it is currently expected to do, as articulated in various plans and strategy documents. A similar argument will hold up for many, if not all, post-conflict countries.

It is thus easy to imagine how premature load bearing can have disastrous effects on the capabilities of a fragile state. As an example, consider Box 3.1 and the case of land registration in Afghanistan—just one of the many tasks expected of this supremely overburdened fragile state.

Table 3.1. Revenue per capita for various governments and time periods, in US$ (not PPP)

Country	Government revenue per capita (including aid where applicable) in 2006	Ratio of US government revenues per capita in 1902 to countries in 2006 (constant dollars)
Nicaragua	204	2.6
India	102	5.2
Uganda	120	4.4
Tajikistan	60	8.8
Niger	67	7.9
Afghanistan	105	5.0

Source: Adapted from Thomas (2009), table 4. Government revenues per capita in 1902 were US$526 in 2006 prices (but not adjusted for PPP)

Box 3.1. LAND REGISTRATION IN AFGHANISTAN, THE FUTURE IS THE PAST

The Afghanistan National Development Strategy has two expected outcomes for land registration under the "governance, rule of law and human rights" pillar:

(1) Mapping of villages and gozars (neighborhoods) and reviewing their boundaries. Target: *by Jaddi 1388 (end-2009), the government will carry out political and administrative mapping of the country with villages and gozars as the basic units and the political and administrative maps will be made available at all levels for the purpose of the elections, socioeconomic planning and implementation of subnational governance policy.*

(2) Modern land administration system established.
Target: *a community-based process for registration of land in all administrative units and the registration of titles will be started for all urban areas and rural areas by Jaddi 1397 (end-2008).*

A quick retrospective shows that the establishment of a land registration system has been attempted before. In 1963 a Department for Cadastral Survey was established in Kabul with USAID funds, and a cadastral survey was initiated in 1966. The process leaned heavily on US support, and its costs were enormous. By 1977 around 45 percent of landowners had been surveyed, and only one-fifth of total arable land had been covered. Not a single title deed was issued. Eventually, in 1977, the process was disrupted by the onset of the revolution.

Gaining Normative Traction (Or, Decoupling de jure and de facto)

The application of "best practices" in low capability environments leads to a decoupling process in which the notional practice (de jure) and actual practice (de facto) diverge, resulting in a loss of what we call "normative traction." A metaphor to illustrate this concept is the image of pulling a brick with a rubber band; one can drag the brick in spurts, but the rubber band is too weak

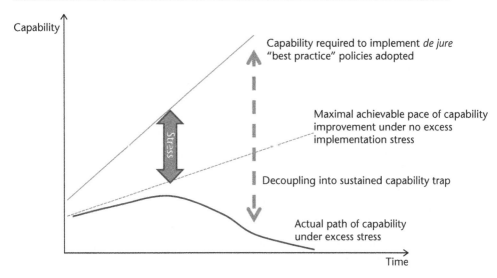

Figure 3.2. Wishful thinking about the feasible pace of improvement in capability can cause implementation stresses that undermine capability and sustain capability traps
Source: Authors

to lift it, and will eventually snap if stressed too far. A reform process gains normative traction when the de jure and de facto practices begin to steadily align. If this cannot happen, an overly optimistic perspective on the level and possible pace of creating state capability amounts to wishful thinking: an organization is overloaded with tasks it cannot perform, and as such the temptation is strong to retreat behind a façade of isomorphic mimicry to justify one's actions and to sustain the flow of resources. Continued over time, this process will eventually reach a point where the de jure ceases having any normative traction on the de facto: any changes made in notional policy will no longer have any real effect on the ground, because the connection between the two realms is completely severed. (See Figure 3.2.)

To illustrate how this process unfolds, consider two examples from the economic realm—each illustrating the deterioration of capability as stress increases.

Example 1: Tariff Rates

An old example comes from customs data, in which the tariff line item is compared to the *ad valorem* official tariff rate and the actual collected rate—the ratio of tariff collected to reported import value. In both Kenya and Pakistan the collected rate increased with the official tariff (not one for one, but did increase) up to a point around 60 percent, after which the collected rate

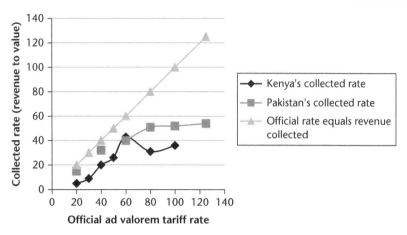

Figure 3.3. When official tariff rates passed a threshold, collections stopped increasing
Source: Adapted from Pritchett and Sethi (1994: table 2)

stopped increasing. After that point, further increases in the tariff just increased the discrepancy between the official rate and collected rate—even in the officially reported data. Including the categories of mis-declaration, under-invoicing, and outright smuggling would almost certainly lead to an even more dramatic deterioration in the collected rate. In this case the stress is obvious, as the tariff rate increases the amount an importer will pay to evade the tariff increases and hence the potential temptations for customs officials to deviate increases. (Of course, these considerations, among others, eventually led countries to reduce tariffs as in many countries they were simply uncollectible.) (See Figure 3.3.)

Example 2: Doing Business vs. Enterprise Survey, de jure vs. de facto

A second example is the comparison of "official" times for how long it would take to comply with various regulations—such as getting a license to operate a business, or to get goods through customs, or to get a construction permit—with how long firms themselves say these procedures *actually* take.

There are two different ways in which the "investment climate" has been measured. The first is via the Doing Business survey, which measures (among many other things) how long it would take the typical firm to get a typical construction permit in practice if they followed the law. This is intended to measure not the worst it could possibly be, but asks local researchers and consultants to estimate typical times if firms followed the existing regulatory procedures—and did not, for instance, hire an agent. In other words, the "Doing Business" surveys record the de jure regulations. The second primary

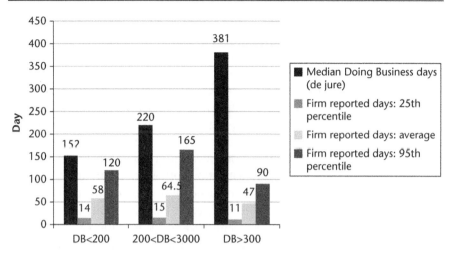

Figure 3.4. In countries with very high official regulatory times to get construction permits, firms actually report taking *less* time to get permits

Source: Author's calculations from data as reported in Hallward-Driemeier and Pritchett (2015)

source for assessing the investment climate is Enterprise Surveys, which just ask firms how long the process actually took for them. The Enterprise Surveys asked firms who recently received construction permits how long it took to get them. For sixty-three countries there is enough data (both a Doing Business measure, and more than twenty firms answering the survey question about a construction permit) to compare the two. Figure 3.4 shows the results comparing countries with different formal measures of regulatory stringency—those with fewer than 200 days, those with 200 to 300 days, and those with more than 300 days (as reported in Doing Business).

There are two striking things about Figure 3.4. First, the quarter of the firms who report the fastest actual times report that it takes about ten to fifteen days, no matter what the Doing Business survey data says the law says. All that grows as the legal compliance times grow is the gap between the legal compliance times and the fast firms' reported times: no matter whether the DB reported days is 100, 200, 300, or 400, there is a set of firms that report no trouble at all getting a permit. Second, the actual reported times—at all points of the distribution of firm responses—to get a permit are lowest in the countries with the most stringent regulations. In countries where Doing Business data says it takes more than 300 days the average reported time was 47 days—lower than the average of 58 days in countries where the regulations were fewer than 200 days. Hallward-Driemeier and Pritchett (2015) argue that once regulations pass the threshold that the country can enforce, the legal and actual compliance times become completely unlinked. In effect, asking about the "investment climate" for firms in countries with weak implementation is like asking what the temperature a person is experiencing when everyone has air-conditioning—it does not matter what the outdoor thermometer says, the temperature is what the indoor thermostat is set at.

While there are obviously a number of ways to interpret this figure, one such interpretation is that when de jure regulations exceed the organization's maximum capability, compliance simply breaks down and outcomes are deal by deal. Once a policy-implementing organization has passed the threshold into collapse, all else is irrelevant. Who wants rules when they can have deals? As such, a first lesson is that putting organizations (whose capability depends at least in part on the background institutions on which it can draw to create accountability on the one hand and intrinsic motivation on the other) under duress before they have developed sufficient capability—not just apparent capability but also robustness to pressure—is a recipe for disaster.

The developing world is in fact now riddled with agencies that have been delegated the responsibility for implementing policy regulations in which the de jure policy and the stated organizational objectives have no normative or positive traction on the behavior of the agents of the organization. While this is perhaps a good thing if the policies themselves are overly restrictive, organizational disability spills over into capability to enforce even desirable regulation.

The Role of External Actors in Organizational Failure

By starting off with unrealistic expectations of the range, complexity, scale, and speed with which organizational capability can be built, external actors set both themselves and (more importantly) the governments they are attempting to assist up to fail. This failure relative to expectations (even when there is positive progress) can lead to erosion of legitimacy and trust, both externally and internally. We will argue that these unrealistic expectations are not merely creating a dynamic of perpetual disappointment, but that there are genuine dangers involved which go way beyond simply not reaching one's goal.

The difficulty is that the de jure can be created with the stroke of a pen—countries can adopt sound policies, create "modern" organizational charts, pass impressive legislation, announce noble "plans." These de jure changes can create the appearance of a positive reform dynamic that is pleasing to external actors and domestic constituencies, but the creation of de jure without a genuine capability to implement creates parallel universes within the organization. One universe is inhabited by a small number of well-educated, often English-speaking individuals, those that "have capacity," who engage actively with a large number of foreign consultants and other forms of technical assistance, and know how to tick various donor boxes. The other

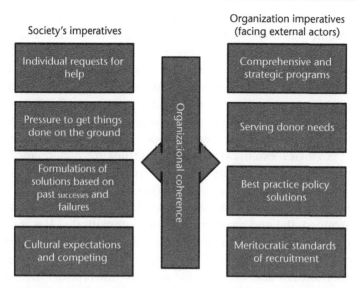

Figure 3.5. Tensions between imperatives of internal and external actors threaten organizational coherence

universe is inhabited by the remaining civil servants, which constitute the vast majority and in particular the front-line agents—those who are in direct contact with the citizens who are continually making demands for real solutions to their real problems. Over time, this logic widens the gap between the demands of domestic society and the demands generated by the internal imperatives of development agencies: the upper-level leaders of governmental organizations become embedded in different value systems than the citizenry, which manifests in various (potentially conflicting) tensions. (See Figure 3.5.)

The internal tensions between the front-line agents and the upper level leaders of the organization creates a situation in which the group of front-line agents, stigmatized as "lacking capacity," becomes increasingly disgruntled and disengaged from the international community, and steadily disassociates themselves from the efforts conducted by the upper layers. They become ever less inclined to carry out the tasks assigned to them by the upper layer—if these tasks were even assigned to them in a comprehensible manner in the first place—or to follow the organizational behavioral norms underpinning them. The temptation for these agents to pursue their own interests (as opposed to those of the organization) thus increases, and the gap widens between what the organization notionally aspires to and what it can actually implement.

In such circumstances, the organization comes under increasing stress and finds itself in a downward spiral toward a severe loss of institutional integrity. Since the organization needs legitimacy for its survival it will need to pretend that it is still functioning. Coercive, normative, and mimetic forms of iso-morphic mimicry all become engaged; the organization will continue to create the illusion of being a capable organization through adopting the outward forms of a capable organization, with little regard for the actual functionality of the organization. The organization survives, but the price it pays is a severe loss in organizational coherence and a subsequent fall in real capability to deliver.

The institutional imperatives of many large development institutions con-tinue to reflect high-modernist mental models, in spite of a changing rhetoric on paper. As a logical extension of this way of thinking, performance tends to be measured in terms of inputs or output indicators—which reflects form, rather than outcomes that can reflect function. There is an automatic assump-tion that when the inputs have been entered, the outputs achieved and the "form" obtained, the end results will follow automatically. Has the strategy document been written? Has the organization been restructured? Have the consultation workshops been held? Have the training and "capacity building" sessions for front-line staff been conducted? Have the procurement rules been faithfully followed? This perspective is heavily biased against implementa-tion, as there are few checks and balances in place to ensure that the policy change has actually been implemented on the ground. In other words, it is quite possible to get away with ticking the donor boxes without the policy change ever reaching the ground. As such, the international aid community itself suffers from—and reinforces—isomorphic mimicry, where ticking the boxes fulfills its need for sustaining its own legitimacy.

There is therefore a genuine risk that the engagement of the international community creates a deepening of the pattern of isomorphic mimicry, and a further loss of institutional integrity. Rather than strengthening the capability of the state—the goal the policies clearly aim to achieve—these well-intended efforts may actually backfire and reduce the capability of the administration. It may be that the more rapidly the appearances presented must conform entirely with "modern" rules systems—in order to garner legitimacy from external actors—the more quickly it will diverge from reality. To illustrate this process with a real-world example, let's return to Afghanistan.

Example 3: Meritocratic Reform in Afghanistan

One particularly painful example of this tension can be found in the "merito-cratic" standards of recruitment that are the foundation of Public Sector Reform. Meritocracy is premised on the notion that all individuals should have equal opportunity and that preferential treatment of individuals on criteria deemed to be "morally irrelevant" (Roemer 1998)—such as gender, ethnicity, or kinship—is unjustifiable. But these are a particular set of values, acquired gradually over time through an organic political and social process.

Box 3.2. APPLYING MERITOCRATIC STANDARDS IN AFGHANISTAN

The Ministry of Public Health in Afghanistan is generally seen as a poster child for public sector reform and capacity building. However, problems remain and are related to the political economy of change, and its lack of social fit with individuals' and society's expectations. The following concerns were identified:

- The overall lack of political commitment to the reform process.
- The corruption of the Lateral Entry Programme. Some individuals have allegedly been hiring their friends and relatives through this program.
- The continued role of patronage networks. Effects of this have included the resignation of a qualified staff member brought in through the priority reform and restructuring (PRR) process who did not have the necessary support from powerful people within the ministry.
- The continued training and "capacity building" of individuals who are never going to have the capacity to carry out their jobs adequately.
- The growth of some departments as a result of PRR beyond the extent planned. This is caused by continued pressures to hire unqualified staff, or, in the absence of a severance package, by the need to accommodate those who did not successfully compete for a PRR post.

Source: Lister (2006)

For agents within organizations with a different internal logic, to apply meritocratic principles is not easy as it can be incompatible with the existing normative underpinnings of many societies, particularly when the stakes are high—e.g. when government jobs are at a premium. Afghanistan is again a case in point.

The difficult point is that meritocratic standards are a worthy goal—just not one that can be achieved immediately by declaring it so. We have no road map on how to get from a system based on patronage and kin-based loyalty systems to a system premised on universal rules and equal access. One might think the "donor community" would learn to not attempt premature load bearing in fragile states from the experience in Afghanistan (and elsewhere). But in the new state of South Sudan, a "South Sudan Development Plan" was issued in August 2011 one month after the country was born into independence with essentially zero capability. The plan bore all the hallmarks of donor-driven premature load bearing: a document 413 pages long with "objectives" in governance like "zero tolerance" for corruption (an objective not achieved by any of its neighbors), and for the "public administration" component of the governance pillar, goals such as to:

- Ensure a strong public administration through the enactment of just and effective laws and the development of responsive and inclusive policies, based on transparent processes and credible information and knowledge.

- Enhance the systems, structures and mechanisms of coordination at (and between) all levels of government to promote professional, ethical, and efficient service delivery to all the people.

- Strengthen and sustain the capacity of oversight institutions to enhance accountable and transparent public administration through effective monitoring, evaluation, and verification.

And this in a "plan" that was intended to run only until 2013. But it wasn't really a plan; it was a paean to premature load bearing.

Robustness to Stress: From Spartans to Paper Tigers

The battle of Thermopylae, at which a small force of Spartans (and others) held off a massive invading force from Persia, fighting to the last man, resonates through the ages. It is remarkable that a relatively obscure battle over 2,000 years ago has inspired various Hollywood movies (including a spoof). There are of course a variety of reasons why this battle is so famous, but the reason we want to focus on it is that the Spartans illustrate the robustness of organizational capability for policy implementation to countervailing pressures.

Ideal Actions vs. Real-World Actions

To begin, we need a definition of organizational capability that includes a notion of organizational robustness to stress. As we've noted elsewhere in this book, the first important distinction to make is that the *individual capacity* of the agents is one, but only one, element of *organizational capability*. All public sector organizations—ministries of education, police forces, militaries, central banks, tax collection agencies—have *stated* objectives. One can define their organizational capability as the extent to which the agents of the organization, both management and front-line agents, undertake the actions which would, contingent on their maximum individual capabilities, pursue the organization's objectives. For instance, a hospital's maximum capability might be limited by the technical knowledge of its nurses and doctors.

The second important distinction is stress, or how well the organization actually performs in "real-world" conditions. As we all know, there is many a slip twixt the cup and the lip; in fact, agents have their own interests, goals, and objectives—and agents choose their actions to pursue those objectives. This is not to say those objectives are exclusively or even primarily pecuniary, as intrinsic motivation or commitments to professional identities or normative desires to help their comrades or not "lose face" (or "honor") certainly play important roles. But there are pressures on agents to pursue other objectives and these can be less or greater. Let us now illustrate these with a military analogy.

Spartans, Keystone Cops, and Paper Tigers

An intuitive example of these two dimensions of organizational capability and stress is to think of armies as an organization. A reasonable measure of their organizational capability is their ability to inflict damage. One can imagine how large this capability would be if the army itself were under no countervailing battlefield pressure and every agent (from officers down) were operating at their maximum individual capacity. This might be larger or smaller depending on the size of the force, the equipment at their disposal, the level of training, experience, etc. But every military leader knows that this definition of organizational capability is irrelevant. The more important question is the *robustness* of that capability to pressure from the opponent. How quickly does the ability of a fighting force to act to inflict damage on the capability of the opponent degrade under actual battlefield conditions?

The US Marine Corps official doctrine *Warfighting* (1997) is publicly available and makes for interesting reading. For the US Marines, "war is an interactive social process" in which one force attempts to impose its will on the other; hence the overwhelming emphasis of their war-fighting doctrine is not destroying the opposing force in material terms (casualties or equipment) but destroying the opposing force's *will to fight*.[2] Their goal is to sufficiently disrupt the opposing forces' organizational coherence such that its individual agents cease to act as a coherent purposive body and instead pursue their own immediate interests; in so doing, the organizational capability of the opposing forces, even with huge numbers of personnel and massive equipment, disintegrates, in effect turning the opposing *army*—a social organization capable of directed action—into a mob of individuals.[3]

One element of this process, and which makes military history fascinating, is that the process is sharply non-linear. That is, in battlefield situations the degradation of organizational capability often does not follow a linear process

---

[2] None of this is particularly original as these are the ideas of B. Liddell Hart, transmuted into the German Army's application of *blitzkrieg* in which the deep penetration of rapidly moving armored units sufficiently disrupts the ability of the opposing army to respond such that the capability of the opposing army disappears, often with small casualties or materiel loss. The German conquest of France in World War II is perhaps the paradigm example. The broad review of the history of military strategy provided by Freedman (2013) is also consistent with our story—as is, more narrowly, the oft-cited conclusion of Helmuth von Moltke, head of the Prussian army in the late nineteenth century: "No battle plan ever survives first contact with the enemy."

[3] Using the example of an army is hardly original; Wilson's classic *Bureaucracy* (1989), for example, opens with a martial example.

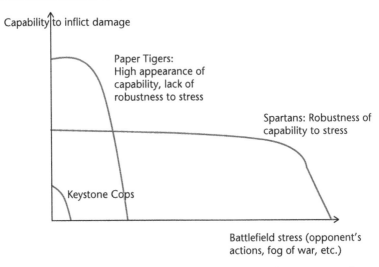

Figure 3.6. Armies illustrate the notion of the robustness of organizational capability to stress

in which incremental units of battlefield pressure yield constant units of degradation of capability. At least at times a small action can cause a ripple effect in which soldiers believe their position is untenable, lose the will to defend it, and a battle becomes a rout (or conversely, a single action prevents the loss of a position that would cause a rout).

These considerations of the robustness of organizational capability with respect to pressure and potentially non-linear dynamics lead to Figure 3.6, which, building on Figure 3.1, contrasts three paradigm cases: Spartans, Paper Tigers, and Keystone Cops. The Keystone Cops were a staple of early silent film comedies; they were a platoon of policemen who, with great fanfare and flurry of activity, would rush around completely incompetently. This is an example of an organization (or disorganization) which even under ideal conditions is incapable of accomplishing anything and hence has low organizational capability over all ranges of pressure. But the Keystone Cops wear uniforms, carry batons, and engage in various policeman-like practices that, on the surface at least, enable them to pass as real police officers.

A contrast to the Keystone Cops is a Paper Tiger. The term "Paper Tiger" refers to an army that appears impressive on the parade ground but is not robust to stress and collapses under even modest battlefield stress. It has trained people with the *individual capacity* to, in principle, recognize states of the world and respond to them. It has the materials with which to work and has, again at least in principle, modes of command and control of the organization that allow it to operate. But, when put under battlefield stress, the capability collapses as the individuals cease to pursue the organization's interests; the organizational integrity and coherence necessary for capability disappears, and a large army that looks fantastic in parades becomes a mob on the battlefield.[4]

This brings us back to the Spartans. Part of the point of Spartan training (indeed Spartan society itself) was to create individuals with high capacity (i.e. who knew how to execute the individual skills) but another part—a part of all military training—was devoted to maintaining that capability as an organization even under the greatest duress: when the actions of the individual put their lives at risk in order to maintain the overall organizational integrity and coherence. The Spartans may have had low total capability but were capable of performing under conditions in which each individual member continues to perform, even when in great personal danger.

Figure 3.6 illustrates this. On the vertical axis is an army's ability to inflict damage on an enemy. Between the three types of army, there is sharp non-linearity of collapse—which can be modeled as a variety of interactive organizational dynamics—at the various points of stress indicated.

These tensions between building capability and stress play out in real time in war. Two examples. When America declared it was entering World War I, England and France were overjoyed; they had suffered horrific rates of casualties for too long. However, the American general in charge of bringing America into the war, John Jay Pershing, wanted to end World War I with a capable *American* army. This created enormous tension with the British and French commanders, who of course wanted relief immediately and as such demanded that the American soldiers come into the existing armies under British and French command. General Pershing, however, knew this would not build a capable American army; he knew that putting fresh American-commanded units under battlefield stress against the battle-hardened German troops could easily lead to premature load bearing and collapse. So, neither side wanted American troops as integrated units under American command too soon, but the British and French wanted to use troops soon to augment the existing capability of their armies while Pershing wanted a capable American army. Pershing's stubbornness led to many more casualties for the British and French as they held the lines waiting, but did lead to a capable US Army.

Similar pressures were present in training air forces at various stages of World War II for both the UK and Japan. Churchill famously praised the Royal Air Force, declaring that "Never in the field of human conflict was so much owed by so many to so few." This raises the question: why were the few

---

[4] A similar phenomenon plays out in team sports. In Australia, for example, elite athletes and coaches often refer dismissively to "flat-track bullies": those individuals and teams who appear intimidating and can perform wonders at training but whose performance falls away rapidly once the demands of a serious, actual contest unfolds.

so few? It is not for lack of volunteers but rather because it takes time to build pilot capacity. Sending pilots into conflict too soon produces a rate of casualties so high that no amount of training of new pilots can keep up. The Japanese, of course, addressed this problem in the last desperate days of their war effort by creating kamikaze pilots with a specialized one-way mission that achieved immediate impact at the expense of future capability.

All of this discussion of militaries is in part relevant, because militaries are large public sector organizations given responsibility for aspects of high-stakes policy implementation (i.e. maintaining national security). But primarily they serve as a useful analogy of more general issues that affect all elements of policy implementation, from direct service provision (e.g. education, health, agricultural extension) to "obligation imposition" (e.g. policing, tax collection) to the implementation of economic policies from the macro (e.g. central banks) to the micro (e.g. prudential regulation).

Failure and "Big Development"

It is alarming that these forces of isomorphic mimicry and premature load bearing can lead so drastically to organizational failure; and it is disturbing that the international aid community often contributes to such processes. But what happens when a development project obviously fails? What is the response of development agencies to such issues of implementation failure and loss of capability?

Providing answers to these questions requires an examination of how responses to failure, as and when it occurs, are pursued within the prevailing development architecture. When policies or programs fail because of implementation failure, there are many seemingly good response options that are actually bad (because they do not change the underlying systemic failure; indeed, they may perpetuate it):

1. *Adopt a "better" policy.* One obvious response to failure is to assume that the reason for failure was that the policy, even if it had been faithfully implemented, would not have accomplished the objective anyway and hence failure requires a new policy. However, even if the new policy is *demonstrably* better—in the sense that when implemented it leads to better outcomes—if it is equally (or more) organizationally stress-inducing in implementation, this will lead, after a number of intervening years, to further failure.

2. *Engage in "capacity building."* One attractive and obvious response to policy implementation failure is to assume that the problem was that the individual implementing agents lacked "capacity," in the sense that

they could not have implemented the policy even had they wanted to. This is nearly always plausible, as policy implementation requires agents to successfully recognize states of the world and to know what to do in each instance (e.g. a nurse mandated to do community nutrition outreach has to be able to recognize a variety of symptoms and know which to treat, inform parents about how they should respond, which symptoms need referral to a doctor). What could be a more obvious response of public sector failure in (say) health, education, procurement, policing, regulation, or justice than to "train" health workers, teachers, procurement officers, policemen, regulators, lawyers—particularly as it will be demonstrably the case that "ideal capability" (i.e. the organizational capability if all individuals worked to capacity) is low?[5] However, if the organization is under excessive stress due to the attempt to implement over-ambitious policies, the achievable increments to ideal capability may neither (a) augment the "robustness" of the organization and hence be irrelevant in practice, nor (b) shift the entire capacity frontier outward far enough to actually avoid the low-level equilibrium. (In Figure 3.6 even substantial outward shifts in the "low" capability case would still lead to the equilibrium of zero implementation.)

3. *Cocoon particular projects/programs/sectors.* Another reaction to implementation failure, particularly when external assistance agencies (whether donors or NGOs) are involved, is to ensure "their" project succeeds in a low capability environment by creating parallel systems. These parallel systems come in many varieties, from project implementation units to "bottom up" channels in which funds are provided directly to "communities." The common difficulty with cocooning is that there is often no coherent plan as to how the cocooned success will scale to become (or replace) the routine practice. In fact, the cocooned implementation modes are often so resource intensive (in either scarce human capital resources "donated" by NGOs or financial resources) that they are not scalable. Again, cocooning can be a valuable technique of persistent failure—one can have long strings of demonstrably successful individual projects while a sector itself never improves.

4. *Throw more resources into it.* It is easy to see how isomorphic mimicry and premature load bearing make a powerful partnership. When governments are carrying out necessary and desirable goals (e.g. building roads, educating children, maintaining law and order) *and* are doing so by pursuing demonstrably successful policies (i.e. policies whose

---

[5] Moreover, as the development saying goes, "A project that gives a man a fish feeds him for a day, but a project to teach a man to fish lets you give your friend the technical assistance contract."

effectiveness as a mapping from inputs to outcomes has been shown to achieve results when implemented somewhere) *and* are doing so through isomorphic organizational structures (e.g. police forces or education ministries whose organizational charts and de jure operational manuals are identical to those in functional countries), then doubling down the bet seems the only viable strategy. After all, this is *known* to work: it works in Denmark. Because most places with low state capability also have low productivity and hence governments are working with few resources, it is hard to not believe that simply applying more resources to achieve good goals by implementing good policies through good organizations is not the obvious, if not only, strategy.

Not only are there many good bad response options but some potentially good options are bad options, on the part of both clients and donors.[6]

- Scaling policies to the available implementation capability is often professionally and normatively unattractive (i.e. scaling to the level of a given system's prevailing capability to implement could be, or appear to be, highly condescending, patronizing, and insulting if that level is actually embarrassingly low).

- Expanding capability in ways that are perhaps more "robust" but which do not expand the "ideal" are often decidedly unattractive to development actors who prefer options that are "modern," "cutting edge," and technically "state of the art."

- Attacking organizational failure is unattractive, as once an organization's goals have been inverted to rent collection these are often subsequently capitalized into the political system in ways that eliminate potential constituencies for organizational "reform."

As techniques that can both produce and allow persistent failure, the dangers of isomorphic mimicry and premature load bearing are pervasive precisely because they are attractive to domestic reformers. But, paradoxically, as already noted, external agents, whose presence is justified by the need to promote (and fund) progress, also play a strong role in generating and sustaining failure. Development agencies, both multilateral and bilateral, have very strong proclivities toward promoting isomorphic mimicry—e.g. encouraging governments to adopt the right policies and organization charts and to

---

[6] Some of these issues were addressed in Chapter 1. See also Banerjee et al. (2008), who demonstrate the resilience of deep organizational failure in attempts to enhance the performance of nurses in Rajasthan. What is striking about these examples is that they all come from India, which is, on average across the four indicators we use of "state capability," in the upper tier of developing countries.

pursue "best practice" reforms—without actually creating the conditions in which true novelty can emerge, be evaluated, and scaled. It is much more attractive for donors to measure their success as either inputs provided, training sessions held, or "reforms" undertaken and in process compliance in project implementation; all of these are laudable activities that can be readily justified and attractively presented at year's end, yet can lead to zero actual improvement in a system's demonstrated performance.

The logic of the broader structures of the international aid architecture and the core incentives faced by staff of the major development organizations, however, largely conspire against local innovation and context-specific engagement. This system instead rewards those who manage large portfolios with minimal fuss (actual accomplishment of objectives being a second-order consideration), is resistant to rigorous evaluation (since such an exercise may empirically document outright failure, which cannot be ignored) and focuses primarily on measuring clear, material inputs (as opposed to performance outcomes). Moreover, the more difficult the country context and the more ambiguous the appropriate policy response, the stronger the incentive to legitimize one's actions—to clients, colleagues, and superiors—by deferring to what others deem to be "best practices" and to assess one's performance in accordance with measurable "indicators," which again tend to be inputs (since, unlike outcomes, those can be controlled, managed, and predicted in relatively unproblematic ways). Given that virtually all developing country contexts are, almost by definition, "complex" and facing all manner of "needs," the systemic incentive to identify "proven solutions" and universal "tool kits" is powerful; those who can provide them (or claim to provide them)—from microfinance and conditional cash transfers to malaria nets and "property rights"—are development's stars.

What to Do? Navigating the Second Jump Across the Chasm

So what is the prognosis for states stuck in a capability trap? Clearly, the standard responses of large development agencies to the failures caused by isomorphic mimicry and premature load bearing do not counteract the negative trajectory of these pernicious processes. Unfortunately, the even more worrisome problem with premature load bearing is that it may be more difficult to fix an organization once broken than to build it from scratch. In the debate over the transition in the post-Soviet era there was a saying used to justify "shock therapy" approaches: "You cannot cross a chasm in two small jumps."[7] If your first jump fails, the second jump is from the bottom of the chasm and your legs are broken.

Hence, whatever the explanation for why the first jump failed, a second jump is different. Models of capability building that may have been correct strategies for implementing first jumps are not applicable to second jumps. To the extent that state capability completely (or nearly) collapsed (as in Liberia or Afghanistan or DRC or Somalia or Haiti) or had been sharply retrogressing from moderate levels (as the data on "Quality of Government" suggest of Pakistan or Kenya or Venezuela) or is merely stuck at a low rate of either retrogression or progression (or a mix) or a moderate level of capacity (as appears to be the case in, say, India), these are all "second jump" situations.

As organizations slip out of de jure control, agents consolidate around a new set of norms and practices. Society's expectations of the behavior of the administration will alter as new behavioral patterns are created. The difficulty of the second jump at the chasm in building state capability is that with failure on the first jump one can end up in a situation in which "things fall apart" (in Achebe's resonant phrase; see also Bates 2008), and while the previous systems of folk accountability and folk norms are eroded they are not replaced with strong systems of external thin accountability or strong internal performance norms in formal state organizations.[8] Rather one has to contend with ingrained—indeed "capitalized"—cynicism inside organizations and alienation and cynicism about state organizations from without.

There are a variety of possible scenarios for capability failure, and different states—and even different ministries within states—can take on different characteristics.[9] State functionality could collapse fully; the state could remain present nominally but simply not perform any tasks; the state could turn into an extractive state where rent-seeking and state capture by individuals is the order of the day; or the agents of the state could respond to the demands of the society as a whole and base its actions on the normative underpinnings of the society as a whole. We conjecture Somalia exemplifies

---

[7] An internet search attributes this saying to David Lloyd George, though variations on it exist in numerous cultures (cf. China, which under Mao argued that "you cross the stream by stepping on the stones" after a previous ill-fated attempt at a "great leap forward"). See also the witty exchange between representatives of these contrasting approaches to institutional reform—single bound versus incrementalism—in the post-Soviet era conveyed in Adams and Brock (1993). As Dani Rodrik has wryly noted, when policy arguments are made with pithy aphorisms one knows the contribution of economic science is limited.

[8] As our opening epigraph from Dewantara conveys.

[9] One might invoke Tolstoy at this point, extending his famous opening line in *Anna Karenina* to propose that happy, high capability states are all the same but that unhappy, low capability states are unhappy in their own way.

the first scenario; Haiti perhaps the second; many sub-Saharan African countries the third scenario.

Each failure makes success the next time around that much more difficult, as it breeds distrust between internal and external actors, cynicism among citizens, and a "wait and see" attitude among existing public sector agents when the next round of "solutions" are announced. Moreover, dysfunction often comes with corruption and this creates powerful private interests for the continuation of the status quo.

What to Do About Premature Load Bearing?

Does the risk of premature load bearing and collapse of state capability mean that the state should take on fewer functions? Does this mean that less aid should be channeled through the state? This is not a conclusion that we would automatically draw. The role of the state is crucial for effective development assistance, and therefore we have to treat state capability as a scarce resource, or perhaps even the binding constraint on development. We argue that state capability should be deployed in those spheres where it is most crucial and strategic, and that tasks should remain within the limits of what can genuinely be accomplished, even as we recognize that a defining feature of development is that states become incrementally more able to implement, under pressure and at scale, more complex, and more contentious tasks.

At the moment, however, the international community is squandering this precious resource by making tremendous demands on state capacity for non-productive purposes, such as reporting requirements and continuous organizational restructuring. Non-strategic functions can be outsourced, and a strategic plan can be put in place for a slow and gradual transfer of responsibility back to the state. Even so, there is the need for a genuine debate about the tasks a government can realistically perform at a given moment in time. When tasks can equally well be carried out by other actors, and the government role in this sphere can be limited, then perhaps this is worth exploring. As Thomas (2015) argues, aiming for a much less ambitious (or at least realistic) role for the state "is not about ideology, this is pragmatism." That is, in states with high levels of capability much of the debate is about what the state ideally *should* do, which sometimes breaks into the familiar left–right ideological spectrum. But in fragile states the main problem is whether the state *can* do even those very limited tasks it *must* do. Adding roles and responsibilities, however attractive those may be in principle and in the long run, can actually be worse than useless.

The dilemma faced by the international community in fragile states and/or conflict situations is a catch-22. State capability is low and clearly needs to be strengthened and reform is necessary to increase capability. At the same time, pushing too hard for reform may put too much strain on the system leading to retrogression rather than progress. This is particularly true for those reforms that are contentious and cause the highest stress on the system.

This is the capability trap in which many fragile states find themselves stuck, and to which the presence of the international community too often unwittingly contributes, in spite of good intentions. But explaining this dire situation is the easy part. Much harder is offering a coherent, supportable and implementable alternative, not least because trenchant criticism per se does not automatically generate one. And the incumbent always has the upper hand. But we argue that development practitioners must redefine their modus operandi; perfectionist project designs and proliferation of templates have not worked.

4

Capability for policy implementation

When one of us (Lant) was working in Indonesia for the World Bank he was tasked with verifying the accuracy of government reports detailing which households were receiving subsidized rice, a program provided to mitigate the impact of a major economic crisis. As he traveled from the state capital to the village he was reassured by officials at each level (state, then district, then local) that all households that reported getting rice were actually getting the total amount, and that only those households were receiving the subsidy. Once in a village, however, it took all of about fifteen minutes to ascertain that, once the village head had received the allotment of rice from the logistics agency, the rice was being spread among many more people than just those on the eligibility list. Lant already had good reason to suspect that this spreading of benefits was happening, as it had been widely reported for months. This was both perfectly understandable (given the village dynamics) and perhaps even desirable in some ways—which is why he was traveling to the village to see for himself. The real insight, though, came when he turned to the officials who were accompanying him on the trip and said: "Why did you keep telling me all was exactly according to the reports?" After some furtive glancing back and forth, one of them said: "Well, you were from the World Bank. None of you has ever wanted to know the truth before."

Defining Organization Capability for Policy Implementation

Chapter 1 documented the low and stagnant levels of state capability using primarily country-level indicators like "rule of law" or "bureaucratic quality" or "government effectiveness." In this chapter we zoom down to specific organizations and ask: what does it mean for an organization to have capability for policy implementation? For that we need to articulate what we mean by "policy" and by "organizational capability."

A study of getting a driver's license in Delhi, India, in 2004 (Bertrand et al. 2007) helps illustrate the key concepts. Researchers solicited participation from people arriving to get a driver's license and documented how the "control" group in their experiment got their license (or not). The official or formal or de jure policy for getting a driver's license in New Delhi looks pretty much like anywhere else: one goes to a government office, proves various personal facts about eligibility (like identity, age, and residence), shows the physical capacities associated with driving (like adequate vision), and then demonstrates driving ability through a practical test. In principle, those that meet the requirements get a license and those that don't, don't.

You might guess that that is not at all what happened. Fully 70 percent of the control group who successfully obtained a license hired a tout (also known as a fixer or facilitator) to help them with the transaction. The touts did more than just facilitate the interaction with the bureaucracy. Only 12 percent of those in the control group who hired a tout actually took the *legally required* driving examination. In contrast, 94 percent of those that did not hire a tout had to follow the law and take the practical road test, and two-thirds of those who took the test without hiring a tout failed the driving test and did not get a driver's license (at least in their first attempt; most of them wised up and just hired a tout in the next round). The intervention of the tout did not just speed the process along, it actually subverted the purpose. The study tested the driving ability of those that hired a tout and got a license—and two-thirds of them could not drive either and, if the policy were actually implemented, should not have had a license. All else equal, those that hired a tout and had a license were 38 percentage points more likely to fail an independent driving exam than those who got a license without hiring a tout.

Knowing the results of this study, what is the "policy" for getting a license in Delhi? One could recite the formal rules or policy formula but equally persuasively one could say the actual policy is "hire a tout, get a license." In our working definition a "policy" has four elements: a *formula* that maps from actions to facts, *processes* for determining the policy-relevant facts, a set of *objectives*, and a *causal model*.

A policy *formula* is a mapping from facts to actions by agents of an organization. This *formula* from facts or conditions or "states of the world" to actions by agents is often what is described as a policy. A fire insurance policy says "if the fact is that your house burned down, here are the actions we the company, via its agents, will take" (though it may say this in a few hundred pages). We call this a policy formula because in mathematics class we all learned that a function maps from a domain to a range; a policy formula is a mapping where the domain is "facts" and the range is "actions by an agent of an organization."

Discussions often conflate the policy *outcome* and the *formula*. For instance, a tariff policy is a mapping from different types and value of imports (the policy relevant facts) to authorized actions of agents in collecting revenue. But the total tariff revenue collected is not the policy formula; it is the outcome of an application of the policy formula to a set of facts. The exact same policy formula can produce very different outcomes: two countries could have exactly the same tariff code and yet different tariff revenue if the composition of their imports varied.

As a policy formula is a mapping from facts to actions, a policy must have a specification of how the *administratively relevant* facts of the formula are to be determined and, if necessary, adjudicated. The driver's license formula says "if the *administrative fact* is that you can drive (and other conditions are met), the action is that you are issued a license." An integral part of the policy is the specification of which organization and which agents have the authority to declare what the *administrative* facts are. These need not have anything to do with common-or-garden variety facts. A property tax policy formula applies a tax rate to the *administratively relevant taxable* value of a property. The value of the property as determined by its market price or its value as collateral can be completely irrelevant to the policy implementation relevant fact of its value for tax purposes (either de jure or de facto) and there is a process whereby that value is determined.

The combination of a policy *formula* as a mapping from administratively relevant facts to actions by agents and the *process* of determining the facts implies that policies and organizations are inextricably linked. Integral to a public policy is a designated organizational mechanism for implementation. Conversely, most public sector organizations are defined by the policies they are authorized to implement.

The emphasis on the organization authorized for policy implementation as an integral part of a policy helps distinguish organizations and institutions. Institutions are commonly defined as "norms or rules or human devices for affecting the behavior of individuals so as to structure the interactions of groups of people." This definition of institutions would include an incredibly broad array of human practices, from those associated with the "institution" of marriage to an "institution" of private property to the "institution" of religion. Some formal institutions may be enforced with official policies and legally constituted organizations responsible for implementation. But institutions can be also be "informal," with no written policy formula and no organization responsible for implementation. The distinction between organizations and institutions and between formal and informal "rules or norms" is crucial because formal organizations often lack capability for implementation because there are informal norms that have more traction on the behavior of implementing agents than formal rules and processes. As we will show in several cases, this leads to policy dysfunction.

While one could regard the specification of the policy formula (mapping from facts to actions) and the organizational processes of implementation (how facts are determined and adjudicated and actions taken) as complete, in our approach a policy has two more elements: *objectives* and a *causal model*.

We define *objectives* as an intrinsic component of a policy. Many policies may lack an explicit declaration of objectives or purposes but, whether these are implicit or explicit, a policy exists to do something—educate a child, limit environmental damage, prevent corruption, resolve disputes to avoid violence. We focus on a policy's *normative* objectives, which may differ from the actual purposes to which the organization or policy is being used. That is, the *normative* objective of a tax is to collect revenue for the government. The actual organization purposes may be to use the authorization to tax to collect some tax and also extract some revenue that flows to others illicitly, but one can still consider a policy and implementing organization relative to its normative objectives.

A policy also has a *causal model*. A causal model is what relates the policy formula (mapping from facts to actions of agents) to the policy objectives (what the actions of the organization implementing the policy are meant to achieve). While the causal model is almost never made explicit by organizations, it is nevertheless a critically important part of the policy as it ultimately serves as part of the organization's claim to legitimacy, both externally to its "authorizing environment" (Moore 1995) and internally to its own agents.

The delineation of a policy into the four elements of policy formula, organizational process for determining facts, normative objectives, and causal model (as illustrated in Table 4.1) highlights two distinct ways in which a policy could fail to achieve its normative objectives. The *policy formula* could be based on a *causal model* that is wrong about the connections between the fact-contingent actions of agents and the normative objectives. In this case, even if the policy formula was faithfully implemented—the policy relevant facts correctly assessed and policy formula stipulated facts taken—this would not achieve (or perhaps even promote) the policy objectives.

The other possibility is that—as in the case of the post office and international mail in Chapter 1, the driver's licenses in Delhi, the examples about healthcare below, or any of hundreds of examples around the world—policy is just not implemented. The driving test may or may not reduce traffic accidents—but people are getting licenses without it so it doesn't matter. Having nurse-midwives in clinics providing antenatal care may or may not decrease child mortality at birth—but if they are not there the question is moot.

Much—almost certainly most, and quite possibly nearly all—analysis of public policy focuses on which policy formula are based on correct causal models such that *if they were implemented* they would produce better outcomes. Economic analysis, for instance, often has very different predictions about the impacts of the expansion of government supply of commodities because it assumes consumers are already acting to secure what they demand. This can mean that policies based on a naïve model of impact of supply will fail to predict actual outcomes even if the policy were perfectly implemented. We are all for more and better scientific analysis of policy impacts. But "black box" approaches to policy/program/project impact cannot distinguish between a failure to produce desired outcomes because of an incorrect causal model linking outputs to outcomes, and a failure of policy implementation—namely, that implementing agents just didn't do what the policy formulation stipulated they would do. Either will lead to the inputs provided not producing the desired outcome; not making these necessary distinctions can thus lead to inaccurate conclusions as to why a given "policy" (or program or project) failed.

Table 4.1. The elements of a policy: formula, administrative facts, normative objectives, and a causal model

	Policy formula		Organizational process for determining administrative facts	Normative objectives	Causal model
	Facts	Authorized actions			
Imposition of obligations					
An 8% sales tax	The firms taxable sales	Collect 8% of total	Tax authority through records and/or audits	Collect revenue to fund government	
Driver's license	Age, eligibility, adequate sight, driving ability	Issue legal authorization to operate motor vehicle	A agency/ bureau that approves, including testing driving skills	Reduce road accidents, injuries, fatalities	Allowing only people capable of driving (ex ante and ex post) to legally drive will reduce the risks of traffic accidents
[Reader's example]					
Delivery of services					
Immunizations	Child of appropriate age, vaccination history	Give child vaccination	Variety—use of healthcare providers or facilities or vertical programs	Reduce child illness/ death from preventable causes	Vaccinated children will be at less risk themselves and less risk of transmitting diseases to others
[Reader's example]					
Operation of the state					
Procurement	Is the bid the least cost qualified bid?	Sign contract with bidder	Procurement unit of organization	Get most benefit to citizens from use of resources, prevent corruption	The procurement process is capable of generating competition among alternative suppliers that reveals lowest costs

Organizational Capability for Policy Implementation

Sorry for the last section. It was kind of like a predatory big cat sneaking up on prey with slow stealthy moves, no one of which seemed particularly threatening, in fact, kind of boring. While it may have seemed tedious, the definition of "policy" as not just formula but also organizational process, objective(s), and a causal model enables us to define strong and weak organizational capability for policy implementation. Strong capability organizations are those in which agents take those actions that promote the organization's normative objectives.

Organizations with weak capability for policy implementation are those that cannot equip their agents with the capacity, resources, and motivation to take actions that promote the organization's stated objectives.

There are two elements embedded in this definition of capability for policy implementation that we need for our overall approach but which we wish to highlight are unusual: the seemingly sudden pounce after the boring stalking.

It might be a big surprise that our definition of organizational capability for policy implementation does not refer at all to the policy formula. One very popular older approach was to *define* the objective of public sector management or public administration as policy compliance. In that frame, an organization with strong capability for policy implementation would be one that implements the policy formula: it ascertains the facts and applies the policy formula to those facts with fidelity. In our view this approach is very attractive—indeed it may seem like common sense, if not definitional, that high organizational capability for policy implementation should be measured by policy implementation. But we feel this approach is deeply wrong about what capability is, indeed that it leads to misguided and counterproductive approaches to achieving capability.

Embedded in our definition of organization capability is that organizations discover and act on a workably correct causal model of achieving the policy's normative objectives. Take an extreme example. Suppose there was a society that believed that the sun would only come up in the morning if during the night a crank was turned. Given the importance of the sun coming up, this society may create an elite organization responsible for the nightly crank turning. This organization may achieve perfection in complying with the policy formula and the crank is turned every night. Does this crank turning organization have high capability? Certainly it has high capability for achieving compliance with the policy formula. But since no reader of this book sincerely shares the causal model that the sun's rising is determined by crank turning the organization has no capability at all for achieving the normative objective of raising the sun.[1] Enabled by the prevalence of isomorphic mimicry (Chapter 2) and overambitious agendas (Chapter 3), the developing world is full of excellent policies (indeed often "best practice" policies) and lousy outcomes. At least partly responsible for this state of affairs, however, is that definitions of organizational capability and its construction have been separated from achieving objectives and instead reduced to compliance.

---

[1] And, as modern academics, we can go "postmodern" and define other social objectives that the crank turning may achieve as defined from within a social context in which all participants do in fact believe a false causal model about the sunrise and that the organization also has capability for those, potentially important, objectives. But it doesn't have capability to raise the sun.

We are defining capability relative to *normative* objectives. This is not a reprisal of the "functionalist" approach, in which an organization's capability would be defined relative to the function it actually served in the overall system. This definition allows an organization engaged entirely in isomorphism to assume the status of being "capable" if it was fulfilling a functional role through that isomorphism.

Using our definition of state capability we delineate five levels.

Ideal capability, in which the agent takes the best possible action available and hence produces the best achievable policy outcome. We assume agents are maximizing the normative objective of the organization. This can produce outcomes better (perhaps much better) than policy compliance. This assumes the agent has a perfect ability to determine the relevant "facts of the world" and has perfect causal knowledge of what action will produce the best outputs and outcomes—which, in our imperfect world, is completely impossible. Even so, ideal capability is the standard to which the best organizations aspire and in reality closely approximate.

Policy-compliant capability means that agents do exactly and only what the policy formula dictates. Agents give drivers' licenses when, and only when, the fact of the world meets the policy formula conditions for a driver's license. The case of the Delhi drivers' licenses, of course, was less than policy compliant. But even policy compliance can be much less than ideal, if either (a) the policy formula is less than ideal (or just plain wrong), or (b) success requires actions that cannot be fully specified in a written policy (see Chapter 5 for a typology). In education it is hard to believe that a policy could dictate exactly what teachers should do such that a "policy-compliant" outcome would actually be an ideal educational experience.

Actual capability is what happens in practice when agents make their own decisions. In Delhi, agents colluded with touts and gave licenses to drivers who had not passed the formally required driving test. In this case, actual capability was less optimal than policy compliance. This is the typical case of "actual capability" in the developing world: agents choose to maximize their own wellbeing, with the objective function that is inclusive of intrinsic and extrinsic motivations and with the incentives presented by their social and organizational context.

But in cases of high-capability organizations, actual capability is preferable to pure policy compliance because agents can take actions to improve outcomes. (In such organizations, "work to rule" is a threat because doing so *lowers* effectiveness, whereas in low-capability environments "work to rule" would be a massive improvement.) Thus, actual capability could be more than policy-compliant capability and nearer ideal, or could be (and often is) much less policy compliant and actually near zero.

Weak capability for implementation manifests in organizational inputs, outputs, and outcomes. The agents of organizations do not do what they are supposed to do—they are absent, they do not put in effort, they take bribes, they are ineffective or even counterproductive in their actions. Weak

capability results in low organizational outputs from policy implementation—
regulations are not enforced, infrastructure is not maintained, mail is not
delivered. The result is teachers who do not teach, police who do not police,
tax collectors who do not collect taxes.

Zero capability is what would happen if there were no organization at all. Actual
capability can be this low—or, as we will see, lower.

Negative capability is a possibility because the state, by the very definition of being the
state, has the ability to coerce. Organizations of the state can use power to exploit their
own citizens and, through the imposition of obligations with no corresponding benefits, make them absolutely worse off.[2]

Capability: More Than Individuals, Less Than Countries

A key task as we move toward a pragmatic approach to building state capability is to shed two common misconceptions that implicitly or explicitly guide
efforts to build capability. One misconception is to not distinguish between
the *capacity* of individuals and the *capability* of organizations. Perhaps the
most common response to low capability, particularly when external agents
get involved, is to propose more technical training ("capacity building") on
the view that organizational capability is limited by individual capacities.
The second misconception is that state capability is completely determined
by broad nation-state (or perhaps state or provincial) level conditions and
hence what is needed to build capability is broad "reform" that affects all state
organizations.

Organizational capability versus individual capacity. Given the overwhelming importance
given to "training" in discussions of building capability, one might imagine that the
capacity of individuals in an organization was (nearly) everywhere and always a key
constraint to the *capability* of organizations. We define the *technical capacity* of individuals as their ability to recognize and act on a correct causal model.[3] But in many
instances it is obvious that the capacity of individuals is not the key constraint—they
know what to do, they just don't do it.

One simple illustration of this is absenteeism. In this case the relevant
policy formula maps from the fact of the world that is date and time to the
action of the agent of being there. A study of teachers in India (again, a middle

---

[2] Leeson (2007), for instance, argues that the typical Somali may well have been better off
without any state than with the predatory state they had. Scott (2009) discusses how various
communities in Southeast Asia have actively avoided "being governed," as anarchy was deemed
preferable to the predatory states that were available.
[3] We could just as easily refer to organization "capacity" and individual "capability"—the only
point is that it is helpful to distinguish the two, in particular the one is not the simple sum of the
other. Using a different word for each helps.

capability country overall) found that teachers were not present in the school 26 percent of the time. A follow-up study, a decade later after much attention to this issue, found it had declined, but only to 23 percent. A recent study of eight African countries found average absence was 20 percent. These rates of absence result in weak organizational capability—achieving the normative goal of student learning is clearly inhibited by teacher absence—but it is ridiculous to imagine that any of this absence is because the teachers either don't understand the policy formula ("be there on Tuesday") or do not know the true facts ("it's Tuesday").

An excellent illustration of the distinction between technical capacity and organizational capability on a more complex implementation issue comes from two different studies of healthcare providers in India. One study in Delhi assessed the technical capacity of medical care providers by analyzing their ability to respond correctly about how to diagnose and act on conditions presented in vignettes (Das and Hammer 2007). They then also observed the same providers in their actual practice. The public sector employed only trained doctors as providers, so their *technical capacity* on the vignettes was much higher than the typical private sector provider (many private sector providers of first line medical care were "less than fully qualified"—some might say "quacks," i.e. people offering medical advice and services with very little or no training at all). But, when examined in their public sector primary health center (PHC) settings the trained doctors did only a small fraction of what they had demonstrated they knew how to do while the private sector knew little but did what they knew.

A follow-up study in rural Madhya Pradesh assessed healthcare providers by training research collaborators to present as patients and report specific symptoms. Some presented with symptoms of myocardial infarction (heart attack), complaining of chest pains. Of the public providers, very few asked even the most basic diagnostic questions: only 45 percent asked about the location of the pain, only 19 percent about its severity, and only 10 percent whether the pain was radiating. (We as middle-aged men are a biased sample, but even we know that location, severity, and radiating pain are key symptoms for recognizing a heart attack.) The "policy formula" when faced with a "fact of the world" of a patient presenting with symptoms of myocardial infarction in rural settings is very simple: (1) aspirin, (2) nitroglycerine, (3) ECG, and (4) referral to a hospital. Fifty-eight percent of formally trained (MBBS) doctors in public primary clinics in Madhya Pradesh did *none* of those things for patients presenting with symptoms of a heart attack—not an aspirin, not an ECG, not a referral.

This outcome was not the result of a lack of technical capacity on the part of those individuals to diagnose; it was the *organizational* setting that determined these outcomes. The distinction between technical capacity and organizational capability was made clear because the study also had the "patients" present themselves with symptoms at the practices of the exact same MBBS-trained doctors who worked in the private health clinics when they were working on the side in their own practices. The result was that, when judged by either the likelihood of checklist completion of the protocol for the disease or by a standardized checklist score, the *worst* medical care in the study was provided by the trained doctors in their public clinics and the *best* medical care was those exact same doctors in their private practices. The differences are astounding, as checklist completion is less than 3 percent in their public practice—which is therefore the *organizational capability*—while in their private practice it is 27 percent—which reveals the *technical capacity* of the doctors as individuals far outstrips their actions when embedded in the organization.

By combining the efforts of individuals in productive ways, organizations can have capabilities much, much higher than individuals alone. Indeed, it might be said one of the very foundations of "modern" economic and political life is the rise of organizations (public and private) that have vastly higher productivity than that of individuals. In such organizations, the whole truly is greater than the sum of its parts. Yet it is also the case that organizations can be so dysfunctional that they become "value subtracting"—i.e. the productivity of the individual when inside such an organization is *lower* than it is outside and the whole is much *less* than the sum of the parts.

Illustrations of this unhappy phenomenon of value subtraction come from studies of contract versus civil service teachers. In an experiment in Kenya, a new teacher was added to early grades to reduce class size. When the teacher added was hired as a civil service teacher the additional teacher had no impact on improving child test scores. When nothing else was different but that the new teacher was hired on a contract renewable at will by the school (and hence with performance and parental input), student test scores improved substantially (Duflo et al. 2007). An observational study in Uttar Pradesh found students learned twice as much from a contract teacher versus a civil service teacher—in spite of the fact that the salary of the civil service teacher was many times higher than that of the contract teacher (Atherton and King-don 2010). It appears that a person with exactly the same technical capacity has their absolute level of productivity *reduced* by being inside the standard civil service-type organization—the organization is value-subtracting.[4]

---

[4] One should not conclude from such a study, of course, that the solution to raising student test scores around the world is to hire lower-cost contract teachers; our point here (and that of the researchers) is that it is the capability of organizations that powerfully influences the performance of its constituent members, and that in the worst situations dysfunctional organizations can literally subtract from, rather than add to, the technical capacity of their members.

Capability varies across organizations in the same country. While in Chapter 1 we use national measures of state capability, these are broad aggregates and of course hide massive variations in capability across the same country. For instance, many of our examples to illustrate low capability in this book come from studies in various states of India and in Chapter 1 we saw that India was an average developing country in aggregate capability. Yet many of the top-tier organizations in India exhibit very high capability. In September 2014 India successfully put a satellite into orbit around Mars. The graduates of India's institutes of technology are highly recruited globally. So the fundamental issue is not that India is a "failing" state with no state capability, rather it is a "flailing" state with highly capable elite organizations and yet very poorly performing organizations in other aspects (e.g. policing, basic education, health).[5]

A study in Bolivia surveyed over 1,000 public officials and asked them to rate the performance and characteristics of other Bolivian public agencies.[6] The results revealed large and consistent patterns in differences across organizations, even within a country with very low country-level measures of capability. For instance, the Ombudsman, Electoral Court, and National Comptroller had service performance ratings by agents of other public agencies over 80 whereas the police in Santa Cruz had a service rating of below 30. On an index of bribery, organizations like the Ombudsman are rated near zero while the worst (again the police in Santa Cruz) are rated over 80.[7]

Any adequate account of organizational capability has to be able to explain both differences across countries in aggregated or average organizational capability as well as differences within countries across organizations. A World Bank study on health and education in the Middle East North Africa region shows this same logic can be deployed to explore and explain how public agencies within the same sector within the same country enacting the same policies can nonetheless generate considerable performance variation—in Yemen, for example, staff absenteeism in health clinics ranges from 8 to 83 percent. Learning from this variation in performance can reveal how the capability can be strengthened.[8]

How Organizational Capability for Policy Implementation Matters

The effectiveness of policy is mediated by the quality of implementation. The example of the (non)returning of misaddressed international mail in Chapter 1 shows that the exact same policy can lead to completely different outcomes—from zero to 100 percent. All countries have policies against

---

[5] See Pritchett (2009).   [6] Kaufmann et al. (2002).

[7] Since the scores are all normed by the mean and standard deviation within Bolivia, it is impossible to compare how large these variations are compared to international differences.

[8] See Brixi et al. (2015).

corruption in public procurement and yet corruption is nearly absent in some cases and ubiquitous in others. When implementation is weak the converse can be true: we show below a case in which completely different de jure policies lead to roughly similar outcomes.

Weak organizational capability for policy implementation leads to two practical consequences: administrative fact becomes fiction; and the consequences of de jure "policy reform," particularly a change in the policy formula, are completely unpredictable. Note that the key point here is not whether these matter for final outcomes; rather, this is *how* weak capability affects implementation. We address each in turn.

1. Facts Can Be Fiction

A policy formula is a mapping from facts to actions. This makes implementation sound easy. But the sad fact is facts are (often) not facts. Public sector organizations do not operate on regular garden variety facts like that the sky is blue, rain is wet, and Tuesday is a workday but on the *administrative* facts. Policy includes the designation of which agents have the authority to declare administrative facts and who and how disputes about administrative facts are adjudicated. One of the ways in which implementation fails is not that the real facts are agreed as administrative facts and implementing agents fail to act on those facts, but rather that the administrative facts stipulated in the policy formula are manipulated to create policy compliance which is a complete fiction.

Living in parallel worlds of administrative facts and actual facts is part of life in most developing countries.[9] A friend of ours was interviewing a girl in rural India about her schooling. Since government schools provide benefits like free uniforms and mid-day meals there are incentives to be enrolled in public school. But learning conditions are perceived to be better in low-cost private schools. The girl regularly attended a private school. But when asked where she went to school she said she went to the government school. Our friend pointed out that she was actually sitting in class in a private school during school time. The girl thought about this for a few minutes then responded: "My *name* goes to the

---

[9] Nearly any ethnographic work (or just work that actually asks people what is going on) finds that "working misunderstandings" (Watkins and Swidler 2013) between the official policy formula, front-line agents, brokers (who often have no formal existence), and "beneficiaries" are rife (as Watkins and Swidler 2013 did in their work on NGOs and AIDS work in Malawi). Robert Wade's analysis of irrigation in India revealed that what was supposedly a bureaucratic agency was really a collection of markets (Wade 1982). Diane Singerman (1995) in Egypt discusses the key roles of networks in securing public services. As pointed out in different contexts by Scott (1998), Ferguson (1994), and Mosse (2005)—among many others and the simple vignette that opens the chapter—it actually takes a special kind of training and mindset to "stabilize the epistemic framing" (Mosse 2005) and *not* see the gap.

government school, but *I* go to private school." In low-capability organizations, even seemingly routine administrative facts like someone's age are often opaque and potentially open to abuse. Gupta (2012) documents in anthropological detail how certain front-line implementers of social programs in rural India exploit widespread uncertainty about people's actual age to their personal advantage, demanding sexual and financial favors from citizens in return for declaring them age-eligible (i.e. over 50 years old) for these programs. In such circumstances, one is as old as the implementer deems you to be; the administrative fact is effectively arbitrary on an issue that in high-capability organizations and contexts is precise and readily verifiable in seconds.

Let us give four other quick examples of where administrative fact is fiction.

Regulation of pollution in Gujarat. The regulation of industrial emissions of pollutants in Gujarat, India, required private firms to hire other private firms as "auditors" to assess their level of emissions. But these environmental emissions auditing firms were chosen, hired, and paid by the emitting firms. A recent experiment looked at what happened to reported emissions before and after the incentives changed such that auditors were not dependent on the goodwill of emitting firms for business.[10]

Not surprisingly, when firms hired the auditors to declare the administrative facts about their admissions, the facts were a complete fiction. The reported facts were that nearly all firms had emissions just below the legal threshold. Again not surprisingly, the actual facts were that many firms had emissions two or three times higher than those reported by the auditor. Perhaps surprisingly, however, many firms had emissions much *lower* than those that were reported by the environmental auditor. One might think that reporting pollution *higher* than your true level makes no sense. But, once it was widely acknowledged that the administrative reports were a complete fiction the only objective was to be cheap (why even visit the plant?) and not attract regulatory attention (so report a value clustered where it seems not in violation but also doesn't seem suspiciously low).

Community development in Kenya. The World Bank has financed "community driven development" (CDD) projects in Kenya.[11] One element of these projects is to create "livelihoods" by providing poor beneficiaries with assets, often livestock like goats or cattle or chickens. Given that this was a World Bank-financed project there were both activities like local meetings intended to provide accountability to the beneficiaries and hence reports on those meetings, as well as the standard reports on procurements. The World Bank had, on the basis of the reported administrative facts, rated the project performance as "Satisfactory" from 2003 right up until a forensic audit in 2010 revealed the facts were fiction and forced the project to be suspended.[12] A forensic audit of seven districts found that in the CDD component of the project, 84 percent of all expenditures were "suspected fraudulent or questionable." The records of "community

---

[10] Duflo et al. (2012).   [11] Ensminger (2013).   [12] See World Bank (2012).

participation" were fabricated and the names of villagers attending were just produced without their actual participation or consent. Ethnographic research found that the project implementers at the district level were able to combine with agents at the village level to almost completely capture the benefits of the project in fact, while producing documents and records creating the fiction that all was well.

Doing Business. The gap between the de jure administrative fact and the on-the-ground reality is evident in many studies of particular issues in particular countries and also in cross-national comparisons. As part of the Doing Business indicators the World Bank ask experts to estimate how long it would take a form or person to obtain a construction permit to build a new building of a specified type *if they followed the law.* In many of the same countries the World Bank also does an Enterprise Survey of a sample of firms. This survey asks of those firms that have recently constructed a building how long it took the firm to get the license to do so. While not a perfect comparison—firms construct many kinds of buildings in many different cities or regions within a country—this provides at least a rough-and-ready comparison between de jure and de facto policy implementation.

The comparison of the two measures of regulatory compliance is revealing. While one might think that it would take longer in countries with stiffer formal regulation, in reality there is almost zero correlation across countries between the Doing Business time and the average or median of what firms actually report. If you wanted to predict how long it would take a firm to get a construction permit, knowing the country estimate of the legal time to obtain a license would have no little or predictive power. Figure 3.4 (see Chapter 3) showed that in countries where the Doing Business measure was fewer than 200 days the average firm reported it took 58 days to get a permit. In countries where Doing Business reported, it took more than 300 days (and in the median country in this category it was 381 days—more than a year), the average firm that got a permit reported it took them *less* time—only 47 days. So an *increase* in 230 days in the de jure time to get a construction permit is associated with a nine day *decrease* in the time the average firm reported it actually took (Hallward-Driemeier and Pritchett 2015).

This isn't to say the law did not matter at all. In the Enterprise Survey data there are responses from many firms so one can compare the times reported by "fast" firms (the 25th percentile) and the "slowest" firms (the 95th percentile). There was a big gap between the "fast" and "slow" firms, such that the difference between "fast" and "slow" firms in the same country was much, much larger than the gap in legal times across countries. In countries where the Doing Business reported de jure compliance times to 200 to 300 days the "fast" firms reported 15 days and the slow firms reported 165 days—a gap of 150 days. One might say that for how much time it will really take a firm to get a permit it matters less where you are than who you are, and that what really matters for firms it not the de jure regulation but the implementation gap between policy and action.

Bank accounts in India. A naïve "public–private partnership" approach that relies on the private sector for implementation to achieve public purposes does not solve the problem of state capability, as it just pushes the question off onto private organizations—which may have capability for some purposes but not for pursuing a policy's normative objective. One illustration is that in order to promote financial inclusion the government, via the Reserve Bank of India, mandated that all banks (both parastatal and private) had to offer a low-cost, low-balance account. One might think that since the law mandated their availability these accounts would be available. A study in the Indian state of Tamil Nadu in 2014 sent "mystery shoppers" into various banks to see if the banks would in fact tell potential customers about the availability of these accounts or open them if asked. Zero were offered the low-balance account at any type of bank. Even when the "mystery shopper" asked specifically about the type of account, only between 10 and 25 percent would admit to offering the account they were legally required to offer. And, as is often the case, the private and foreign providers

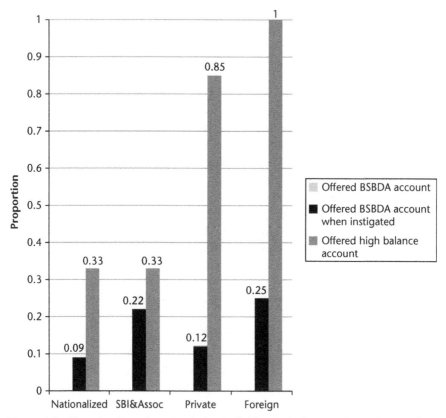

Figure 4.1. Changing law, changing behavior? A law in India mandating banks offer a basic savings account didn't lead them to offer it—even when asked directly—even in public sector banks

Source: Adapted from Mowl and Boudot (2014: table 2)

were better at doing what was in their interest—85 percent got offered a high-balance account versus only one-third in public sector banks—but less likely to do what is not in their interest (see Figure 4.1). So capability for implementation is not solved by pushing implementation into the private sector, which can maintain the same fact–fiction gap in the absence of capable regulation enforcement.

2. Weak Capability Makes It Impossible to Predict the Impact of Changing a Policy Formula on Policy Actions, Outputs, or Outcomes

Since weak capability for policy implementation often implies both that the policy formula is not being followed (and will have little or no traction on the behavior of the organization's agents) and that the normative objectives of the organization are being undermined, this means that the impact of "policy reform"—particularly of the type that changes the policy formula—has completely unpredictable impacts. Sensible sound policies—and even policies that have been rigorously "proven" to work in other organizational settings—may produce zero, or even perverse, results.

Some examples illustrate this point. Three different studies of attempts to reduce front-line worker absences by introducing technology to track attendance and incentives produced three different results. Working in partnership with a local NGO, researchers looked at the impact of using date-stamped cameras to verify the attendance of teachers at the NGO's schools. They found that the improved technology to verify attendance increased teacher attendance and that increased teacher attendance improved child learning (Duflo et al. 2012). So one might conclude that better technology to monitor attendance improved attendance, and thus that better technology improves the quality of service delivery. But no.

One of the same researchers worked with the same NGO to attempt to improve attendance of auxiliary nurse midwives (ANMs) at local clinics. This program introduced new technology to monitor attendance of the ANMs, introduced the possibility that their pay would be docked if they were present less than half the time,[13] clarified responsibility for attendance on a "clinic day" that ANMs should not have other field duties, and utilized the NGO in spot checks to "ground truth" the reliability of the technological monitoring of attendance (to check incentives to damage the new machines, etc.). Moreover, with a realistic nod to the difficult politics of changing the behavior of existing staff, this new policy applied only to newly hired ANMs.

---

[13] Previous extensive fieldwork by the researchers had revealed that the average absence in subcenters and aid posts was 45 per cent so this was only a moderately ambitious target (Banerjee et al. 2004).

The outcome of this wonderful policy reform that drew on the rigorous knowledge from the previous paper ("Monitoring Works") is aptly summarized by the title of the new paper: "Putting a Band-Aid on a Corpse."[14] What is interesting is *how* the program failed. Eighteen months into implementation the rate of ANM *administratively recorded* absence had *fallen* in the treatment versus control group. Unfortunately the actual physical *presence* rate of the ANMs in the treatment group also fell. The program actually, if anything, increased *actual* absence while decreasing *administrative* absence. How? The category "exempted from duty"—ANMs not in the clinic but not counted as absent—rose dramatically. This attempt at improving health through better attendance of health workers failed because organizational capability for policy implementation was so low that putting increasing pressure on the recorded absence merely increased the manipulation of the administrative facts.

Another example comes from the Indian state of Karnataka, where the government introduced biometric monitoring of attendance with the threat that healthcare workers would be docked their leave days if they were excessively absent. This experiment had even more curious implementation and results (Dhaliwal and Hanna 2014). For one, the "treatment" was never fully implemented as, while the biometric machines were installed and the data reported, it was never actually the case that this data was used to discipline any worker (nor did it appear it could be implemented given the internal political objections and legal challenges). But birth outcomes improved in the "treatment" areas where the PHC introduced biometric recording of attendance—but not at all for the reasons hoped. The introduction of biometrics did not change doctor attendance at all, but did raise the attendance of other workers (e.g. nurses, pharmacists) at the clinic. Even so, this outcome was actually associated with *worse* perceptions of clinic quality by users, which in turn led *fewer* people to use the biometric treatment PHCs and instead they switched into higher-quality facilities—bypassing the PHCs for larger hospitals. Hence the better birth outcomes was the result of *lower* utilization of the PHCs in favor of facilities with better birth outcomes.

So, three rigorous experiments, all in India, each introduced some form of improved technology for tracking attendance into a low capability for implementation environment. The result is that pretty much anything that could happen, did happen: in one—which was an NGO provider—attendance went up and outcomes got better; in another, attendance didn't change (or, if anything, got worse) as the policy was completely undermined; and in yet another the policy wasn't implemented, the impact on attendance was mixed, patient-perceived quality got worse, but outcomes got better—because they used the clinics *less*.

---

[14] See Banerjee et al. (2007).

Contract teachers. A policy formula that works when implemented by one agency may fail when implemented by another agency, even when the "policy reform" seems an exact replica. A randomized experiment in western Kenya showed that reducing class size by hiring contract teachers, whose contracts might not be renewed at the discretion of the local community and school, improved children's learning.[15] In that same setting, reducing class size by the same amount by adding additional civil service teachers did not improve student learning. Not that surprisingly, contractual status affected teacher performance which improved child learning. This policy reform had been tested in the most rigorous way and proven cost-effective.

When Kenya went to take this policy to scale nationwide, other researchers measured the impact of the scaled program. Fortuitously for social science, neither a major NGO nor the ministry of education had the ability to take the program to scale nationwide, so in part of the country an NGO was responsible for implementation and in other parts of the country the ministry was. The new researchers[16] found that when the new contract teachers' policy was implemented by an NGO it had exactly the impact the previous research had found. However, then the *exact same policy formula* was scaled by the ministry of education, reducing class size by hiring contract teachers had the same impact as reducing class size with civil service teachers—zero. That the policy was "proven" to work with one organization's capability was not evidence the same policy would work when implemented by an organization with different capability.

Improving the "Doing Business" Indicators. As we argued above, there was very little association between the rules on the books as recorded by the Doing Business indicators and the responses firms gave. Many countries have pursued reforms to aggressively reduce the times to compliance—as measured by the Doing Business indicator. What effect does that have on firms? Figure 4.2 shows that two-thirds of countries that reduced their de jure times to get a construction permit saw the time reported by firms either stay the same or increase. The impact of policy formula reform with low initial compliance is unpredictable (Hallward-Driemeier and Pritchett 2015).

* * *

Organizational capability for policy implementation is not the achievement of policy compliance. Organizational capability is the ability of an organization to equip, enable, and induce their agents to do the right thing at the right time to achieve a normative policy objective. Reductionist approaches to organizational capability often attempt to reduce this to compliance with policy formula, which easily leads to isomorphism (see Chapter 2) or to

---

[15] Duflo et al. (2007).   [16] Bold et al. (2013).

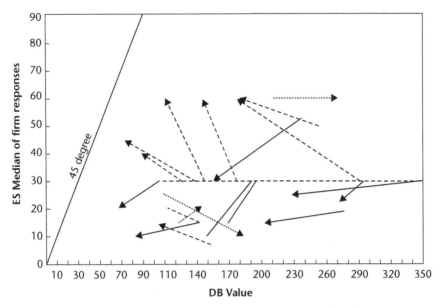

Figure 4.2. Evolution of days to get a construction permit: Doing Business and Enterprise Survey results

Source: Hallward-Driemeier and Pritchett (2015: figure 2b)

emphasis on the inputs deployed by the organization rather than the outputs and outcomes achieved, or reduce organization capability to individual capacity, which leads to an over-emphasis on technical training. Conversely, the conflation of state capability with country-level legal or institutional features, like laws against corruption or good looking civil service legislation, assume that creating functional organizations begins with country-level action.

Achieving better outcomes requires better organizational capability for implementation. Before moving on to describe a pragmatic approach to building capability, we first need to examine the different kinds of capability various types of activities require. It is to this that we now turn.

5

What type of organization capability is needed?

Socrates: Suppose someone came to your friend [who is a doctor] and said "I know treatments to raise or lower (whichever I prefer) the temperature of people's bodies; if I decide to, I can make them vomit or make their bowels move, and all sorts of things. On the basis of this knowledge I claim to be a physician; and I claim to be able to make other physicians as well by imparting to them." What do you think they would say when they heard that?

Phaedrus: What could they say? They would ask him if he also knows to whom he should apply such treatments, when and to what extent.

Socrates: What if he replied, "I have no idea. My claim is that whoever learns from me will manage to do what you ask on his own"?

Phaedrus: I think they'd say the man's mad if he thinks he's a doctor just because he read a book or happened to come across a few potions; he knows nothing of the art.

(Plato, *Phaedrus*)

Capability Matching

Imagine you are an athletic trainer and someone comes to you and says: "I want to build my athletic capability to compete successfully in a sport." The first question you would ask is: "What sport?" If a person wants to be a badminton champion then quickness, agility, and flexibility are key capabilities. If a person wants to be a long-distance runner then cardio-vascular conditioning is a prime concern. A weightlifter's capability is single repetition maximum power. Capability needs to be matched to the task at hand.

In the private sector high-capability organizations take a variety of shapes and sizes. In some domains high-capability organizations grow very rapidly and become very large while in others high-capability organizations stay very small. In others, organizational reach is large but not through direct expansion but through relationships. The company Facebook was founded in 2004 and ten years later had 1.2 billion active users. Walmart was founded in 1962 and fifty years later had 2.1 million employees—it is surpassed as an employer only by the US Department of Defense and China's People's Liberation Army. Yet Harvard University was founded in 1636 and 380 years later still has only 6,722 undergraduate students out of a US total undergraduate enrollment of over 28 million. McDonald's serves 68 million customers *a day* in over 35,000 restaurants but it only owns and operates about 20 percent of those; the rest are franchises. Clearly in the private sector, where organizational form can freely adapt to function, there are a wide variety of ways, types, and scales at which organizations build capability.

Discussing how to build "state capability" independently of the answer to the question "capability to do what?" is bound to end in disappointment. The art of building the capability of state organizations has to begin with a taxonomy of the types of activities to be accomplished and the capabilities those activities need. Is an organizational building capability to deliver the mail? Set monetary policy? Deliver first contact curative care? Regulate point source pollution? This chapter delineates an analytical typology that uses four questions to classify tasks or activities into five types of organizational capability it requires. The five types are: *policymaking/elite services*, *logistics*, *implementation-intensive delivery of services*, *implementation-intensive imposition of obligations*, and *wicked hard*.

A Basic Framework of Accountability

What motivates a teacher to teach well, or a doctor to give his best effort in treating patients? What is the difference between a tax collector who performs his job effectively, and a tax collector who takes bribes? Organizational capability often boils down to a functional system of accountability. There are two important dimensions of accountability: direct formal accountability to the organization, and indirect and informal accountability to a broader social and associational (e.g. professional, religious) norms.

Formal accountability is a relationship between two entities (person to person, organization to organization, many people as collective to organization leadership, organization to person). Formal accountability is embedded in an ongoing relationship that creates set of norms and expectations for both parties. Economists have used one type of accountability analysis, "principal–agent" models, to examine features of organizational size, scope, and incentive design as problems of contracting. In a purely market organization there are principal–agent problems that deal with resources (what does the agent work with?), information (how does the principal observe agent effort and outcomes?), decision-making (which decisions are made by the agent, which by the principal?), delivery mechanisms (who does the agent interact with?), and incentives (to what extent do payoffs to the employed agent depend on his/her performance?).[1]

Within any formal accountability relationship, there are four elements that structure agents' choices. The World Bank's World Development Report 2004 (World Bank 2004) calls these the "design elements" of an accountability relationship. Based on these, the agent chooses actions and hence the

---

[1] This is not to say, of course, that a principal–agent analysis exhausts the complexity of the service provision problem.

performance of the agent is endogenous to (a function of) the design elements but cannot be directly controlled.

The four elements of any formal accountability relationship are:

- Delegation: A specification of what is wanted from principals to agents.
- Finance/support: A flow of resources from principals to agents.
- Information: Once the agent carries out the required task some information is created that is available to the principal—although the essence of a principal–agent problem is that the information is necessarily incomplete as many other factors determine success or failure at the observable output/outcome than just the agent's effort.
- Motivation: Based on the information the principal takes actions that affect the agent, which can affect the agent's intrinsic and extrinsic motivation.

Life is full of garden variety accountability relationships. When your sink is clogged and you contract a plumber, you delegate and finance the plumber (by telling him to fix the sink with the promise of paying him if he does), he chooses his own preferred level of performance (by either fixing the sink well or not well), thereby providing you information (was the sink fixed?), and you are left with some control over motivation through the power of enforceability (to call the same plumber next time your sink clogs, give a tip for exceptional service, spread negative reviews if performance was bad, sue the plumber, or just to call a different plumber the next time). Every time you go to the doctor you become a principal in a potentially fraught principal–agent relationship, as many things could go wrong with each of the elements of the relationship.

Delegation. We go to a doctor for treatment when we experience symptoms. But as doctors have specialized knowledge and expertise we cannot tell them exactly what to do: which tests to run, how to interpret the results, and what treatments to give. Rather, we *delegate* in a way that gives broad discretion to the doctor: "Make me feel better."

Finance. A doctor has to be compensated adequately to make her effort worth the time (and repay the years of training) but the structure of the financing arrangement creates different incentives. In a "fee for service" arrangement the doctor gets paid depending on the actions taken (diagnostics done, treatments given): this creates incentives for doctors to over-treat patients, and in turn creates a tension between the interests of the patient as principal (make me feel better at reasonable cost) and doctor.

Information. After whatever the doctor does, you as principal now ask how you feel. But it may well be the doctor does the best he or she can and your condition doesn't respond. Alternatively, many visits to doctors are for "self-limiting" conditions that would have gotten better whether the doctor did any treatment or not. Hence the course of your own perceived health is not a good signal at all about whether the doctor treated you appropriately or not. Das and Hammer (2007) found massive amounts of over-treatment by private sector health care providers, particularly the provision of quack treatments like steroid drips that have temporary "feel good" benefits to make patients *think* the provider was responsible when in fact the provider's service is of no real medical value.

Motivations. Based on the information from the doctor's visit the principal may take actions intended to either enhance or reduce the doctor's wellbeing. These can be either extrinsic or pecuniary motivations—like repeat business or referring the doctor to others that increases the doctor's income—or extrinsic motivators like direct praise of the doctor's behavior.

Economists and other social scientists have used analysis of principal–agent relationships to examine how for-profit firms behave, as there are generically three principal–agent problems. One is between owners of firms (as principals) and those who manage the firm on their behalf (as agents). Owners have to design incentive mechanisms that deter managers from utilizing the assets of the firm to reward managers rather than the shareholders. This is complex because in modern corporations ownership is often quite diffuse and so many principals must coordinate to motivate few executives. The other generic principal–agent issue for a large private firm is how the management (now acting as principals) structures the employment relationship and compensation structure to motivate workers (as agents). Finally, firms must generate revenues and this is by the firm (as agent) providing a service demanded by another, with the firm's clients now acting as principals.

The issues of accountability facing public sector organizations are considerably more complex than for private firms. When the public sector acts it has four continuously operating relationships of accountability between different numbers and types of actors. Each of these relationships of accountability has the four accountability elements of delegation, finance, information, and motivation.

- Politics: Citizens, as principals, act to hold politicians, as agents, accountable for how they exercise sovereign power.
- Compact: The executive/legislative powers of the state, as principals, act to induce public sector organizations (central banks, police forces, environmental regulators, teachers, courts) to provide functions.
- Management: The top management of public sector organizations, as principals, act to induce front-line workers, as agents, in the organization to carry out their functions.
- Client Power: Citizens, as principals, act directly on front-line providers and organizations to hold them, as agents, accountable for delivery.

Weak organizational capability can be the result of weakness or incoherence in accountability relationships *within* the organization, in particular the *management* relationship. But just because a tire is flat does not mean the hole is on the bottom. Weak performance of organizations can be symptomatic of weak elements of the *system* of accountability relationships into which an organization is embedded. Weaknesses in state organizations can start from weakness in *politics*, such that politicians and policy makers are not concerned with functional organizations, or from weak *compact*, in which the executive apparatus of the state does not provide the conditions for organizations to succeed.

There are four typical ways in which accountability in state organizations is incoherent.

Mismatch of what is asked (delegation) and resources (finance). This mismatch happens at all levels. As we say in the discussion of "premature load bearing" in Chapter 3, often the goals articulated by the state for the organization, the *delegation* element of the *compact* relationship, are far beyond what is possible with the *finance* actually provided. Many developing country governments just have control over far too few resources to do all of the functions as well and as universally as they claim to (and as they are pressured to by outside support). Thomas (2015) describes the situation of Afghanistan after the US invasion in which the Afghan state was expected to provide a wide array of services—from security to health to education to infrastructure—with a tax base per person that was a small fraction of what the USA had *even in 1900* when the US federal government took on very few tasks. This mismatch sets up governments and organizations for failure, as they cannot possibly be held accountable to do the impossible.

Mismatch of delegation and information. Another common accountability incoherence is that the *delegation* is at least nominally oriented to normative objectives but *information* is only collected (at best) on input utilization and process compliance. This is a common feature both of the relationship of the state to organizations (*compact*) and inside state organizations (*management*). For instance, a study of regulation of labor safety in Brazil found that the agency's goal was safer work places but that their only information was about inspector visits and citations to firms about violations. For years, they never actually tracked—and hence could not motivate workers to pursue—workplace safety (until they did; more on this example later). Anyone who has worked in a public bureaucracy knows that at times all that matters is that what gets measured gets done—even if everyone knows that what is being measured doesn't really matter. As discussed in Chapter 2, when delegation is vague or just inconsistent with the information collected then organizations can—and in many instances must—rely on isomorphism rather than performance as performance isn't measured.

Mismatch between delegation and motivation. Another common failing is that even with *delegation* expressing laudable normative objectives, neither the organization (in the *compact* relationship with the state) nor front-line workers (in the *management* relationship with the organization) are given the latitude and scope of autonomy to act, nor is there alignment of extrinsic and intrinsic motivation. That is, often organizations will get the same resources year after year whether they perform well at achieving their normative objective or badly.

Mismatch in objectives across actors. Even if there is one strong and coherent relationship of accountability the organization can nevertheless lack capability if there is incoherence between the true accountability relationships across the different accountability relationships. For instance, the leadership of an organization might attempt to strengthen the *management* relationship by collecting better information on outcomes and output and attempting to motivate (with carrots and sticks) providers to do a better job. However, this may conflict with other motivations of politicians in the *delegation* function. Politicians may want to use public sector organizations as a means to give patronage jobs to political supporters. This is clearly incompatible with removal of dysfunctional workers. This is incoherence across the rows of Table 5.1—the different actors in their role as "principal" to "agents" really have very different objectives. Again, one can expect failure out of a public sector system in which the citizens, politicians and policy makers, leaders of public sector organizations and front-line workers all have completely different notions of what "success" would look like.

But before one can discuss in detail how to construct effective and coherent relationships of accountability within organizations, governments, and in broader systems, there first has to be a clear analytic of what kind of capability is required, and how that capability aligns with accountability.

Table 5.1. Four relationships of accountability (columns) by four elements of each relationship of accountability between Principals(s) (P) and Agent(s) (A) (rows) as a diagnostic for the systems of accountability within which state organizations operate

Four design elements of each relationship of accountability (Principal (P) to Agent (A))	Principal–agent relationships			
	Politics: Citizens to "the state"/politicians (many P to one A)	*Compact:* "The state" to organizations (one P to one A or one P to many A with non-state providers)	*Management:* Organizations to front-line providers (FLP) (one P to many A)	*Voice/ Client power:* Service recipients (parents/children) direct to FLP/ organizations (many P to one A)

Delegation: Specification of what P wants from A

Finance: Resources that P provides to A (either in advance or contingent)

Information:
P collects information on performance of A

Motivation:
How is A's wellbeing contingent on performance?
Change to motivation?
 • Intrinsic
 • Extrinsic
 • Exit (force out)
Performance of agent (endogenous)

Classifying the Type of Organizational Capability Needed: Four Questions

We ask the reader to think of any concrete public policy objective. The more specific the task and the more specific the context specified, the better. "Education" is too broad, whereas "remediating reading proficiency deficits in Bihar, India" or "vocational training in rural Sindh, Pakistan" is the desired level of granularity. "Public financial management" is too broad, whereas "management of procurement of medium-sized goods and services in Mozambique" is fine. "Microfinance" is too broad whereas "micro-savings programs for urban informal workers in Durban, South Africa" or "providing finance to promote entrepreneurial finance medium-sized enterprises in Saudi Arabia" is better.

It will help if you, as a reader, take time to write down a policy objective that interests you before proceeding. (We'll wait while you find a pen and paper. Back with pen and paper? OK.)

We want you to answer four questions about what it will take to accomplish your policy objective. The goal is to classify the type of capability an organization would need to be successful. This classification scheme cuts across sectors as within each sector (education, regulation, justice, infrastructure, health) there are analytically very different types of tasks.

Each question begins: "Does the successful accomplishment of your policy objective require actions or activities that are ... ?"

1. Transaction intensive? The first question is whether the accomplishment of the task is going to require many people or few people (or at least many transactions). For instance, a central bank can set some macroeconomic and monetary policies with decisions of a few individuals that are, more or less, self-implementing. So even though the USA's $20 trillion economy is unfathomably complex, key elements of monetary policy are made by a dozen or so individuals who themselves draw on remarkably few people. This is not transaction intensive. In contrast, primary schooling requires that lots of teachers work with lots of students every day. Teaching in primary schooling is transaction intensive. There are also elements of primary schooling, like setting the curriculum or creating textbooks, which may involve relatively few experts and hence are not transaction intensive.

Policing is transaction intensive. Passing laws is not transaction intensive. Dispute resolution is transaction intensive. Appellate courts are not transaction intensive. Procurement and spending budgets are transaction intensive. Setting a budget is not transaction intensive.

"Does the successful accomplishment of your policy objective require actions or activities that are transaction intensive?" Write down the answer. (And yes, we realize many readers' answer will always be "But it is more complicated than

that"; even so, we ask the reader to shake that impulse off for now and just write down yes or no.)

2. Discretionary? Services are *discretionary* to the extent that their delivery requires decisions by the agents responsible for implementation to be made on the basis of information that is important to success but inherently imperfectly specified and incomplete, thereby rendering them unable to be mechanized. Returning to Chapter 4's definition of a "policy formula" as a mapping between "facts" and "actions of an agent," whether or not achieving the policy objective requires agents to exercise discretion depends on three aspects of the policy formula:

- Does successful implementation require agents to use professional training, experience and judgment, or are the relevant facts of the policy formula obvious or easily ascertainable? Can policy implementation be reduced to a script that relies nearly exclusively on "hard" or "thin" information?

- How costly is it for a third party to verify and adjudicate in a contractually enforceable way what the "true" facts of a given situation are?

- How sensitive is the link between facts, actions of the agents, and outcomes?

Vaccinations and ambulatory curative care illustrate the difference in "discretionary." Both are transaction intensive, as they involve a face to face meeting between an agent (health care provider of some type) and the person receiving the service in order to be successful. But ambulatory curative care requires that the action taken be tailored to each patient so that a diagnostic process arrives at the right treatment (if any) can be discerned. A person presenting with severe pain radiating from their chest must be treated differently from a person presenting with pain in their knee for the curative care to be effective. In contrast, nearly every child gets the same vaccinations for childhood diseases. The relevant policy formula fact for vaccinations is the age of the child and their vaccination history, neither of which involves information which is difficult to ascertain or hard to verify.

Nearly all sectors and activities involve some elements that do and do not require local discretion. Policing requires that agents go into complex, often dangerous and tense situations and make hard, sometimes life-and-death decisions. No matter how finely specified the law, policemen operate with discretion. In contrast, giving traffic tickets is transaction intensive but need not involve discretion.

In primary schooling, getting textbooks delivered to each school on time and one to each child is an important task, but not one that requires discretion. In contrast, quality classroom instruction and teaching requires an ongoing interaction in which teachers tailor their actions to the students, individually and as a class, on a near-continuous basis. As such, these locally discretionary decisions usually entail extensive professional (gained via training and/or experience) or informal context-specific knowledge.[2]

"Does the successful accomplishment of your policy objective require actions or activities that require implementing agents to exercise local discretion?" Write it down. If some elements of accomplishing the policy objective do and others do not require discretion, specify which. We'll wait. OK.

3. Service or obligation? When the government's agents interact with citizens in the course of implementation they are either *providing a service* or *imposing an obligation*. Taxes, for instance, are the price of civilization and in democracies "the people" collectively agree to be taxed (Pritchett and Aiyar 2015). But in the act of collecting a property tax or sales tax or income tax the agents responsible for tax implementation are imposing an obligation. Similarly, the police necessarily interact with criminals. While this is a service to the society at large, to those who seek to avoid the law the role of the police is to impose obligations.

This distinction of whether the implementing agents are providing a service or imposing an obligation in their typical interaction is key for two reasons. One, it structures the possibilities for how the "client" interaction can be used for accountability. When "service delivery" is the goal then incorporating the feedback of direct users (of water, of schools, of health services, of roads) into the accountability of agents expands the range of inputs and information available to assess performance. In contrast, it is much more difficult to survey criminals about how the police treated them or put too much emphasis on "customer satisfaction" for tax auditors or environmental regulators (Chapter 4 reported how putting "clients" in charge of contracting for the reports of their own emissions lead to the predictable result of biased reporting). Two, in the imposition of obligations the decisions made in implementation can be high stakes and hence the pressure brought to bear on the agents of implementation to mis-declare the "facts" of the policy formula in order to produce an outcome desirable for the citizen but which thwarts the policy objective are high. Corruption is the ever-present risk in the imposition of obligations. Chapter 4 showed that even compliance with very mild obligations like demonstrating driving skill to get a driver's license can be undermined by payments to implementing agents.

---

[2] Forgive us the potential confusion, as "discretionary" more appropriately refers to the *mode* of the arrangement of an activity (which, at some level, is an endogenous choice) while we are using the term to refer to the underlying characteristics of the activity that lead it to be provided in a discretionary manner (or suffer losses from *not* being provided with arrangements that provide for discretion).

"In their routine activities are the implementing agents providing a service or imposing an obligation?" Write it down.

4. Based on known technology? Many tasks, like ambulatory curative care, are complicated and require agents to exercise discretion. But doctors can rely on bodies of knowledge and training and handbooks and even protocols to follow for diagnosis and treatment. Running a central bank is not an easy task, but there is a body of knowledge and empirical evidence and a strong professional consensus about many components of the decision making that central bank leaders and staff can rely on (or ignore at their peril). But often success requires that the agents of an organization go beyond following established protocols; they must actually innovate and move beyond the frontier of known technology and accepted practice to achieve success.

This need to go beyond the known technology and actually innovate can arise for a variety of reasons. One is that new situations and new technological shifts may mean that what was the known technology no longer applies but no one is (yet) sure what does. The other reason is that human beings are just enormously complex and how to motivate them to do certain things and not others cannot be reduced to a formula. So, while the technology of weight loss is relatively well known there are very few successful *programs* to induce weight loss in others. This isn't to say nothing is known but just that, for instance, ambulatory curative care, or treating specific disease conditions that patients present with at facilities, is based on a known technology while inducing populations to reduce risk has proven enormously more complex. A final reason an activity might be wicked hard is that one is promoting something like "entrepreneurship" that itself means individuals need to innovate.

"Does successful implementation require innovation from agents as opposed to reliance on an agreed upon technology?" Write it down.

A Typology of Tasks by Capability Required

Based on these four questions (illustrated in Figure 5.1) we create a taxonomy with five principal types of tasks based on the type of organizational capability and how the task facilitates or complicates building this capability: *policymaking and/or concentrated (elite) services, logistics, implementation-intensive service delivery, implementation-intensive imposition of obligations,* and *wicked hard* (illustrated in Figure 5.2)

Policy formulation (and elite concentrated services). The first category is distinguished from all of the others by its nature of not being transaction intensive. This is really a combination of categories of those for which implementation requires relatively few people. The task of policymaking itself—of articulating the policy formula, objectives,

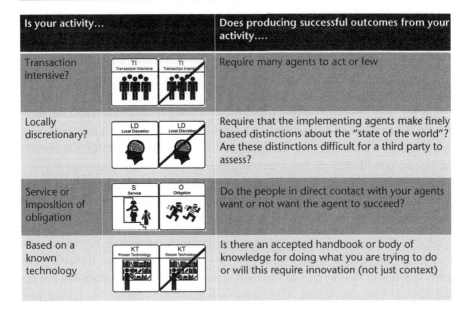

Is your activity...			Does producing successful outcomes from your activity....
Transaction intensive?	TI Transaction Intensive	TI Transaction Inten...	Require many agents to act or few
Locally discretionary?	LD Local Discretion	LD Local Discretion	Require that the implementing agents make finely based distinctions about the "state of the world"? Are these distinctions difficult for a third party to assess?
Service or imposition of obligation	S Service	O Obligation	Do the people in direct contact with your agents want or not want the agent to succeed?
Based on a known technology	KT Known Technology	KT Known Technology	Is there an accepted handbook or body of knowledge for doing what you are trying to do or will this require innovation (not just context)

Figure 5.1. Four key analytic questions about an activity to classify the capability needed

and causal model—is nearly always possible (if not desirable) to do with relatively few people.

This category can also include apex or elite institutions in many sectors as, in the larger scheme of things, these require very few agents. Nearly every sector has apex institutions—the tertiary hospital, the research university, the highest appellate court, the central bank, for example—that may only involve a few hundred core professionals and hence are not transaction intensive. Even within organizations there are often "elite" units, as in most militaries. When these are in separate organizations or distinct within an organization this creates a different dynamic for organizational capability as their concentrated and apex nature makes peer monitoring and *esprit de corps* the primary accountability mechanisms. Heart surgeons care about what other heart surgeons think of them, Navy SEALS about what other SEALS think of them. We mention this because many countries maintain impressively strong elite or apex institutions even in otherwise largely dysfunctional and/or corrupt environments. However, these successes don't necessarily point to a potential for broader success at building capability for more transaction-intensive activities.

Logistics. A second type of capability is the ability of organizations to induce large numbers of agents to follow relatively simple scripts that rely on easily observable

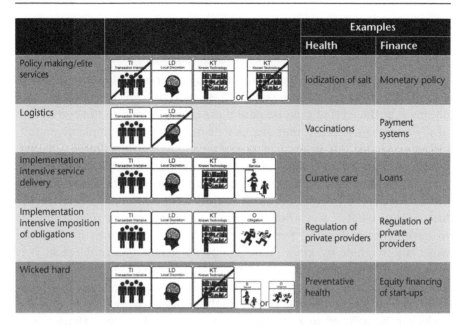

				Examples	
				Health	Finance
Policy making/elite services				Iodization of salt	Monetary policy
Logistics				Vaccinations	Payment systems
Implementation intensive service delivery				Curative care	Loans
Implementation intensive imposition of obligations				Regulation of private providers	Regulation of private providers
Wicked hard				Preventative health	Equity financing of start-ups

Figure 5.2. The five types of activities that have different capability needs in implementation

and judicable facts. In financial matters, an example is retail banking transactions, many of which can be carried out by a junior clerk (or for the most routine transactions, a machine).[3] To implement a "program" the agents of the organization need only to stick to a relatively fixed "script" (Leonard, 2002; Dobbin, forthcoming), in which the choices are few and judging the choice appropriate to the situation is relatively easy.

Implementation-intensive service delivery. Tasks that are discretionary (unlike logistics) and transaction intensive (unlike *policy/elite services*) we classify as "implementation intensive" as they require large organizations with agents engaged in complicated actions. The key distinction is whether these actions are devoted to "services" in which agents interact with people who (in principle) directly benefit from successful implementation.

Implementation-intensive imposition of obligations. The imposition of obligations can be implementation intensive, like policing, taxation, or regulation. Implementing such tasks entails overcoming the resistance of those upon whom obligations are being imposed; recipients may seek to use everything from passive resistance to physical threats to material incentives (bribes) to induce agents to be less than diligent in carrying out their duties.

Wicked hard. The most difficult tasks that combine *transaction intensive* (a large number of agents need to participate), *discretionary* (the decisions made by agents are based on

---

[3] The name "programs" has the advantage of following the usual development nomenclature (of policies versus practices) but also invoking the idea of a computer program.

difficult-to-verify knowledge) and *not based on a known technology* require a category all their own. As we are based in Boston we call these "wicked hard" tasks (where "wicked" is the local vernacular for "very," not "evil").

Going one level of specificity further, our taxonomy allows us to think analytically about the diverse range of tasks within a given sector. The taxonomy is at the level of tasks because these classifications do not correspond neatly to sectors; it is not that case that "education" is all "implementation-intensive service delivery" or "finance" is all "concentrated/elite." Rather, within every sector and subsector there are examples of each type of task.

For instance, a girl turns up at elementary school eager to learn: What has to happen to provide her with high-quality instruction? The teacher has to know what to teach her and when, which means the curriculum has to have been established, preferably along with some norms for learning expectations grade by grade. This is a *policy formulation* problem as it is primarily technocratic and not transaction intensive. The girl has to be near a school with adequate facilities and learning materials. This is primarily a *logistical* problem as building schools and buying blackboards and desks can be reduced to a (reasonably) standardized process. There has to be a teacher there that know what to teach, knows the material, and knows how to teach it. This is *implementation-intensive service delivery*, as teachers exercise local discretion, hour by hour, class by class, and child by child. There are also elements of the *wicked hard*, as innovations are needed to not just keep learning levels constant but increase them over time. Similarly with procurement: the formal rules may be determined by a select committee (*policy formulation*), but ensuring that all relevant staff members in an organization know what these rules are might entail preparing a handbook and an online tutorial that can test knowledge (*logistics*). Knowing how to apply the rules in response to marginal, novel or ambiguous cases, however, will entail considerable discretion on the part of adjudicators (*implementation-intensive service*), while enforcing them in instances where there might be potentially lucrative kickbacks on offer (*implementation-intensive obligations*) is likely to entail adherence to strong professional norms and internalized codes of conduct.

Implications for Organizations of the Capability Taxonomy

The purpose of the foregoing sections was to create an analytically grounded classification of types of organizational capability. This taxonomy is necessary because there is a tendency, in practice if not academically, to distinguish between policy formulation and policy implementation. Capability in policy formulation is the ability to frame objectives, analyze options and, based on the relevant methods and evidence, choose the best policy. Capability in policy implementation is regarded in strictly logistical terms as creating organizational procedures that produce the process compliance of agents with the policy as formulated.

If everything the public sector did was "logistical" in our sense, and the organizations already had adequate capability, then this wouldn't be a terrible approach. In Wilson's (1989) classic on bureaucracy he points out that the US Social Security administration was roughly as cost-effective in the task of delivering old age pension checks to eligible recipients as any organization, private or public, could hope to be. This is because the task is entirely logistical: the policy formula for eligibility is well defined in hard facts (based on age and duration of contributions) and maps to a simple clear action (mail a check of a certain amount). Full stop. At logistical tasks like that, nothing beats a bureaucracy.

Carpenter's (2001) history of the emergence of the US Postal Service (and others) as a modern Weberian bureaucracy recalls a period in which the bureaucracy was seen by forward looking reformers as the solution to the problems that riddled existing systems, which at the time were captured by local political interests and patronage networks. It struggled its way into existence by legitimizing stronger bureaucratic control over the post based on its superior efficiency. Indeed, even as post offices around the world are being corporatized and many functions shifting to private sector firms, those firms are competing to be more effective bureaucracies. But if one compares FedEx or DHL or UPS to the US Postal Service they are nearly identical in the way they are organized and operate—because they are competing to be a better bureaucracy at doing logistics.[4]

We have yet to meet anyone who can name a large firm of dentists. Everyone knows their dentist, but almost always in market economies their dentist works alone or in a partnership with one or two other dentists. Dentistry isn't policy-making and dentistry isn't logistics. Dentists have practices.[5] A "practice" is the organizational form for implementation-intensive service delivery when it is not in the public sector. Most law firms, physician practices, universities, household contractors, therapists, marriage counselors, music teachers, and sports coaches[6] are incredibly small relative to the national market. Even

---

[4] Indeed, the slogan of UPS for a time was "We Love Logistics"; interestingly, for our purposes at least, it is currently "United Problem Solvers."

[5] Our rendering of "practices" should not be confused with Sunstein and Ullmann-Margalit's (1999) intriguing notion of "second-order decisions," which they define as the various strategies adopted in complex environments (by key actors such as judges, politicians, administrators) to *avoid* actually having to make discretionary decisions. Our discussion is more akin to, and in some senses builds on, Heifetz's (1994) useful distinction between "technical" and "adaptive" decision-making.

[6] The exception that proves the rule in the "coaching" industry (e.g. music lessons, sports instruction) is the emergence of large organizations that provided courses that prepare students for a *standardized* exam.

though they are transaction intensive, the need for "local discretion" makes these tasks a mismatch with the logic of the logistical imperatives of large-scale, routinized, administrative control of agents to produce process compliance.[7]

The classic bureaucracy is appropriate for logistical tasks for which simple accountability is sufficient for adequate performance; "delegation" (what it is the agent should do) and "information" (measurement of the agent's performance) are completely reducible to easily judicable facts. The post office is the quintessential example, as everything about what each agent should do to each parcel is easily contained in a few bytes (the address and the class of service). This creates compatible internal (management) and external (politics, compact, client power) formal and folk cultures of performance. What the postal clerk is expected to do by his managers (did he deliver the mail?) is measurable in exactly the same terms that clients can measure it (did my mail arrive?), the overall organization can be measured (what percentage of parcels were delivered on time?), and the political system can talk about it (is the post office doing its job at a reasonable cost?).[8] Note that this is a characteristic of task, not sector, and not whether it is in the public or private sphere. In the United States the internal mechanics and size and structure of organizations that deliver packages in the private sector (FedEx, UPS, DHL) look organizationally nearly identical to the post office—same trucks, similar uniforms, similar thin accountability tracked with thin information.

Everything about the way an organization tends to work depends on that task it confronts at its "operating core" (Mintzberg 1979). All large organizations have multiple elements and these elements have different capability requirements, but the "operating core" is the part of the organization that is the unique producer of value and *raison d'être* for the organization's existence. Law partnerships, universities, and architectural firms all have units that handle accounting but accounting is not their "operating core"; it is a service function deployed in the interests of the technical core—legal services, teaching and research, designs of buildings respectively. When organizations can choose their structure the overall size, scope, and culture of the organization is driven by the characteristics

---

[7] In policing, for example, Goldstein (1990: 8) concludes that "studies identified the enormous gap between the practice and the image of policing. They identified problems in policing that were not simply the product of poor management, but rather reflections of the inherent complexity of the police job: informal arrangements... were found to be more common than was compliance with formally established procedures; individual police officers were found to be routinely exercising a great deal of discretion in deciding how to handle the tremendous variety of circumstances with which they were confronted."

[8] The postal service itself, it should be noted, rightly seeks to convey a more noble account of its activities. Literally chiseled in stone on the National Postal Museum in Washington, DC is the following inscription, reminding visitors that a postal worker is actually a: Messenger of Sympathy and Love/Servant of Parted Friends/Consoler of the Lonely/Bond of the Scattered Family/Enlarger of the Common Life.

of the operating core. If the operating core is logistics, the organization reflects that. When the technical core is a "practice" the organizational structure reflects that, while incorporating service functions operating as logistics.

The major risk of not having an adequate taxonomy of organizational capability is the risk of mismatch between the approach to building an effective organization and the task at its technical core. As we articulate in the future chapters, the dominant tendency in public sector organizations has been to impose the Procrustean bed that public sector organizations are either "policymaking" organizations or "logistical." Organizations that are responsible for implementation are treated as standard Weberian bureaucracies—which is fine if tasks that are logistical are in the technical core, but not at all fine (i.e. can fail badly) when more implementation-intensive activities are in the technical core.

Pritchett (2013, 2014) illustrates this mismatch in primacy education. As we saw above, primary education requires tasks of different capability types: *policymaking/elite* (standard, curriculum, assessment), *logistics* (building schooling, delivering inputs), and *implementation-intensive service delivery* (classroom teaching). It is clear that when delivered outside of public sector contexts that if instruction is the technical core then organizations are typically organized as "practices" because it is implementation intensive. However, for a variety of historical, political, and intellectual reasons primary education came to be dominated by "spider"[9] organizations which approached public education as a logistical problem of expanding enrollments. This mismatch between an organizational structure well adapted to logistics led to a situation in which the goal of expanding enrollment—through the construction of buildings, buying of inputs, hiring of teachers—has been met but many countries are admitting to a "learning crisis" as the quality of teaching and student learning is, not at all surprisingly, given the inversion of the operating core, very weak. In one state of India, enhanced budget and programs were able to improve all of the measures of facilities and logistics—and yet in less than a decade the system lost a million students to providers as parents chose to pay for private education rather than enroll children in the public system for free (Pritchett 2014).

Accounting and Accounts in Accountability

Let's return to accountability relationships and systems of accountability in light of the taxonomy we've just outlined. Packed into "accountability" are

---

[9] The terminology of "spider" and "starfish" as types of organizations comes from Brafman and Beckstrom (2006).

two fundamentally different notions embedded in different variants of the same word: *account* and *accounting*.

An "account" is the justificatory narrative I tell myself which reconciles my actions with my identity: am I fulfilling my duties? An account is the story of my actions I tell to those whose opinion of me is important to me (including most importantly, myself, but including family and kinsmen, friends, co-workers, co-religionists, people in my occupation and other people whose admiration I seek) that explains why my actions are (or, if the account is a confession, are not) in accord with a positive view of myself as an agent.[10]

Following the notion elaborated by Geertz (1973)[11] of a "thick description," we create the distinction between "thick accountability" (the *account*) and "thin accountability" (the *accounting*).[12] Thick accountability is inevitably a folk process in which behavior is shaped by norms that are unwritten and informal, while thin accountability can be (re)produced within formal sector organizations.

Our argument is that successful organizations rely on a combination of thin and thick accountability, both internally and externally. Once agents have lost the sense that their account, either to their organization or to their fellow citizens or their fellow professionals, depends on their carrying out their formal duties, no amount of *accounting* can make a difference. A strong *account* and indeed *thick accountability* is required in public service delivery that is implementation intensive (and more so for the wicked hard).

As we saw in Chapter 4, when accounts and accounting diverge, organizations can often "fix" the accounting and thereby make the "administrative facts" of accounting a complete fiction. A public agent's *account* actually rests squarely on many *folk* understandings. What is the *account* of the doctor in the Madhya Pradesh study, who doesn't get off the phone when dealing with a patient presenting with chest pains? What is the *account* of a teacher who doesn't smile at the students (much less laugh, joke, or talk to them)? What is the *account* of a policeman who takes bribes from motorists? Or the bureaucrat who issues licenses without the compliance? Fixing the *accounting* cannot fix the *account*, and the *account* is in the realm of the *folk*.

Our argument is that successful organizations are built on internal and external accounts for which accounting provides some support and plays some role. Think of any organization with a long track record of success (on the organization's objectives): Oxford University, the Catholic Church, the

---

[10] Our views and description of an "account" is strongly influenced by MacIntyre (2007) and his views on Aristotelian notions of virtue.

[11] Geertz himself acknowledges the priority of Gilbert Ryle in the idea of "thick" description but he popularized the notion as a methodological stance.

[12] The term "thick accountability" is also used in Dubnick (2003), who describes the idea with many of the same meanings and implications we use here.

Red Cross, the US Marine Corps, Exxon. These organizations survive and thrive because key agents believe it is important that their account of what they do (indeed perhaps who they are) accords with the purposes of the organization. Indeed, the three of us can attest from experience that high-capability universities do not thrive because professors do accounting for their behavior, but professors at thriving universities do have an account of what they do because they are professors and this account is important to them.

Moreover, to some external audiences the organization has to justify itself for legitimacy and ultimately resources. This external accountability is not driven by accounting or detailed measures of cost effectiveness or proven impact or reducible to precise figures, but they have to continually prove to key constituencies that they work because there are competitors for their support base (students and faculty for universities, adherents for religions, donors and volunteers for philanthropic organizations, funding among other public uses for marines, capital markets and customers for Exxon) and if these external actors no longer believe the organization's account then they lose traction with their internal agents and external constituencies no matter what the accounting says.

Consider for a moment the thickness of information.[13] "Thin" information can be thought of as information that is easily amenable to being reduced to "information" in the Shannon (1948) sense of information as messages encoded in bits and bytes. "Is it Tuesday (right here, right now)?" is a "thin" question on which we all can readily agree and, if necessary, have third-party adjudicators agree to what the fact of the matter is. It is easy to create high-powered incentives on thin information: "I will pay you $10 if it arrives on Tuesday and only $5 if it arrives on Wednesday" is an enforceable contract because the fact of "Tuesday" is easily judicable and hence Tuesday is a contractible.

The world is, however, immensely thick. Only a tiny fraction of our every-day existence can be reduced to thin information. Was Tuesday a nice day? Was the bus driver rude to you on Tuesday? Was the Starbucks clerk friendly to you on Tuesday? Were you in a good mood on Tuesday? Was your lunch delicious on Tuesday? Were you attentive to your partner on Tuesday? Did you do your best at work on Tuesday? All of these are potentially important determinants of our wellbeing, but none of these are easily contractible. They

---

[13] The central issue in the "economics of information" is the costliness of the adjudication of information. The economics of information as an explanation of institutions and organizational behaviors starts with Williamson (1975), then builds through principal–agent theory to organizational compensation schemes (Lazear 1995), organizational strategies (Milgrom and Roberts 1992), allocation of authority (Aghion and Tirole 1997), and the theory of the boundaries of the firm itself as a problem of contracting (e.g. Hart and Holmstrom 2010). The economics of information approach has also been applied to delegation, contracting, and the scope of public sector organizations (e.g. Hart et al. 1997; Laffont and Tirole 1993).

are not judicable because the difficulty of establishing third-party intersubjective agreement on just what the facts on Tuesday really were about: nice, rude, friendly, delicious, inattentive, best effort, etc.

How does this "thick" versus "thin" distinction relate to the capability of the state for policy implementation?

When attempts at thin accountability—making agent rewards depend on judicable "facts" (like attendance, like were actual taxes owed)—are impossible because the overall institutional environment is weak, then even using incentives will not work.[14] Besley and McLaren (1993) used a model of tax collection and tax inspection to note that when punishment based on observed actions was sufficiently difficult (the probability of an effective audit with punishment was low) there was no advantage of paying a fixed wage high enough to deter corruption or encourage honest inspectors. In their model when actions cannot be contracted then a "capitulation wage"—paying low wages and admitting all tax inspectors who were not monitored would be corrupt, which results in a cynical and entirely dishonest set of tax inspectors—was the net revenue generating strategy.

Besley and Ghatak (2005) explore this issue referring to organizations with "mission" (what we call *internal folk culture of performance*) and show that if organizations can be matched to mission then this non-pecuniary form of motivation reduces the need for (if not desirability of) high-powered pecuniary incentives. The better organizations are able to recruit individuals motivated by mission (individuals whose personal thick accountability is strong) the less the organization needs to rely on thin accountability.

As mentioned earlier, logistical organizations such as FedEx can rely on thin accountability to function. In organizations that perform tasks that are predominantly of more difficult, non-logistical types (e.g. concentrated, implementation-intensive service delivery, implementation-intensive imposition of obligations, wicked hard) the internal folk culture required for performance is at odds with a formal culture of thin accountability (see Table 5.1). A high-performing university or hospital (either in the public or private sector) requires a culture of accountability for performance. But this does not translate into professors being tracked minute by minute by GPS. You cannot reduce the delegation of what a professor should do to be a high-quality professor to a sequence of bytes. The same is true of nurses. The same is true of policemen.

While there might be some minimal performance criteria that are thin (like attendance), what has been learned from decades of studies of schools, for

---

[14] One of the key insights of principal–agent theory is that the less precisely the desirability of the actions of the agent can be measured, the less high-powered the incentives should optimally be (e.g. Holmstrom and Milgrom 1991, and for an application to civil service Klitgaard 1997).

instance, is that the thin accountability parts of schooling do not affect education very much. While good teachers—as measured by their performance—matter a lot to student learning what being a "good teacher" means is not reducible to thin criteria like degrees or age or years of service (Chetty et al. 2011; Rivkin et al. 2005), or even, we would argue, student learning alone. Similarly, inputs alone, the kinds of things that education management information systems can measure and track, just do not have a very strong connection with the education a child receives—or the inequality in outcomes across schools (Pritchett and Viarengo 2009)—as "implementation-intensive service delivery" good schools require thick accountability as well as thin accountability, internally and externally.

Valuable local *folk* practices—idiosyncratic knowledge of variables crucial to the welfare of the poor (e.g. soil conditions, weather patterns, water flows)—get squeezed out, even lost completely, in large centralized development programs designed to address these issues (see Ostrom, 1990; Scott, 1998). The myriad informal "practices" that indigenous communities in particular have evolved over the millennia to address these concerns may be clearly ill-suited to the complexity and scale of modern economic life, but the transition from one set of mechanisms to the other cannot be made in a single bound. While not attempting the transition at all is a prescription for continued poverty, revolutionaries from Stalin to Mao to Nyerere to contemporary "shock therapists" have imagined that it was actually possible and desirable to ruthlessly "skip straight to Weber"—but with patently disastrous results. In the murky middle ground between the public services and risk management systems of "Djibouti" and "Denmark" lies the need for a much more delicate articulation of the two, an articulation that the technocrats and bureaucrats of large development (and other) agencies inherently and inevitable struggle to resolve.

These more graphic examples of large-scale bureaucratic disaster, however, have their counterpart in a host of smaller everyday instances of repeated failure by standardized delivery mechanisms to provide basic services to the poor. Some of these problems, of course, stem from the fact that in many instances the state itself (for whatever reason) was unable and/or unwilling to provide the services that citizens wanted. Our concerns, however, apply to systemic services failures that routinely occurred even in settings where intentions and resources were reasonably good.

In our taxonomy of the capability requirements of activities we want to stress that *moving* an organization from lacking capability to capability is itself *wicked hard*. That is, if one has a dysfunctional post office that is not delivering mail in an effective way the capability needed is pure logistics but *moving* an organization from lacking the capability to do logistics to having the capability to do logistics is wicked hard. Why? Because building capability, even using our approach of PDIA is not a "known technology." Changing organizations is changing the behavior of people and many aspects of human behavior are just too complex to pretend it can be reduced to a simple formula.

The same is true of moving from organizations with capability for logistics but not for the implementation-intensive components of what the organization needs to do. For instance, in building out a system of basic education capable of producing learning some elements—like building the school buildings or assigning teachers to schools, or ensuring attendance—can be reduced to logistics but other elements, like teachers displaying concern, cannot. Getting a large-scale organization from logistics to implementation-intensive capability is itself wicked hard and requires something like PDIA.

In Part II of the book we turn to the practical task of building the capability you need for success.

Part II

A Strategy for Action—Problem-Driven Iterative Adaptation

6

The challenge of building (real) state capability for implementation

There is an old story of a doctor who prescribed aspirin to her patients every time they complained of head pain. Where pain medication was the appropriate solution, the treatment led to positive results with many patients. It helped some patients avoid heart attacks and strokes as well, often as an unseen (and unforeseen) side effect. It did not work for all the doctor's patients, however. Some returned with continuing head pain, which did not go away after even repeated and extensive aspirin treatment. These patients typically suffered from other ailments that needed different, more complex, treatments—aimed, for instance, at cleaning sinuses, reducing stress, and even removing tumors. The doctor failed many of these patients because of her limited approach and inability to adapt diagnoses and treatment. Her failure was more direct with patients whose bodies did not have the capacity to handle the aspirin treatment (and suffered from severe bleeding disorders, asthma, and liver and kidney disease). These patients experienced complications after receiving the aspirin treatments, which sometimes brought on life-threatening medical problems and even death.

This simple story helps to summarize our views on why many development interventions have limited impacts, and especially why efforts to build state capability have regularly had muted effects (as we saw in previous chapters). These efforts often take the form of commonly used, highly designed and engineered best-practice solutions (like aspirin) that have worked in many other places and that we suspect (and hope) will work again in many contexts. Modern internal audit is an example. This is a relatively recent management tool (codified only in 1979) that bolsters an organization's ability to manage risk and ensure accountability, both of which ostensibly foster greater capability. It emerged as a useful practice in mostly Anglo-Saxon countries and is now a staple of state capacity building initiatives around the globe (Andrews 2011, 2012, 2013).

Such interventions do sometimes work, especially when the treatment actually addresses problems that fester in the context. Where the contextual problems are different, however, the treatment is just isomorphic mimicry—it looks good but will not be a solution to problems that actually matter. Many internal audit reforms have been just this, with governments introducing new laws and audit requirements that are not acted upon. Development organizations often cannot see this, however, and offer the same solution again and again—hoping for a different outcome but imposing a capability trap on the policy context, where a new diagnosis and prescription is actually needed. In some countries the treatment has an even worse impact, fostering premature load bearing—where the designated institutions cannot handle what is prescribed. Just like the patients who bleed after aspirin, countries in this situation find that external solutions overwhelm their limited capabilities, compromise the possibility and legitimacy of institutional reform and policy implementation, and undermine efforts to build confidence and capability in the context. We see this in some countries even with something as apparently innocuous as internal audit, where governments that try to use the tool sometimes find it to be extremely disruptive and alien in their extant management systems.

Given that you were interested in reading a book on building state capability for implementation, we assume that you are also asking what can be done to improve the impact of efforts to build state capability, and if there are approaches to doing development that can be applied when aspirin does not work. This chapter offers an introduction to thinking about this approach, which we call problem-driven iterative adaptation (PDIA).[1] The chapter builds up to a discussion of this approach and its core principles, taking you through our own journey toward identifying PDIA, and showing why we think it is an appropriate tool for building state capability, and when it is most relevant. We start with a simple classroom exercise to do this, focused on designing a strategy to travel from east to west in the United States of America in 2015 and 1804. The exercise may seem a little removed from your development experience, but it leads into a discussion of the different challenges in building state capability in developing countries—and the importance of having different strategies to face up to these different challenges. One of these strategies is PDIA, which we see as appropriate in addressing complex challenges that are common when trying to build state capability. We conclude by asking you to reflect on which of your challenges fall into this category, and where you can start applying the PDIA principles.

Building Capability to Go West

We take many of the development professionals we work with through a simple exercise when introducing PDIA as a new strategy for building state capability. It is designed to illustrate why different approaches are needed when building state capability in developing countries, and to introduce PDIA as a particularly useful approach.

The 2015 Challenge

We start by asking professionals to create a plan that will get them, as quickly as possible, by car, from St Louis to Los Angeles in the United States in 2015. They are given a road map and a table showing distances between cities. You might want to try it out, using Figure 6.1 and Table 6.1 to assist. Do not hesitate to draw on the map, showing the precise details of your journey—roads you will

---

[1] Our initial work on PDIA was published as Andrews et al. (2013).

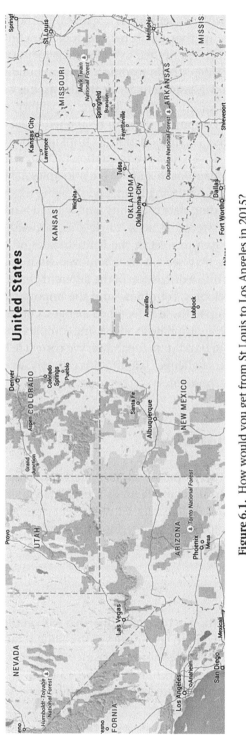

Figure 6.1. How would you get from St Louis to Los Angeles in 2015?
Source: Google Maps

Table 6.1. Distances of various cities from St Louis

City	Grand Junction CO	Denver, CO	Dallas, TX	Albuquerque NM	Wichita KS	Reno NV
Distance	1103	858	633	1041	443	1849
City	Oklahoma City OK	Los Angeles CA	Las Vegas NV	Kanas City, MO	San Diego CA	Phoenix AZ
Distance	496	1840	1606	253	1858	1504

drive on, distances, times, and so forth. Think of it as your strategy to build 2015 capability to travel west.

Ultimately, all the professionals we work with manage to produce a solution in quite a short time period. Interestingly, they typically identify one of two routes, going through Denver to the North or Albuquerque to the South. These, apparently, are the "best-practice" options in this case (being the shortest and most direct). Perhaps you identified the same routes?

We then ask what the professionals assumed when coming up with the solution. The list is always long, and includes things like the following: "we assumed the map was real"; "we assumed the distances shown were for the routes on the maps"; "we assumed the roads really exist"; "we assumed there would be rest rooms and gas stations en route"; and "we assumed there would be police officers providing order (and not holding us up to extort bribes)." We ask them why they are comfortable making so many assumptions. The answer is usually something like, "These assumptions are safe to make because we are dealing with the United States, where we know such things are really true." They also note that the assumptions were possible because they had firm start and end points. Some will also reflect on the fact that they have followed the same kind of map before and this experience lends credibility to the assumptions ("Maps in the United States are dependable, so we expect this to be dependable too").

We conclude this part of the exercise by asking what kind of capability they need to complete the journey, whether it is a risky journey, and what kind of leadership will be required to make it happen. The answers are again quick and common: "a pair of individuals with driving licenses, a cellphone and some kind of mapping software can easily complete this, with no real risk." We ask how many people in the room have the requisite capabilities, and just about every hand goes up. This demonstrates how accessible the journey is, requiring common capabilities, and proceeding relatively risk-free along a best-practice route that we know exists. The leadership discussion is short-lived as a result: "You just need someone to oversee the drivers, and make sure they follow the route as it has been identified." A single individual can do this if they are given authority over the drivers, with basic oversight capabilities, facing very little risk of failure and very little resistance from the drivers.

Table 6.2. A strategy to Go West in 2015

What drives action?	A clearly identified and predefined solution
How is action identified, carried out?	Reference existing knowledge and experience, plot exact course out in a plan, implement as designed
What authority or leadership is required?	A single authorizer ensuring compliance with the plan, with no other demands or tensions
Who needs to be involved?	A small group of appropriately qualified individuals

Source: Authors' work, based on Andrews (2015a)

We summarize this discussion by asking participants to break down the key elements of the strategy they propose to get from St Louis to Los Angeles in 2015 ("how would you build the capability to do this?"). They do so by answering four questions: What drives action? How is action identified and carried out? What authority or leadership is required? and, Who needs to be involved? Table 6.2 shows the common responses to each question. These show, essentially, that action will be driven by a predefined solution, which is identified with reference to existing knowledge and experience, planned out in detail and implemented as planned. This requires only one authorizer or leader (given the narrowness or specificity of the task) and the person authorizing or leading such work simply needs to ensure she can ensure full compliance with the plan, involving very few individuals in the process (ensuring they have appropriate skills, but facing few other personnel problems—like having to motivate their engagement or incentivize them to take on extra risk).

The 1804 Challenge

Then we turn the tables a bit, and give the professionals we work with a map of the United States in 1804, before the west had been fully explored. St Louis was one of the western-most cities at the time, and there was no fixed or commonly shared knowledge about where the west coast was or what lay between St Louis and that coastline. With a (nearly) blank map in front of them, we ask the professionals to imagine they are in St Louis in 1804 and then work out a strategy to find the west coast. You may want to take the challenge yourself, with the map provided in Figure 6.2. It actually shows more than you would have known in 1804 (given that we have added a west coast boundary into the figure, but no one actually knew where this coastline was at the time). Think of it as your strategy to build 1804 capability to travel west.

Hopefully that was not too tough a task! It is for many of those we work with, incidentally. Some of them try to retrofit the 2015 strategy into the 1804

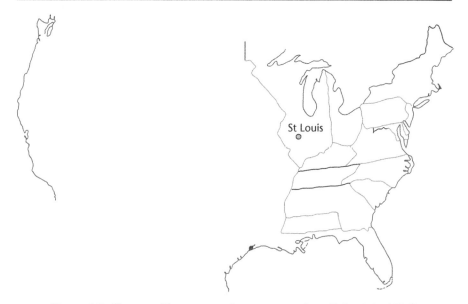

Figure 6.2. How would you get to the west coast from St Louis in 1804?

context: "take the same route up to Denver, and then down to Los Angeles."
We remind them that Denver and Los Angeles do not exist, and the route from
St Louis is also not yet in place. This clarity is often greeted with frustrated and
confused questions: "how do we determine a solution without roads, or a
map?"; "surely someone knows where the west coast is and can direct us
there?"; "you must have some more information to share."

Once the participating professionals realize that the unknowns are all
intended—and that they were really unknown to the adventurers of the
time—some of them immediately declare the task impossible: "if we don't
know where we are going, how can we identify a strategy to get there?"; "how
do we identify a route if there is no route to choose from?"; "if no one knows
anything, why are we even trying to go the west coast?" Others say that a
strategy must be possible—after all, someone did find his way to the west
coast—but that any strategy is heavily dependent on luck. The most common
suggestion by such participants is the simple, fatalistic strategy: "identify
where west is on your compass and walk . . . hoping everything turns out OK!"

We acknowledge that luck must play a part in any initiative involving
fundamental uncertainty and weak (or nonexistent) knowledge and information. At the same time, we ask if a strategy could have more detail to it than
"face west, walk, and hope for the best." In essence, we ask if any process could
be set in place to maximize one's luck in such an expedition (or even create
luck as one moves west).

Faced with this challenge, participants tend to start thinking a bit more laterally, and offer interesting ideas about potential strategies for action. Most participants begin by noting that a team is needed to do this work, for instance, comprising a broad set of agents with different skills and playing different functional roles. The list of necessary functions they offer usually includes a doctor, cook, soldier, and builder. We often add a few roles to this list, including a cartographer (to map the route, so that everyone can go back afterwards), a local guide (to help the team navigate routes that have not yet been codified but can be traversed if one has the tacit knowledge of their existence, gained through hands-on experience), and an authorized spokesperson representing whoever is sending the team (to negotiate with other political representatives en route and ensure the journey is continuously supported).

Typically, some of the professionals we work with will reflect on the need for regular changes in the team's composition. They argue that one cannot know upfront exactly what skills are required, or who will fall away during the journey, or when a new guide is needed: So the team needs to have a way of adding and changing its membership given emerging challenges. This observation usually gets the whole class thinking about more general limits to pre-planning the journey: One cannot predefine the exact composition of the team or the exact path to take. Some participants will comment that this kind of task warrants a step-by-step approach, where the team progresses in a set direction for a few days, determined at times by a "best guess" method—using whatever knowledge or experience is available and then deciding which direction to take. The team would map the territory as it progresses and then stop and set up camp, reflect on progress, send injured members back, access reinforcements (to join via the same route), and think about what the next step could be (given lessons learned along the path, and any unexpected opportunities and difficulties encountered). They may be surprised by how open their chosen path is and walk for days before having to stop, or they may encounter unknown challenges (like rivers) that require stopping soon and maybe even turning back or changing direction dramatically.

Some of those we work with note that the journey will probably comprise a number of these steps, which we would call experimental iterations. The steps would combine into a new path leading from a known starting point to an aspirational destination that emerges as one progresses (given that it is unknown at the start). Some point out that the team would probably need more steps like this on longer journeys. They note, as well, that the steps would tend to be shorter and require more variation when passing through demanding and surprising terrain (like mountains or rivers, where the team would need to try multiple potential routes of passage, return to a base camp to discuss which worked and why, and then decide on which one to take).

We reflect on this idea in depth, noting how different it is to the strategy identified as appropriate to go west in 2015. Going west in 2015 simply requires a few individuals using common technical skills to follow a well-established and reliable best-practice map. Going west in 1804 requires having a multi-skilled group that moves step-by-step into the unknown, learning and adapting in a continuous manner, and making the map as it goes along.

Professionals we work with note that the 1804 expedition is undoubtedly more risky and demanding than the 2015 challenge. As a result, they point out that we should expect the journey to test the resolve of authorizers (funding and supporting the journey) and team members in a way that the 2015 journey will not. Anticipating this, we typically ask what they would do to keep the journey funded and supported and to ensure the group members do not mutiny or leave somewhere along the path. Some participants suggest using monetary payments to incentivize everyone involved, but others indicate that this will probably be very expensive (given the high level of uncertainty and risk involved in the exercise) and may not be effective in getting participants to do really risky things. Some suggest that these incentives may even lead to strikes along the journey, where some group members demand more money to take specific "next steps."

Another common idea many participants offer is to inspire the authorizers and group members by emphasizing the importance of the work, and particularly how the work will reduce threats and problems faced by them and their families, friends, and neighbors. Most agree that authorizers and group members will remain engaged if they see their journey in this significant manner, as addressing a problem they care about and need to see solved. They note that this approach will require creating and maintaining a motivating narrative about the problem being solved, and providing ongoing feedback along the route about how the problem is actually being solved (to the authorizers and group members, to keep them motivated). Participants note that this motivation will be needed at repeated points in the journey, and would need to target many diverse groups of authorizers and team members. There would be many agents acting as authorizers, for instance, including those providing

Table 6.3. A strategy to Go West in 1804

What drives action?	A motivating problem that is felt by those involved
How is action identified, carried out?	Through experimental iterations where teams take an action step, learn, adapt, and take another step
What authority or leadership is required?	Multiple authorizers managing risks of the project (by motivating teams, and more) and supporting experimentation
Who needs to be involved?	Multi-agent groups (or teams) with many different functional responsibilities and talents

Source: Authors' work, based on Andrews (2015a)

initial funding and those allowing the team to pass through new territory, or to access new resources. These different authorizers would all need to be motivated differently, as would team members from different backgrounds and with different personal and professional interests. This kind of motivation is not needed if one is driving from St Louis to Los Angeles in 2015, given that the journey is not risky and demands very little of both authorizers and implementers (who are also individuals rather than groups).

We draw this discussion to a close by asking those we work with to identify the strategic elements emerging from the discussion, given the same questions posed in respect of Table 6.2. Table 6.3 summarizes the common answers, which suggest, for instance, that the action needs to be driven by a highly motivating problem that is felt and owned by those involved. Action cannot be predefined but must rather emerge through experimental iterations where teams take a step, learn, adapt, and take another step. Multiple authorizers will be needed to manage risks of the project and support experimentation. Finally, the work will require engagement and effort from multi-agent groups (or teams) with many different functional responsibilities and talents (not just a few appropriately skilled individuals).

We posit that this approach was actually adopted by the 1804 Lewis and Clark expedition in the United States, which found a trade route to the United States' west coast under the primary authorization of President Thomas Jefferson (but with additional authorization from various Native American leaders along the way).[2] This expedition focused on a multi-faceted problem, centered on the need to establish an all-water trade route to the Pacific. This trade-related problem was a high priority in Congress, which needed to authorize funding for the journey even before it began. It was an urgent problem, which Congress felt quite significantly, given that some newly created Midwest communities needed expanded trade opportunities—and there was a sense that other nations were looking for the same routes. The expedition involved much more than the two men after whom it is remembered (Lewis and Clark) as well. There was an entire corps of people, with varied backgrounds and responsibilities. Their numbers were also expanded as the journey unfolded, with local guides proving vital (especially Sacagawea, the Native American renowned for assisting the expedition). The team also iterated significantly as they moved along, using maps that existed to guide the initial steps but adding to these as they progressed, continually learning and adapting their path. Records show that they split into multiple smaller teams when faced with unexpected challenges (like rivers and mountains), for

---

[2] The best resources to reference for those unfamiliar with this initiative are at the PBS website, in an active section where one can learn about the "Journey into the Unknown." This is what motivated the exercise. See http://www.pbs.org/lewisandclark/into/index.html

example, to gain lessons about the possibilities and limits of different routes along the way.

From Going West to Building State Capability

We commonly conclude with two interesting observations from the Go West exercise:

- First, there are different capability building challenges in the world. One (the 2015 challenge) involves doing things we know, using knowledge that has already been acquired, with very few unknowns about the context and very few risks. Chapter 5 calls this a logistical challenge (while others might call it a simple or complicated challenge; see Glouberman and Zimmerman 2004).[3] A second (the 1804 challenge) involves doing things we do not know, given a lack of knowledge about what to do, with many unknowns about the context, many different interests, and many interactions that heighten risk. This is like the wicked hard challenges we discussed in Chapter 5, or what some call complex challenges (Glouberman and Zimmerman 2004; Snyder 2013).
- Second, different strategies are needed to address the different challenges. The relevant strategy to address a simple 2015 challenge is itself simple: identify a solution, plan its implementation, and implement it as planned, with strong oversight and the right people. The appropriate strategy to address a more complex 1804 strategy is also more complex: identify motivational problems, allow solutions to emerge from experimental iteration, ensuring continued and expanding authorization for work by teams of agents with highly varied skill sets and functional roles.

Whereas these observations arise from a basic exercise, we find much food for thought when reflecting on the challenge of building state capability in development. These manifest in two questions: (1) Do efforts to build state capability involve 2015 or 1804 challenges, or a blend of both? and (2) Do 2015 or 1804 strategies work better when trying to build real state capability for implementation?

---

[3] Where a simple challenge is one that we know how to address and can address without specialized or expensive resources—like following a map in a cross-country journey, which anyone with a common driving license can do—whereas a complicated task is also something we know how to do, but which requires some specialized resources—like building a rocket to go into space, which requires hiring the right (expensive) people to use a known technology in a precise manner.

Is Building State Capability a 2015 or 1804 Challenge?

We believe that all challenges tend to have both 1804 and 2015 dimensions. We have found empirical evidence supporting this argument as well, in a case survey study of 30 public sector reform initiatives that are considered sufficiently successful to be included in Princeton University's Innovations for Successful Society (ISS) case database (Andrews 2015a). We constructed the sample to be representative of a significant slice of the state building initiatives in development. The initiatives it includes range from efforts aimed at improving tax collection agencies to strengthening municipal management, providing better local government services, improving central government policymaking, and beyond. These are common reforms in countries across the world, and reflect successful efforts to build capabilities considered important in many contexts. As such, we felt that a study of the challenges involved in these initiatives would provide a useful perspective on the nature of state building challenges in general.

We tried to code each case to see whether they resembled 2015 logistical or 1804 wicked hard challenges. This involved assessing the degree to which each case exhibited the characteristics listed in Chapter 5: being transaction intensive (or not), discretionary (or not), a service or an obligation, and based on introducing a known technology (or not). The coding proved extremely difficult, however, in that each case had numerous dimensions that all exhibited different characteristics. Building a new tax agency involves some logistical challenges, for instance (like passing a new tax law that creates the agency) and many wicked hard challenges (like building the capability to actually collect taxes from itinerant but wealthy citizens). Similarly, establishing a high-level policy unit is partly logistical (identifying a location and a legal basis for operation) and partly wicked hard (determining what policies to examine, and how to build support for new policy ideas).

The study found that every single case involved a blend of challenges, some resembling going west in 2015 (being logistical) and others resembling going west in 1804 (being wicked hard, or complex). This validates our view that all efforts to build state capability involve various types of challenge, such that one never finds a pure logistical or wicked hard challenge. Interestingly (and importantly), however, we found that twenty-five of the thirty cases were dominated by wicked hard dimensions (i.e. that were transaction intensive, discretionary, involving obligations, with no known solution). This means that the challenge of building state capability is likely always a blended challenge but has common, and commonly dominant 1804 dimensions that need to be addressed for real impact.

This finding resonates with our own experience in building state capability, where it is difficult to find any policy, program, or project that does not involve a mixed set of challenges. We also find that most initiatives are dominated by wicked hard 1804 challenges, which commonly manifest in the downstream activities of the initiative (after 2015 logistical challenges have been addressed). For instance, education projects commonly include some school building initiatives, which are largely logistical (and hence 2015 in nature) but also include efforts to improve teacher and student performance in the schools that have been built (which resemble 1804 challenges). Internal audit reforms pose logistical challenges (in passing new laws and introducing circulars) that are often completed well before the many wicked hard 1804 challenges emerge (building buy-in to the idea of internal audit, establishing units across government to perform the audits, and ensuring managers use the audits once done). Many health sector projects focus on building capabilities to procure pharmaceuticals centrally (which is largely a logistical, 2015 challenge) and then focus on getting the pharmaceuticals distributed across provinces and districts, dispensed at health posts, and used as required by doctors and patients (all of which involve many 1804 challenges).

What Strategies Lead to Success in Building State Capability?

Given the dominance of 1804 challenges in building state capability, we should expect that 1804 strategies are more prevalent in successful efforts to build such capability. This is indeed what we found when our coders examined the ISS cases (Andrews 2015a), but with some caveats. The coders were asked to register a score between 1 and 5 reflecting whether (1) the effort was driven by a known solution or a problem, and (2) if action was predetermined in a plan or emerged through experimental iteration (contrasting ideas in the 2015 and 1804 strategies, as shown in Tables 6.2 and 6.3). They were also asked to assess whether leadership and authorization was provided by one agent or multiple agents, and if the initiative involved a small homogenous team or a varied, multi-agent group (also probing differences in Tables 6.2 and 6.3). Table 6.4 shows their results.

Interestingly, all of the cases received points for having both types of strategy in place, suggesting a blended approach to building state capability. However, as Table 6.4 indicates, evidence also shows that the successful initiatives exhibited more of an 1804 strategy than a 2015 one. These cases were more commonly motivated by problems than solutions, for instance (as reflected in average scores of 4.2 and 2.4 on these dimensions). Similarly, successes emerged more regularly from a process of experimentation and learning than through a predesigned, planned out process (manifest in scores of 3.4 and 2.3 on these dimensions). Finally, most successes involved multiple leaders (or authorizers) and broad groups of agents, with only a few led by individuals working in small groups of agents.

Table 6.4. PDIA as the strategy required for 1804 state capability building challenges

	A 2015 strategy (SLDC)	An 1804 strategy (PDIA)
What drives action?	A clearly identified and predefined solution *Average score: 2.4 out of 5*	A motivating problem that is felt by those involved *Average score: 4.2 out of 5*
How is action identified, carried out?	Reference existing knowledge, plot exact course out in a plan, implement as designed *Average score: 2.3 out of 5*	Through experimental iterations where teams take an action step, learn, adapt, and take another step *Average score: 3.4 out of 5*
What authority or leadership is required?	A single authorizer ensuring compliance with the plan, with no other demands or tensions	Multiple authorizers managing risks of the project (by motivating teams, and more) and supporting experimentation *Multiple leaders in all cases; average number of leaders: 19*
Who needs to be involved?	A small group of appropriately qualified individuals	Multi-agent groups (or teams) with different functional responsibilities *Evident in all cases*

In reflecting on these results, we found that different strategies were introduced to address different challenges in most of the cases, which is why we saw a blend of strategies being adopted. An initiative that focused on reorganizing Indonesia's Ministry of Finance adopted a solution-driven 2015 strategy to develop standard operating procedures (SOPs), for instance (where the minister worked with a small team to define these procedures and ensure they were made available to the 64,000 employees) (ISS 2012). A more 1804, problem-driven process was employed to ensure these procedures were accepted and used in the organization, however (where multiple teams were created to experiment with the procedures, gathering constant feedback on what worked and why, adapting procedures based on this feedback, and working gradually to a final product). We noticed further that the 1804 strategies were more emphasized in the cases because they were crucial in ensuring success in the initiatives. Indonesia's problem driven, experimental 1804 strategy made the difference between having SOPs and having an organization that ran according to SOPs.

This evidence points to the fact that strategies must be mixed in efforts to build state capability, but also that 1804 strategies are crucial in these efforts. This makes sense, given that the challenge of building state capability blends both 1804 and 2015 dimensions, but with dominant 1804 dimensions. One cannot address these complex challenges with a simple 2015 strategy (at least not on its own), but must rather embrace the realities of complexity with an equally complex 1804 strategy. In reflecting on this kind of strategy, one is reminded again of Hirschman's writing on implementation in development and the importance of thinking about development projects as journeys, as cited as one of this book's epigraphs: "The term 'implementation' understates the complexity of the task of carrying out projects that are affected by a high degree of initial ignorance and uncertainty. Here 'project implementation' may often mean in fact a long voyage of discovery in the most varied domains" (Hirschman 1967: 35).

PDIA and Your Challenges

You will notice that Table 6.1 provides acronyms for the 2015 and 1804 strategies that tend to emerge from our class discussions (and were shown in Tables 6.2 and 6.3). The first, SLDC, stands for solution and leader-driven change. This is where an intervention emerges from a fixed solution, is implemented through a well-developed and disciplined plan, and led by a highly authorized individual working with a small group of experts. The second, PDIA, is the approach that we find most relevant in addressing complex, wicked hard challenges commonly involved in building state capability. PDIA is a process strategy that does not rely on blueprints and known solutions as the key to building state capability. In contrast, PDIA combines four key principles of engagement into a way of thinking about and doing development work in the face of complexity: (1) Focus on specific *problems* in particular local contexts, as nominated and prioritized by local actors; (2) Foster active, ongoing *experimental iterations* with new ideas, gathering lessons from these iterations to turn ideas into solutions; (3) Establish an "authorizing environment" for decision-making that encourages experimentation and "positive deviance"; and (4) Engage broad sets of agents to ensure that reforms are viable, legitimate, and relevant—that is, politically supportable and practically implementable. You will probably recognize these as the key dimensions of an 1804 strategy, required to address complex challenges with many unknowns and risks. As Table 6.4 shows, these principles also feature prominently when examining successful efforts to build state capability in development.

We will explain each of these principles in detail in the next chapters—and describe how they foster an effective way of building state capability in the face of complex challenges. We are mindful that you are probably familiar with some of these principles, however, which are not altogether new to development. This is because PDIA draws on and synthesizes the ideas of others, and should thus be seen as building on a foundation of past work. Others who have made similar arguments includes those whose work uses expressions such as "learning organizations" (Senge 2006), "projects as policy experiments" (Rondinelli 1993), "adaptive versus technical problems" (Heifetz 1994), "positive deviance" (Marsh et al. 2004), institutional "monocropping" versus "deliberation" (Evans 2004), "experimentation" (Mukand and Rodrik 2005; de Búrca et al. 2014), "good-enough governance" (Grindle

2004), "democracy as problem-solving" (de Souza Briggs 2008), "problem-driven political economy" (Fritz et al. 2009), "the science of muddling through" (Lindblom 1959, 1979), the "sabotage of harms" (Sparrow 2008), "second-best institutions" (Rodrik 2008), "interim institutions" (Adler et al. 2009), "good intentions" versus real results (Easterly 2002), "multi-agent leadership" (Andrews et al. 2010), "rapid results" (Matta and Morgan 2011), "upside down governance" (Institute for Development Studies 2010), challenges of "governing the commons" (Ostrom 1990, 2008; McCay 2002), "just-enough governance" (Levy and Fukuyama 2010), "best fit" strategies (Booth 2011), "principled incrementalism" (Knaus 2011), "radical institutional change" (Greenwod and Hinings 1996), and "experiential learning" (Pritchett et al. 2012), among others.

PDIA also draws on many existing implementation modalities, given that others have developed practical methods to act on ideas that underpin the four principles. Examples include design thinking, rapid results implementation modalities, agile policymaking, the use of problem trees and Ishikawa or fishbone diagrams in problem analysis, problem-driven political economy diagnostics, double-loop learning methods, and more. Some of these approaches (and others) are evident in the successful interventions we studied as part of our thirty case ISS sample. Many of these foundational ideas and implementation methods have not been widely adopted in development, however, or operationalized for routine use in efforts to build state capability. Most such policies, programs, and projects adopt 2015 strategies exclusively (or as the dominant strategy) by pre-specifying solutions, locking implementation plans in place through rigid logical framework mechanisms, and relying on the authorization and work of individual reform champions. This bias toward 2015 strategies leads, in many cases, to gaps in state capability—where governments have the capabilities associated with 2015 challenges but lack the capabilities involved in getting 1804 challenges done (Andrews 2011, 2012). We see examples of this all over the world, and in different areas of development:

- An expensive state-of-the-art courthouse in the Solomon Islands was effectively built (as a 2015 challenge, according to a 2015 strategy), but it sits only a few times each year and responds inadequately to the types of justice problems that most citizens face most of the time (which are predominantly 1804 challenges, requiring an 1804 strategy).

- A financial management information system was introduced to better control expenditures in Malawi (a 2015 challenge, adopted through a 2015 strategy), but money still flowed into the wrong places, given underlying political and social challenges (which are 1804 in nature, and will only be effectively addressed through an 1804 strategy).

- Brazil's Fundescola reforms introduced new management tools in the country's education sector (largely a logistical, 2015 challenge that was achieved through 2015 strategies), but these tools have often gone unused in the poorer schools of the northwest, given capacity constraints, political complexities, and other challenges (which are all 1804 in nature and need to be addressed using 1804 strategies).

We believe that the PDIA principles combine into a useful 1804 strategy that can help close these kinds of gaps in building state capability. We believe, further, that PDIA can be applied in various ways, using a wide range of implementation options and modalities. PDIA is therefore not a single program or "solution" in itself, but requires a lot of engagement from you—the potential facilitator, policy entrepreneur, or reform catalyst—in determining what tools to use, who to engage with, and what to focus on. We will ask you to engage in this manner in coming chapters, chewing on the ideas we offer for all four principles and trying out some tools we commonly use to bring these principles to life. In order to do this, it would be useful for you to think about the challenges you are currently facing—and particularly about challenges where PDIA would be most relevant. These are the 1804 challenges in building state capability, where you do not know what to do, face real uncertainty and weak information, and need to work hard in motivating broad groups of agents. Chances are these are the challenges you are struggling with the most, where you see low achievement and are most concerned about gaps in state capability. Take a minute to identify these challenges in Table 6.5.

Table 6.5. What do my challenges look like?

My challenges	The 2015 challenges	The 1804 challenges

7

Doing problem-driven work

In the 1990s, anti-corruption commissions were a common "best practice" solution for countries wanting to tackle corruption. These countries were following the model of Hong Kong, which started a commission in the 1970s. Malawi is an example. Its Anti-Corruption Bureau (ACB) was conceived in 1994, when the country underwent democratic transformation and donors pushed for an anti-corruption agenda (Anders 2002). It has not been very successful, however, achieving few prosecutions and operating in a time when corruption crises seem to have accelerated (Andrews 2013). Political leaders have not supported the commission or given it the independence needed to operate effectively and tackle the country's entrenched bureaucratic and political corruption. This experience contrasts with that in the Hong Kong "model," where the commission emerged in response to a corruption crisis in the police force. Political powers supported the commission because they had to address this crisis, and therefore they gave the commission independence to investigate and aggressively pursue prosecutions.

We often observe that more successful efforts to establish complex state capabilities (like anti-corruption efforts in Hong Kong) are problem driven; they focus relentlessly on solving a specific, attention-grabbing problem. In contrast, many less-successful initiatives (like that in Malawi) often seem to be more solution driven, paying little attention to the problem or the context in which the problem is felt. In fact, this seems to be the biggest difference between "best practice" experiences and those that try to replicate such practices: the best practices emerged as responses to specific problems and this is often why they succeeded, whereas the copies commonly do not have a clear problem focus and ultimately struggle to gain traction or impact behavior in the manner expected. We believe the lack of a problem focus commonly leads to repeated failure with reforms like the Malawi ACB: every few years someone notes that the commission is not working and tries to improve it by "doubling down" on the design, and doing it better—only to experience similar frustration. Using the metaphor from Chapter 6, this is a little like assuming that a 2015 road exists in 1804 America, and insisting that adventurers drive down that road—even though it obviously does not exist and the problem 1804 adventurers face is in getting west without roads (Andrews et al. 2015).

This chapter discusses the importance of focusing on problems that key agents care about when trying to build complex state capabilities. This is the first principle of problem-driven iterative adaptation (PDIA), and in this chapter we consider why problems matter as entry points to complex state capability building challenges. The next sections use the Malawi example (and others we have researched or engaged in) to show how problems can be used to drive processes of state capability building in practice; given the need to construct problems, deconstruct problems, and then promote problem-driven sequencing.

Why Is a Problem-Driven Approach Necessary?

A study of forty-four health sector projects pursued by the World Bank and Global Fund in the late 1990s and early 2000s demonstrates the value of problems as drivers of effective state capability building (Andrews 2013). In trying to explain why some projects were considered more successful than others, we found evidence pointing towards two crucial dimensions, one of which was the "problem focus" in project design and implementation: the successful projects pursued locally defined, specific problems in a demonstrable and continuous fashion. This meant that the projects were initiated as responses to locally defined problems, baseline indicators of these problems were measured in the early stages of the project, project activities were directly determined as solutions to these problems, and progress in solving problems was routinely evaluated and considered in adjusting project content. The problem-driven nature of these projects ensured that they focused on actually solving specified problems as the goal (rather than introducing a pre-designed solution). They were adaptive as a result, allowing continuous changes in the design to ensure the problem was effectively addressed.

Various literatures help explain why problem-driven processes are important in addressing complex problems like those involving corruption or in the health sector. Management scholars like John Kotter (1990), for instance, are famous for noting the importance of crises in fostering deep organizational change. Another prominent management theorist, Kim Cameron (1986: 67), posits similarly that "Institutional change and improvement are motivated more by knowledge of problems than by knowledge of success." He argues that bureaucratic agents are more likely to support change initiatives aimed at "overcoming obstacles to basic institutional effectiveness" than looking for ways to improve already-effective institutions (Cameron 1986: 69). In the same vein, institutionalist author Christine Oliver (1992: 564) argues that "performance problems" foster political, social, and functional pressures for institutional change because they "raise serious questions about the appropriateness or legitimacy" of the status quo. Seo and Creed (2002) similarly observes that a problem-driven process forces a reflective shift in collective consciousness about the value of extant mechanisms, which is needed to foster change.

In light of these and other views, we believe that problems force policymakers and would-be reformers to ask questions about the incumbent ways of doing things, and promote a search for alternatives that actually offer a solution (rather than just providing new ways of doing things). Reflecting such view, Sparrow (2008) discusses how getting the right grip on the characterization of the problem can unleash efforts to solve the problem. Beyond this, problems provide a rallying point for coordinating distributed agents who might otherwise clash in the change process. In this respect, coalitions are sometimes defined as groups of strange bedfellows who work together to solve problems that they share but cannot solve on their own (Zakocs 2006; see also Pires 2011).

These arguments suggest that problems provide common windows through which agents are forced to examine their contexts, identify necessary changes, and explore alternatives to find appropriate solutions. The idea of "problem windows" is reminiscent of Kingdon's (1995) work on policy change. Applications of his "multiple streams" theory posits that an awareness of problems brings issues onto the change agenda (Barzelay and Gallego 2006; Guldbrandsson and Fossum 2009; Ridde 2009). Faced with problems they can no longer ignore, agents across the social and political spectrum become aware of structural weaknesses they usually do not consider and work together to solve such.

Given this thinking, we believe in taking a problem-driven approach to any complex reform or policy initiative like the 1804 capability challenges we frequently encounter in development (Andrews et al. 2015). We do not just mean identifying problems at the start of an intervention, however. Simply saying one is identifying a problem does not mean that the impacts necessary to foster effective change will be felt. Indeed, we find that many reformers claiming to be problem-driven are in fact not problem-driven at all. They define the problem as the lack of a preferred solution, rather than a performance deficiency, and their strategy has no real means to draw attention to the need for change, provide a rallying point for coalition building, or offer a "true north" destination of "problem solved" to guide, motivate, and inspire action. For instance, many donors in Malawi continue to argue that the problem with corruption is that the ACB does not work. This kind of problem definition entrenches the capability trap discussed in earlier chapters (where countries do the same reforms repeatedly but continually face failure) and is unlikely to generate the kind of behavioral change theorists like Kingdon propose. This, we believe, is because such problem definitions do not meet the characteristics of a "good problem" that motivates and drives change:

- A good problem cannot be ignored and matters to key change agents.
- A good problem can be broken down into easily addressed causal elements.
- A good problem allows real, sequenced, strategic responses.

Constructing Problems That Matter

We advocate a problem-driven process because it provokes reflection, mobilizes attention, and promotes targeted and context-sensitive engagement.

In order to achieve these impacts, however, we believe that the focal problem needs to reflect on a performance deficiency that cannot be denied or ignored and that matters to key change agents. Think, for instance, of the kind of problem statement that would draw a skilled team together to go west in 1804—where the challenge was uncertain and risky, and the likelihood of the adventurers' deaths was high.

Work is often required to craft problems that can motivate such groups, and draw awareness to failures that commonly fester but are routinely ignored or accepted as normal or unavoidable (or too difficult or risky to address)—as is the case with many challenges in development and in government in general. These challenges resemble what Kingdon (1995) calls "conditions" that agents complain about but also accept—like a nagging hip pain one learns to live with. One does nothing to resolve such pain as long as it is a condition one can endure. When one wakes up and cannot walk, however, the condition becomes a problem demanding attention and individuals find the strength to accept needed change (like a hip operation). Similar to this example, Kingdon notes that many social, political, and economic conditions have to be politically and socially constructed to gain attention as "problems" before we should expect any real change. We believe it is similar for many challenges in building state capability, where weaknesses persist for years and never draw the attention they demand. The construction process involves raising the visibility of persistent weaknesses through spectacular "focusing events" like crises, the use of statistical indicators, or manipulation of feedback from previous experiences.

This is the first step in doing PDIA: Constructing problems out of conditions, drawing attention to the need for change and bringing such change onto the social, political, and administrative agenda.

The construction process involves gathering key change agents to answer four questions: "What is the problem?," "Why does it matter?," "To whom does it matter?," "Who needs to care more?," and "How do we get them to give it more attention?" It is important—in principle and practice—to think about who answers these questions (and frames the problem). In principle, one should be aware of the power dynamics at play in gathering some agents to do this work and not others, for instance, and include some who are out of power (and potentially more aware of the problems). In practice, it is vital to ensure that agents who can foster necessary next steps in the change process are engaged to do so. Balancing these tensions requires including both agitators (commonly not in power) and decision-makers (commonly in power) in the problem construction process. Crucially, these agents are all internal to the context targeted for change (such that this process cannot be done by outsiders but must involve those directly affected by future change).

Answers to the questions should be informed by evidence at all times, to convince agents of their validity and empower the group to have a problem statement that others will find compelling. We provide actual examples in Chapter 8, but the following helps to illustrate the principle in practice:

A would-be reformer in Malawi might be concerned about the failure of Malawi's Anti-Corruption Bureau (ACB). She could try to convince others that serious reform is needed, focusing on improving the "preferred solution" and creating a better ACB (in an example of "doubling down" discussed earlier). Some might argue that the ACB is emerging, however, and will work one day. Others might note that corruption has always been there and is too politically difficult to address. Noting this, our reformer would recognize the need to turn a condition into a problem, through problem construction. She would need to gather a small (to start) group of agitators and decision-makers and ask the questions listed above. Imagine the kind of conversation that would ensue, and how it would focus the reform agenda:

- "The problem is that the ACB does not effectively address corruption."
- *Why does it matter?* "Because we still have a lot of corruption in government, which we can show in various indicators."
- *Why does it matter?* "Because we lose money from the corruption, which we can estimate using basic financial reporting data."
- *Why does it matter?* "Because the lost money leads to reduced services, which we can show in various sectors—including education, healthcare, and water."

Now we have a problem definition that refers to a real performance deficiency that cannot be ignored and that we think will matter to key change agents.

- *To whom does it matter?* "All those receiving the services, including citizens and the politicians who are meant to represent them. These are key change agents, especially at the local level."
- *Who needs to care more?* "Key government decision-makers like the minister of finance and local budget and policy officials."
- *How do we get them to give it more attention?* "By providing data showing the loss in money from corruption, and how this translates into service delivery weaknesses. These data could include stock-out statistics in clinics, or textbook access in schools, and could be provided for different constituencies to convince individual politicians that they should care."

This problem construction process helps to steer one away from defining the problem as the "lack of a preferred solution." Rather, this kind of conversation focuses would-be reformers on service delivery failures that arise because of corruption, which is a functional problem of performance that many agents are likely to care about; and which is likely to mobilize attention and effort to address festering weaknesses in state capability. Contrast this to talking about the problem of a failing ACB, which was where our would-be reformer began. (Which many agents may not care about and which will probably yield little more than a technical fix to a technical condition. Much like giving our friend with the sore hip a walking stick instead of a more necessary but demanding operation. He may accept the help but it assists and perpetuates the problem, rather than forcing our friend to actually confront and deal with the problem.)

Given the way it focuses attention on the need for change, a construction process like this can help to transform a solution and process-oriented condition into a "good problem" that fosters real state building (and the broad and deep reflection and change this often requires). We see the importance of this kind of construction exercise in the example of Swedish budgeting reform:[1]

Technicians in the ministry of finance had been trying to introduce technical reforms since the 1960s, looking to improve the management of public monies, clarify relationships between central and local governments, and discipline policymaking processes (to contain the growth in financial commitments). They tried many international best practices between the 1960s and 1980s, including program budgeting, multi-year budgeting, performance, and results budgeting, different types of accounting reform, intergovernmental reforms, and management by objectives. These mostly fell flat, and by the early 1990s Sweden still lacked fundamental elements of a modern budgeting, accounting, or management system (including a coherent budget calendar, ministry of finance responsible for spending, shared accounting system, and more).

This all led to what theorists call a soft budget constraint, where public spending was allowed to grow with very little control. This was a real problem for Sweden, yielding it vulnerable to any shock and warranting far reaching changes in the make-up of government (to provide capabilities for expenditure control). It was treated largely as a technical condition, however, until 1991, when the country was hit by a major economic crisis. The crisis emerged in European financial markets but spread rapidly to Sweden and wrought havoc on public finances, given the vulnerabilities

---

[1] The discussion on Sweden's case draws on work undertaken for Andrews (2015a) and reflecting various sources, including von Hagen (1992), Premfors (1991), Olson and Sahlin-Andersson (1998), Fudge and Gustafsson (1989), Burkitt and Whyman (1994), Brunsson (1995), Lundquist (2001), Molander (2000), Mattisson et al. (2004), Wehner (2007), Pollittt and Bouckaert (2004), Paulsson (2006), Miyazaki (2014), Molander and Holmquist (2013).

that had worried experts. Welfare commitments could not be adjusted quickly enough to respond to decreased revenues and soon the country faced major deficits (at about 11 percent of GDP in 1992).

Most observers associated the "problematic" deficits with the broader European crisis and high spending levels in the country (leading to calls for spending cuts as the solution). A group of budgeting experts started to construct a parallel narrative, however, that associated the soft budget constraint "condition" with the crisis—in the hope of fostering deeper reforms in the budget system. They worked with a respected German economist to show that Sweden had the second lowest score on a key index of budget system capability, on a par with Italy and Greece (neither of which was considered a desirable comparator), proving that "we have a problem." Beyond this, they helped decision-makers understand the academic studies showing that countries with higher scores on the index had more capability to control spending (and avoid deficits). This helped decision-makers see "why the problem mattered," associating weak systems with the painful deficits Sweden was enduring. They focused attention on parliamentarians in this effort, knowing that these were the agents whose support was most needed for change. Ultimately, these agents (and others) came to care more—and see the conditions as problems—and a sense of urgency entered the reform process, allowing far-reaching reforms.

This is a powerful example of how reformers can energize capacity building efforts to go beyond mimicry and technical fixes and instead address the real problems warranting change. We see problem construction achieve this focus and attention in other engagements as well:

- One country, which we will call Nostria, was struggling to manage the imbalance of demand and supply for justice, which manifest in a large backlog in cases. The country lacked capabilities to manage this backlog, and particularly to allocate public resources to the places where demand was greatest. Donors had supported a project to create a case management system that would help shore up such capability, but after five years the project yielded nothing. Part of the reason was that the reform had been framed as addressing a technical condition ("we do not have a case management system") that did not mobilize enough attention or engagement across a broad section of affected agents whose support was needed for reform. A small set of these agents remained committed to reform even after this experience, however, and tried to reignite a case management system project. Faced with a lack of enthusiasm amongst other agents, they began constructing the problem as we suggest here, asking why the lack of a system mattered, to whom it mattered, and how it could be made to matter more. The process was interesting, and went something like this: "the system matters because we cannot determine where we need new resources (judges, buildings, prosecutors, and more) without the system"; "this matters because we cannot create effective budget requests without knowing what to ask for (and being able to back our requests up with real evidence)"; "This matters because we never get the kind of money we need to manage justice, and our budget requests are routinely turned down." This characterization reflected on a performance problem—rather than a technical condition—that was felt by a number of agents involved in providing justice. It could be framed using real data (showing gaps between budget requests and allocations) and personal narratives (where agencies reflected on the frustration of repeatedly asking for and not receiving funds). As such, the reform team found this framing very effective in drawing important agents into the reform process, and in gaining support to kickstart a new reform process.

- Another government, in a country we will call Mantio, had been trying to strengthen its capabilities to support private sector development. A small group in the ministry of industry was focused on energizing a specific underperforming sector of the economy, and identified the need to improve the business climate faced by firms in this sector. It emphasized policies aimed at improving the Doing Business indicators in this sector (decreasing various kinds of regulatory burdens). This initiative was quite difficult, partly because the group did not have authority over many of the regulations it was trying to change: the regulations were under the control of ministries like finance and land management, and various municipal offices. These other agencies were not part of the reform process, and did not see the need for the regulatory reforms. In essence, they saw the poor performance of the sector as an accepted condition, and not something that warranted major attention (or at least not something that warranted their attention). The ministry of industry's would-be reformers initiated a problem construction process to address this malaise. They started by identifying the problem as "having a weak Doing Business score, given inefficient regulations." When probed as to why this mattered, however, they started offering new ideas: "Firms cannot grow in this environment...and if they cannot grow we will not get enough jobs or exports...and jobs and exports are sorely needed." The group members were asked to provide data showing the gap between where they thought employment levels should have been in their chosen sector and where employment levels actually were. These data were then used to convince high-level government ministers and administrators and local officials of the problem. Constructing the problem like this ensured that these agents supported change, which accelerated in pace and deepened over the next few months.

Effectively constructed problems like these are intended to mobilize action, but they could have the opposite effect if the groups involved in the construction process dwell only on the problem. There needs to be a positive balance to such reflection; something that inspires and encourages vision. This is a lesson we draw from the work on appreciative inquiry, which often presents itself as the antithesis to problem-driven work. It advocates "collective inquiry into the best of what is, in order to imagine what could be, followed by collective design of a desired future state that is compelling and thus does not require the use of incentives, coercion or persuasion for planned change to occur" (Bushe 2013: 1). We do not believe that this approach is in fact antithetical to the problem-driven approach presented here, but rather emphasizes the importance of the "other side of the coin" in doing such work—what will the problem-driven work deliver? In reflecting this, groups doing such work should follow their questions about the problem with an extra one designed to foster positive views: "What will the problem look like when it is solved?" In the Malawi example provided, the group should mention the fact that school and health sector services would be stronger, and money would be flowing to schools and clinics more effectively. The group would focus on specific targets for improved stock access in clinics and textbook provision in schools, once again reflecting on these targets for individual constituencies to ensure the support of individual political representatives. Getting this support allows a start to real action in the change process, which is crucial.

We saw evidence of this in the way the budgeting problem was constructed in early 1990s Sweden. The group of officials who led this construction did not leave decision-makers in a gloomy situation faced with just a problem (of a system that that was prone to deficits). They used the data they had developed to show that while Sweden looked like Greece and Italy at the time (and shared these countries' problems in controlling spending), reforms could help the country produce systems like those in other European countries, where deficits were under control. This allowed them to construct an aspirational goal of "problem solved"—where the country would not have deficits of 11 percent of GDP but would rather enjoy low deficits or even surpluses. This communication did not downplay the urgency of the problem, but infused the urgency with hope and vision. Similar visionary "problem solved" constructs proved vital in the two examples just discussed:

- The Nostrian judicial reform group was quite overwhelmed by the size and scope of the problem they faced (in accessing and organizing case data). Their apprehension was also influenced by the fact that a prior project had failed. This was partially overcome by asking them to construct a vision of what the problem would look like when solved, however. This empowered positive discussion, where the group identified exactly what kinds of data would be available, noted that the data would help in determining what resources would be needed, and explained further that the data would help in requesting budgetary funds. Ultimately, they came up with estimates of how much their budgets would expand because of the work, and how many more cases would be passed each year because of these funds. This measure of "problem solved" became what some leadership gurus would call a "true north" goal for the group—foundational, motivational, and a true measure of success.

- The Mantian officials also balanced their problem construction with a vision of "problem solved." This was done by estimating how many of the missing jobs could be generated in the underperforming sector they were looking at, in six months, a year, and beyond, if reforms were forthcoming. These estimates allowed the identification of a range of new job creation levels that the group thought was possible from its work. It was the first time that some members of the group actually saw their work impacting something as significant as jobs (given that they tended to see their work as administrative and bureaucratic). It was thus inspirational, and injected some enthusiasm and added purpose into the exercise. The "problem solved vision" was also crucial in getting support from politicians who were motivated to support a problem-driven process but needed a positive vision to frame the initiative.

We find that many efforts to build state capability do not construct problems in this manner. These initiatives assume that problems are accepted and will

Table 7.1. Constructing a problem out of your 1804 challenge

What is the problem? (and how would we measure it or tell stories about it?)	
Why does it matter? (and how do we measure this or tell stories about it?)	
Why does it matter? (and how do we measure this or tell stories about it?) • Ask this question until you are at the point where you can effectively answer the question below, with more names than just your own.	
To whom does it matter? (In other words, who cares? other than me?")	
Who needs to care more?	
How do we get them to give it more attention?	
What will the problem look like when it is solved? Can we think of what progress might look like in a year, or 6 months?	

draw attention, and also that those working in the context have a vision of problem solved. This assumption often proves incorrect, however, and agents in the context lack motivation or disagree on what they should be doing. This frequently plays out in failures to gain and maintain support or change or to provoke the reflection needed to address wicked hard challenges. Given this, we want you to take a few minutes (or more) to construct a problem out of one or more of the 1804 challenges you listed in the previous chapter (on 2015 and 1804 challenges). Use Table 7.1 as a guide in this process. We suggest doing the exercise on your own first and then asking some involved colleagues or associates to do it as well. Then you can integrate each other's work and develop a combined version. This exercise will probably unleash some creative insight that will help all of you better understand what you are dealing with. Good luck.

Deconstructed Problems Are Manageable Problems

Change processes that begin with this kind of problem construction will likely yield immediate questions about solutions to employ. These questions can be difficult to answer, because the problems are complex and the "right" solutions are hard to identify. Reformers can get stuck at this point, given the intractable nature of the problem: it is often just too big and thorny to make sense of. This might lead to a push for preferred best practice solutions that reformers are pretty sure will not build real state capability but at least offer something to do. Our reformer in Malawi might still advocate a stronger ACB as the solution to the defined problem, for instance.

To mitigate this risk, one needs to ensure that would-be reformers break the problems down into smaller components that are more open to localized solution building. This involves deconstructing the problem to reveal its causes and then choosing solutions that address these causes. Deconstruction like this helps to make a "good problem" (where one can effectively "frame the grievances of aggrieved constituencies, diagnose causes, assign blame" and identify immediate *options* for redress (Snow and Benford 1992: 150)). In essence, it turns a set of unmanageable challenges associated with any given problem into a manageable set of focal points for engagement, where one can ask what is going wrong and why, and look for workable solutions to these problems. Deconstructing problems in this manner also helps one identify multiple points at which to pursue short- and medium-term successes (or quick wins), which are vital when dealing with a big problem that will likely only be solved in the long run (and which is therefore not likely to attract the needed short- and medium-term political support).

We propose using tools like the "5-why technique" and fishbone diagrams in such deconstruction. These tools emerged from production process theory,

Table 7.2. An example of "5 why" conversations in action

Why is money being lost in service delivery?	Answer 1.	Answer 2.	Answer 3.
	Funds budgeted for services are disbursed for other purposes.	Procurement costs are inflated, leading to fund leakages.	Local officials divert resources to personal purposes.
Why does this happen?	Loopholes in disbursement systems allow reallocation.	Procurement processes are often half implemented.	Officials feel obliged to redistribute money.
Why does this happen?	Disbursement systems are missing key controls.	Procurement processes are often rushed.	Constituents expect officials to redistribute money.
Why does this happen?	Disbursement system designs were insufficient and have never been improved.	Decisions to procure goods are delayed and delayed again, every year.	Local norms make it appropriate to "share" in this way.
Why does this happen?	We lack resources and skills to improve system designs.	Budget decisions initiating purchase decisions are delayed.	Local communities are poor and depend on this sharing.

Source: Authors' example, intended for demonstration purposes.

especially from the experience of Toyota (Liker 2004; Ohno 1988). Toyota uses the tools to scrutinize problems encountered in making cars, to ensure that any remedies treat the root causes of these problems and allow production facilities to introduce solutions that are sustainable (and mitigate against the recurrence of the problem). This is how real capability is built in the Toyota Corporation, where teams learn to "encounter a problem, break it down and scrutinize it, solve the root causes, and lock in the solutions so that the problem does not repeat itself." The tools require those involved in building state capability to ask, repeatedly, "why" the problem was caused, and then chart the answers in a visual manner to show its many causal roots. This allows one to identify multiple root causes and to interrogate each cause in depth. Consider Table 7.2 to see how this might focus the Malawi corruption in service delivery problem (reflecting on just three potential lines of answers to the "why" questions).

The discussion encapsulated in Table 7.2 is only partial, of course, and one could expect a number of answers to the leading question, "why is money being lost in service delivery?" These strands or causal dimensions might emphasize process failures, political interference in money flows, and more. Each strand breaks down into a variety of sub-causes, which will all need attention if change is to succeed and capability is enhanced. Different agents will initiate different strands of thinking, leading to a more robust deconstruction of the problem when one works in groups rather than just doing the exercise alone. We advocate including as many strands of thinking as the group offers, and challenging those who suggest new "causes" and "sub-causes" to provide evidence supporting the inclusion of such. For instance, one might ask if there is evidence to show that "procurement costs are inflated, leading to cost leakages." This allows one to inform this dimension of the problem, which is necessary to convince others that it requires attention. We would caution against prematurely excluding any causal issues because they "don't make sense" or "we lack evidence," however. This is not an academic exercise but rather a practical one—designed to flesh the problem out as much as possible. If proposed causes seem difficult to defend, include them with an asterisk (suggesting they are pending further evidence) and keep them in sight and mind (they just may end up emerging as important).

The many different strands or causal dimensions can be shown graphically in what some call a fishbone diagram, which provides a visual deconstruction of the bigger problems (as in Figure 7.1). The fishbone diagram specifies the problem effect at the right, using data that helps stimulate attention. Potential causes and sub-causes are shown as "bones on the fish," with three illustrated in the example—reflecting problems in fund disbursement processes, procurement processes, and the private use of public funds by officials. Allowing the identification of multiple bones will empower more agents to engage in discussions of solutions, as it breaks often intractable and complex problems down into manageable, bite-size pieces. For instance, it is easier to think of potential solutions to close gaps in the disbursement system than it is to think of solutions to the larger problem of "corruption." This procedure will also disabuse many of the notion that there is any one, cover-all solution to a complex problem (as is implied in starting a commission to deal with

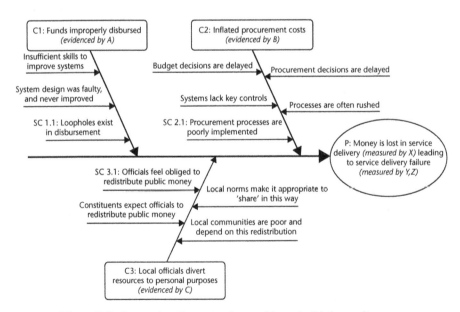

Figure 7.1. Deconstructing complex problems in Ishikawa diagrams

corruption problems). A real solution to big problems actually comes in the form of many small solutions to the many causal dimensions of the problem.

We see exactly this kind of thinking in the way Swedish officials pursued their budgeting reforms in the 1990s. As already discussed, a small group of technical experts constructed the problem in a manner that ensured the support of parliamentarians, ministers and managers. Once this support was in place, however, it would have been easy to despair; the budgeting problems were expansive in size and scope and it was difficult to know where to start or what to do. The officials did not use 5-why methods or fishbone diagrams, but their strategy at the time shows a conscious effort to deconstruct the problem. This involved identifying the main factors considered "causal" to the soft budget constraint problem (which included weak control over spending decisions, duplication of spending, and confusion over roles in the budget process). The deconstruction process involved various new actors, all contributing their views on "why" the budget constraint was so soft. The process led to a manageable agenda of action, and a broader constituency committed to make the agenda a reality.

This process proved vital in the Nostrian and Mantian experiences already described above, where "5 why" and fishbone methods were explicitly used:

- The deconstruction activity was a first for many in the Nostrian context, and served to bring new agents into a fledgling team that included members from a variety of affected agencies. These agents all had views on why the justice sector could not create data-driven budgets, all of which led to the identification of various "bones": "we do not have some of the data we need"; "the data we have are not reliable"; "we do not share the data that exists"; "we do not know how to analyze the data that we have." The team members were asked to illustrate each cause with real evidence (showing, for instance, which data were actually missing and which data were simply in different non-sharing agencies). This evidence was often less than perfect but helped to convince everyone that the nominated cause was indeed worthy of attention. The team then went into depth on each fishbone to further interrogate the causes. In discussing "why" data were not being shared, for instance, the team pointed to communication failures between organizations, which stemmed from political and bureaucratic tensions but also from technocratic issues (like the fact that different organizations used different statistical software that limited sharing potential). Ultimately, within a few days, the team identified a number of causal strands in which they could start thinking about action. They could see that there was no single solution to the overall problem as well (and hence that the "case management system" they had initially wanted was not a panacea).
- The Mantian officials were initially convinced that they could kickstart their focal economic sector by addressing regulatory issues embedded in

the Doing Business indicators. They decided not to simply assume this "solution," however, and embarked on a process of asking businesses "why" employment was lower than it could be. The exercise yielded few responses that related to the Doing Business regulatory issues. Instead, it produced a list of over forty-two challenges that businesses in the sector were facing, which the team of officials organized into a five bone fishbone diagram (where "bones" referred to causal topics like costs of employment, difficulties at the interface with government, costs of engaging in trade, and constraints to innovation). Each major bone represented a major cause of the problem, and additional bones showed the sub-causes (as in the Malawi example in Figure 7.1). The officials were quite amazed at the end of this exercise, especially by what they had learned from asking "why" the problems were persisting (rather than settling for a ready-made solution). Many of the forty-two challenges were new to the officials and had not been on policy agendas before.

We find this kind of problem deconstruction both illuminating and empowering. It forces would-be reformers and policymakers to interrogate the problem that they often think they fully understand. This often leads to a different—and more accurate—understanding of the problem. Beyond this, the deconstruction process helps would-be reformers break the problem down into smaller, manageable parts. This is encouraging to many reformers and empowers practical thinking about where real reform can begin in the short run (the kind of thinking one cannot do when reflecting on overly demanding problems).

We do not want you to take our word on this, however. The value of this approach is appreciated most when actually using the tools in an applied context. Given this, we invite you to go through a basic exercise in deconstructing your 1804 challenge (discussed in Table 7.1). Once again, we propose working on your own initially and going through a "5 why" process to identify as many causes and sub-causes of the problem as possible (use the full-page Box 7.1 to do this). Then, build your fishbone diagram, showing the causal strands (in blank Box 7.2). Get affected colleagues to do this as well, and then come together and compare notes. Try and build a common fishbone diagram, learning from each other's ideas and building a fuller narrative of the problem than any of you had at the start (in Box 7.3).

How does your challenge look now, compared with what you wrote down in Table 7.1? It should be much more fleshed out or broken down than it was before, into causal elements that you can seriously consider addressing. The deconstructed problem should raise immediate questions: Where do I start in trying to solve the problem? What do I do? How do I ensure that all causal strands are addressed? The next steps in PDIA tackle exactly these questions.

Box 7.1. MY "5 WHY" THOUGHT SHEET

Box 7.2. MY ISHIKAWA DIAGRAM, DECONSTRUCTING THE PROBLEM I AM FACING

Box 7.3. OUR COMBINED ISHIKAWA DIAGRAM

Problem-Driven Sequencing Orders the Engagement

Deconstruction provides the basis for problem-driven sequencing in the change process, where sequencing refers to the timing and staging of interventions and engagement. Sequencing matters a great deal in the development process and effective sequencing is key to doing PDIA. A failure to sequence effectively could lead, in principle and practice, to premature load bearing (where change demands are introduced before they can be managed by a targeted country or organization). Most sequencing decisions in the development community are solution-based, however, and involve introducing the "basics first" of a pre-specified new policy or practice (often identified in an isomorphic way). Such an approach does not ask whether these interventions address the problems in place, however, or if "basics first" are even possible in the change context (or if the "basics" are indeed always "basic" across different contexts) (Andrews 2006).

In contrast, problem-driven sequencing involves ordering engagements based on a progressive approach to tackle problems, given contextual opportunities and constraints. The basic approach to doing this begins with recognizing that most deconstructed problems take the form of meta-problems (with many dimensions and indeed many problems making up the larger problem). Solving these problems requires multiple interventions, which allows multiple entry points for change. Each cause and sub-cause is essentially a separate—albeit connected—point of engagement, and each causal dimension offers different opportunity for change. We refer to this opportunity as the "space for change" (other authors might call it "readiness"). This change space is contingent on contextual factors commonly found to influence policy and reform success, shaping what and how much one can do in any policy or reform initiative at any time. These factors have been well discussed in the recent literature on politically smart, locally led development (Booth 2011), and in Brian Levy's research on "working with the grain" (Levy 2014). We simplify the observations from such work into a heuristic that reformers can use in assessing "space for change" in any causal dimension area. This heuristic is not intended as a scientific approach to assessing readiness for change, but generates a set of important questions that reformers can ask when trying to assess where to start an engagement and what kinds of activities to pursue. The heuristic points to three key factors influencing the opportunity for change, authority, acceptance, and ability (triple-A factors) (Andrews 2008; Andrews et al. 2010):

- "Authority" refers to the support needed to effect reform or policy change or build state capability (political, legal, organizational, and personal). Some change needs more authority than other change, and it is always important to assess the extent of authority one already has—and the authority gaps that need to be closed.

- "Acceptance" relates to the extent to which those who will be affected by reform or policy change accept the need for change and the implications of change. Different types of change require different levels of acceptance (from narrow or broad groups and at different depths) and the key is to recognize what acceptance exists and what gaps need to be closed to foster change.

- "Ability" focuses on the practical side of reform or policy change, and the need for time, money, skills and the like to even start any kind of intervention. It is important to ask what abilities exist and what gaps need to be closed.

We assess these questions with different degrees of rigor, depending on the context and availability of evidence on the status of each "triple-A factor." At the most basic, we will ask—for each sub-causal strand—what the authorizing environment looks like and where authority for intervention will come from, whose acceptance is needed to move ahead, and what kinds of abilities are needed to make real progress. This calls for a descriptive discussion where would-be reformers and policymakers are forced to reflect on the contextual factors that actually shape what is possible. Various tools can be used in this discussion, with a simple example provided in Table 7.3. This is meant to structure a discussion on these factors amongst would-be reformers and policymakers and solicit estimates of the authority, acceptance and ability realities they face. This kind of discussion is often quite novel for many, and the resulting estimates are seldom if ever fully or even sufficiently informed. Indeed, they require making assumptions about the behavior of others. We believe these assumptions are part of doing complex policy and reform—where we face uncertainty and opacity and do not really know all that we need to know. The goal is to make as good an estimate as possible, in transparent a fashion as possible, so that we allow ourselves to progressively learn more about the context and turn uncertainty into clearer knowledge. As such, we strive to record these assumptions as effectively as possible (to feed into the learning discussed in the next chapter) in the last column of Table 7.3.

Findings will vary when these triple-A factors are considered in respect of each causal dimension in the deconstructed problem. When considering some sub-causes, for instance, reformers are likely to perceive that high levels of authority, acceptance and ability are already in place, which suggests a large change space or readiness for engagement. This is shown in the left Venn diagram in Figure 7.2 (which provides an easy way to visualize change space estimates and which shows that it is about having all three triple-A factors in place, not just one). These large change space areas allow engagements that can be heavily frontloaded, with bold efforts to resolve the causal issue in question. In other words, they are entry points for aggressive reform. Perhaps

Table 7.3. A basic triple-A change space analysis

	Questions to help you reflect on the contextual change space	AAA estimation (low, mid, large)	Assumptions
Authority to engage	Who has the authority to engage: • Legal? Procedural? Informal? Which of the authorizer(s) might support engagement now? Which probably would not support engagement now? Overall, how much acceptance do you think you have to engage, and where are the gaps?		
Acceptance	Which agents (person/organization) have an interest in this work? • For each agent, on a scale of 1–10, think about how much they are likely to support engagement? • On a scale of 1–10, think about how much influence each agent has over potential engagement? • What proportion of "strong acceptance" agents do you have (with above 5 on both estimates)? • What proportion of "low acceptance" agents do you have (with below 5 on both estimates)? Overall, how much acceptance do you think you have to engage, and where are the gaps?		
Ability	What is your personnel ability? • Who are the key (smallest group of) agents you need to "work" on any opening engagement? • How much time would you need from these agents? What is your resource ability? • How much money would you need to engage? • What other resources do you need to engage? Overall, how much ability do you think you have to engage, and where are the gaps?		

these are areas related to slow procurement processes in the example we are working through here (as shown in Figure 7.3), where significant change space is thought to exist to address the key sub-causes: Procurement processes are often half implemented; Procurement processes are often rushed; Decisions to procure goods are delayed and delayed again, every year; Budget decisions initiating purchase decisions are delayed.

Reformers will probably find less change space in other sub-cause areas, however, where there are gaps in one or more of the triple-A factors. There may be questions about authority and ability to tackle the crucial sub-causes in strand 3, for instance (as shown in the right hand Venn diagram in Figure 7.2 and in the applied Venn diagram in Figure 7.3), where it is tougher to engage on the sub-dimensions: officials feel obliged to redistribute money; constituents expect

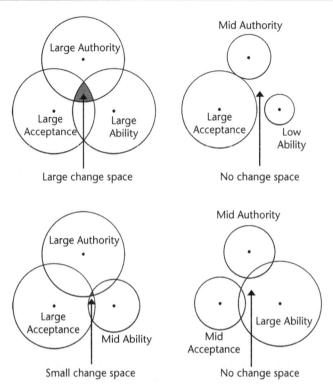

Figure 7.2. Showing the change space graphically

officials to redistribute money; local norms make it appropriate to "share" in this way. This kind of observation should not lead to reformers dropping the area for reform or policy engagement. Rather, it points to the need for early activities that shore up the change space for more far-reaching second or third phase engagements. These could include initiatives to sensitize local communities about the costs of local patronage, or establishing coalitions among appropriately located councilors and officials who might authorize some reforms. Essentially, one needs to grow the change space in such areas before filling this space with something new (whether a new policy or idea or process). Growing the change space is itself a key engagement in the reform process, involving specific activities that need to be purposively thought out and introduced.

This approach will help reformers identify the kind of activities they need to pursue in all cause and sub-cause areas of their deconstructed problem. Many of the areas will warrant activities that grow the change space, whereas others will allow more aggressive reform or policy adjustment because the change space is already perceived as sufficient (as in the procurement area, shown in Figure 7.3). Reformers should look for "quick wins" in this latter set of engagements, which will be crucial to building the authorization for reform

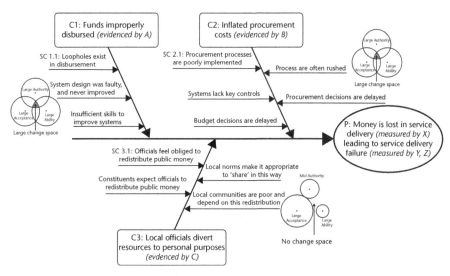

Figure 7.3. Examining change space in different causal/sub-causal strands of a problem

(discussed in more detail in Chapter 9) and will likely help to grow the change space in other areas.

We learned about this kind of sequencing when looking at cases like Sweden's budget reforms in the 1990s. While the reformers in this case were not using the exact tools or approaches we recommend (they did not examine the triple-A situation, for instance) they certainly took a similar view to sequencing. They consciously front-loaded their early reforms in areas where they had political acceptance and authorization, for instance, and where they were building on ideas and abilities from past reform initiatives. They began with substantive efforts to reignite 1980s initiatives to clarify intergovernmental spending rules, for instance, and to introduce a new budget calendar and mechanisms to cut spending (where the calendar and austerity measures had been piloted before). These provided quick wins, and built momentum for the broader reforms. Other areas only saw visible change five to ten years after the initiation however, when new laws shifted budgetary responsibilities from the Parliament to the ministry of finance and introduced fiscal rules and related innovations. The change space was not large enough to accommodate these reforms in the early 1990s—because political acceptance was still only emerging, the reformers needed to bolster their authority to act, and ideas and other abilities had to be proposed, discussed, and tried out. Early steps to build acceptance, authority, and ability yielded more change space in the mid and late 1990s, and this was when more far-reaching change occurred. While interventions were gradual, the entire reform process was always problem-driven and involved constant progression—not periodic innovation.

A similar sequencing approach also guided efforts to build state capability in the other cases we have been discussing—Nostria and Mantia:

- The team working on building judicial capability recognized that some of the causal areas in their fishbone diagram were not accessible for immediate change. They could not, for instance, introduce ideas to improve data sharing across the sector. This required them first building political acceptance for the idea. They could also not immediately work to address data gaps, given a lack of abilities to collect certain kinds of data in the field. They could, however, start building these abilities to expand their change space for future reform. They could also do more immediate visible work identifying what data existed and using that data—even when unshared—to construct a preliminary evidence-based picture of the sector. This first step was intended to build change space in other areas and help set the reform on a path towards solving the bigger problems.

- The Mantian officials went to work immediately on its five-bone fishbone, identifying the change space in all of the forty-two sub-causal areas. It did this by listing the key agents needing to act in each area, noting whether these agents enjoyed authority to act and would likely accept the challenge, and determining whether policy vehicles already existed to enable action. In a number of areas, this search showed the team that some of the forty-two challenges had already been addressed—through past policies or projects—and provided opportunities for "quick wins." In other areas policy vehicles existed and the team could push for quick action to allow a second stage of these quick wins. In other areas the team needed to build authority and acceptance to move ahead, which meant starting with careful communications initiatives to engage other parties and draw support to reform. Overall, this exercise helped the team identify what it was doing in all forty-two areas, stage some of these areas for immediate action (and, hopefully, success) and prepare other areas for more aggressive future engagement. The team built a spreadsheet to note their assumptions in each area and to indicate the "next steps" they proposed for each (which we will discuss in Chapter 8).

Problem-driven sequencing like this is both strategic and realistic, focused on staging interventions to *progressively* solve the problem, given contextual realities (rather than assuming these away or ignoring them). The focus is, overall, on getting the problem solved—and this should be locked in as an aspirational goal as early as possible, with specified metrics that show what "problem solved" actually looks like. Every entry point activity is intended to lead to this goal, with some early steps growing the change space needed for future steps and some aggressively filling the already-extant change space with new policy or

Table 7.4. A change space analysis for each sub-cause on your Ishikawa diagram

	Describing your context (use questions from Table 6.5)	AAA estimation (low, mid, large)	Assumptions
Authority to engage			
Acceptance			
Ability			

reform initiatives. These aggressive early steps should yield the "quick wins" that show the gains of change and point to the promise of more far-reaching change in future. This helps to satisfy the twin need for reform plans that are grounded and practical (addressing "what's next" and "what's possible") and visionary (tackling the big picture issues that authorizers often focus on).

Before moving on, take some time to think about the change space in which you are acting with regards to the challenge identified in prior exercises in this chapter. As with past exercises, use Table 7.4 to work on your own and then with a group or team to reflect on, estimate, and note assumptions about the authority, acceptance, and ability conditions in each sub-causal dimension of your problem. Then modify your fishbone diagram (as in Figure 7.3) to show the kind of change space you have in each area—and noting the kind of engagement implied by such (aggressive engagement with new solutions in existing space, or more strategic engagements to build space, for instance). Use Box 7.4 for this.

Where Does This Leave You?

Adopting a problem-driven approach to building state capability is quite different to the normal approach of pursuing a solution from the get-go. It is vital when one does not know what the "solution" is, however, and where there are no easy or direct routes to building the state capability needed for implementation. We believe that these complex situations demand a different approach, where one identifies problems and finds solutions to the problems and then institutionalizes those solutions. In a sense, this is like finding success before one

Box 7.4. CHANGE SPACE IN OUR GROUP ISHIKAWA DIAGRAM: WHERE SHOULD WE START, WITH WHAT KIND OF ENGAGEMENT IN EACH AREA?

institutionalizes such (which is the opposite of many efforts to build state capability, which focus on introducing success through a new institutional solution).

We expect that anyone actually pursuing the problem-driven approach in this chapter will already find themselves looking at their state capability challenges differently. In many of our engagements with development professionals, we find colleagues enter with challenges that really reflect a missing solution: "we don't have a state of the art budget process" or "we don't have modern teacher monitoring mechanisms" or "we don't have a functional anti-corruption bureau." Given this view, they tend to enter with some knowledge of the "right solution" to their challenge: we can build state capability by modernizing the budget process/teacher monitoring mechanisms/an anti-corruption bureau.

These colleagues leave the problem analysis phase of this work with a completely different perspective on their challenge. They have constructed the challenge to draw attention to the need for change and for real capacity building, and deconstructed the challenge to make it more manageable, and considered the contextual opportunities and constraints in determining where to start and how to sequence engagements. Typically, this kind of problem analysis empowers participants—especially working in their own countries—to feel as if they can actually contribute to solving the problem. This empowerment is itself a product of the PDIA state capability building process, in that capability centers on confidence to do—and desire to do well. Participants empowered in this manner are also impatient about what's next, however, and ask where the solutions are and how quickly they can start implementing them. We hope that this chapter leaves you in a similar place, ready to move on to thinking about iterative processes of finding and fitting solutions that actually work. It is to these issues that we now turn.

8

The Searchframe

Doing experimental iterations

One of Matt's students was a consultant working on a local government project. He came to Matt with a specific concern. "I have a well thought-out project design, based on a solution my firm adopted in a similar place a year ago," he said, "but I cannot get the community in this new locale to support the work." Matt encouraged him to start constructing and deconstructing the problem that warranted his involvement in the community—first on his own and then, when he felt he could state what the problem was, why it mattered, and why it was festering, to engage with the community. He did this, and after a month came back and said that he had learned various invaluable things: first, the community could be mobilized around a problem they cared about— and he had managed to identify such a problem with them; second, his initial assumptions of the problem were mostly wrong, and the "solution" he hoped to introduce would not have been possible or even effective; third, the community members themselves had a bunch of great ideas to work with. Motivated by this experience, he engaged different groups to try some of their own ideas out, and some that he introduced based on his past experience. Altogether, four different work streams emerged with groups trying different "solutions." They met monthly to discuss progress, and all four groups adjusted their work based on the cumulative learning. After six months they were focused on only two streams of work, where ideas had been merged together and lessons accumulated into two potential solutions the community was already implementing. The story is not complete, but progress is being made.

As in the example, we believe that good problems mobilize actors to find solutions to complex challenges like the one you have been working through in prior chapters, partly because such problems point to "feasible remedial action [that] can be meaningfully pursued" (Chan 2010: 3). The deconstruction and sequencing work helps to foster such action, allowing reformers and policymakers to think about *where* they should act (where do we have large change space, and where is it limited?), and even *how* (how do we build change space or fill extant change space?). The challenge is still to determine "*what*" to do when acting, however.

This is a serious challenge when dealing with complex problems, given that the *what* answers are usually unclear—when we are honest about it, we have to admit that we often do not know what to do when faced with complex challenges in complex contexts. It is an even bigger challenge when an externally identified best practice "solution" is offered to us, promising the answer but quite likely to lead into a capability trap. This challenge can leave one wondering what to do and how to manage the lure of best practices (or isomorphic pressure to adopt such).

In response to this tension, we propose a core PDIA principle to inform a strategy of finding and fitting the *what* answers in your situation. Put simply, we hold that the *"what"* answers to complex problems do exist and can be found, but must emerge through active iteration, experimentation, and learning. This means that answers cannot be pre-planned or developed in a passive or academic fashion by specialists applying knowledge from other contexts. Answers must be found within the change context through active engagement and learning.

This is not to say that ideas from the outside (and so-called "best practices") should not be considered as potential answers or pathways to building state capability, but rather that even the most effective best practices are unlikely to address all of the specific problem dimensions needing attention. If completely new to a context, they are also likely to lack the political acceptance required to work effectively (see Andrews 2006, 2012). As such, these "answers" must still be experimented with and adapted, through a process that empowers the search for "technically viable solutions to locally perceived problems" (Greenwood et al. 2002: 60). But what should this "find-and-fit" process look like?

Why Experimental Iterations?

In trying to answer this question, we have been influenced by the literature on incrementalism. This work is attributed primarily to Charles Lindblom (1959), who referred to the policy-making process as one that entailed "muddling through"—i.e. groups "find" institutional solutions through a series of small, incremental steps or actions that are gradually introduced to address specific, targeted parts of a problem. As Lindblom (1959: 301) explains, "A policy is directed at a problem; it is tried, altered, tried in altered form, altered again and so on." Incrementalism can be linear, where one step leads to the next predicted step and to the next step until a pre-planned solution is fully adopted. This kind of incrementalism, however, will not hold up in the face of the uncertainty of complex challenges, given that such challenges seldom allow one to identify many steps ahead. Rather, these challenges demand an iterative incrementalism, where the latter also involves taking small steps to address problems—but where each step leads to some learning about what works and what does not, which informs a next (and potentially different) step to see if an adjusted action works better.[1] The process is thus not perfectly linear, because every step depends on what is learned in the step before—which could be that a radical shift is needed or that the proposed path actually makes sense.

---

[1] Sabel and Jordan (2015) use the word "recursive" to describe a similar process.

Iteration like this is similar to what some call the "try, learn, adapt" method used by some lean management gurus (e.g. Radnor and Walley 2008; Womack and Jones 2010). The hallmarks of this process are simple: targeted actions are rapidly tried, lessons are quickly gathered to inform what happened and why, and a next action step is designed and undertaken based on what was learned in prior steps. Think of an application in the 1804 journey westwards: a team spends three days moving in a westerly direction, and then makes camp, taking time to reflect on the obstacles and opportunities encountered and lessons learned, and then decides on the next step (how long it will be, where it will be, and who it will involve). Iterations like this continue until the problem has been fully addressed (or, using the language of agile software development, "requirements have been met" in the search for a solution).

The process should be seen as experimental, and probably involve acting on multiple potential solution ideas at a time (instead of just one). It can also be accelerated to ensure the change process gains and keeps momentum (to more or less degree, depending on where one is in the change process and what problems, causes or sub-causes are being addressed). Trying a number of small interventions in rapid "experiments" like this helps to assuage common risks in reform and policy processes, of either appearing too slow in responding to a problem or of leading a large and expensive capacity building failure. This is because each step offers quick action that is relatively cheap and open to adjustment; and with multiple actions at any one time there is an enhanced prospect of early successes (commonly called "quick wins").

The blend of cheapness and demonstrable success characterize what some might call "positive deviations"[2] in the process of building state capability, and are important in contexts where change encounters opposition, which is usually the case with government reforms in developing countries. The small steps also help to flush out (or clarify) contextual challenges, including those that emerge in response to the interventions themselves. Facilitating such positive deviations and contextual lessons is especially important in uncertain and complex contexts where reformers are unsure of what the problems and solutions actually are and often lack confidence in their abilities to make things better.

This approach is quite different to the conventional way state capability initiatives are structured, in which specialists initially conduct studies to decide on a "solution," then design how the solution should be introduced into a context, and then initiate implementation. Such phases in a linear process, we believe, yields limited learning or chance for adaptation (whether

---

[2] See Pascale et al. (2010) for broader applications of the concept of "positive deviance" to difficult policy problems.

it is slow or big-bang in nature). An experimental, iterative process, in contrast, has the following characteristics:

- Multiple solution ideas are identified and put into action.

- Experimental, iterative steps progressively allow real (locally legitimate) solutions to emerge.

- Disciplined, experiential learning and flexibility foster adaptation to the idiosyncrasies of the local context.

Crawling the Design Space for Multiple Potential Solutions

Many reform and policy initiatives limit themselves to a narrative of two parts when thinking about *what* to do in the face of a problem: (a) there is the status quo, or the way things are currently done in the target context, that those in the context know how to do but it has not solved the problem; and (b) there are best practices in other contexts that are deemed to have solved similar problems in those other contexts, but we are not sure how to do them in the targeted place and time. Reform and policy change often centers on replacing the internal current practices with external best practices. We believe that there are more options for reformers to work with than just these two, however. A key principle of PDIA is to look for and experiment with multiple alternatives.

We liken the idea to crawling the design space available to policymakers and would-be reformers. Drawing from the ideation stage of design thinking (Gruber et al. 2015; van Manen et al. 2015),[3] the basic strategy here involves requiring change agents to identify at least two ideas for change in the various sub-causal dimensions they are trying to address. The ideas they are looking for will vary in substance, depending on the available change space: new practice ideas might be required where significant change space exists and can be exploited; ideas to improve authority, acceptance or ability will be more pertinent where change space is limited.

Change agents need to identify these various ideas, and then put them into action to foster change. These agents might search for ideas, in different areas of the "design space" shown in Figure 8.1, which helps to explain our approach. It shows a stylized design space that policymakers and would-be

---

[3] The initial steps of PDIA share a lot with design thinking process, where ideation follows phases in which problems are better understood and constructed, through empathizing and defining (similar to the construction and deconstruction processes discussed here). See the brief poster by UNICEF's Natalia Adler on design thinking for Doing Development Differently at http://matthewandrews.typepad.com/the_limits_of_institution/2014/10/design-thinking-and-unicef-in-nicaragua-natalia-adler-will-be-presenting-at-doing-development-differ.html.

reformers face when introducing new policy and reform ideas in response to a complex problem (or when trying to build state capabilities to address these challenges). There are two dimensions to this space, reflected in the axes of the figure: horizontally, we reflect on whether an idea is administratively and politically possible in the targeted context (have the solutions proved to work in this context, such that the people in the context know how to implement them?); vertically, we consider whether the ideas have proved technically correct (such that they have been seen to solve the problem being considered).

Existing practice is the first area of opportunity in the design space—denoted by an "A" in the bottom right corner of Figure 8.1. We believe there is always some existing practice or capability—whether this is a way of procuring text books, reporting on finances, organizing classroom behavior or managing pharmaceutical stocks in a district clinic. People in the context know this practice, but we also know that the practice has fallen short of solving the focal problem(s). Existing practice provides an opportunity, however, in the lessons it holds about what works in the context (and what does not) and why.

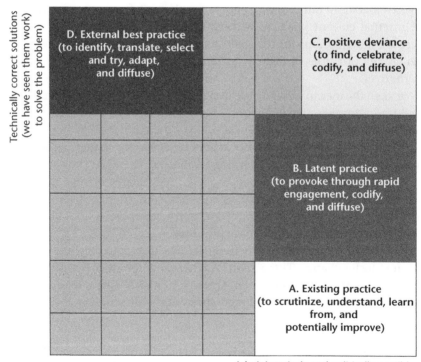

Figure 8.1. The design space: where do we get ideas from?

Initial work to find deficiencies in current practice thus identifies useful starting points in the finding and fitting process. Common tools to help in this process include gap analysis, program evaluation, site visits, immersion and inspection initiatives (where would-be reformers and policymakers spend time interacting with existing practice to get a better sense of how it works, where it has failed, and why). Our would-be reformer in Malawi could suggest examining current procurement processes to identify exactly where gaps exist, for instance, and then try and close the gaps (see the approach to this in Andrews and Bategeka 2013).

In many cases, existing practice also offers improvement opportunities that could be used to initiate action. These opportunities can be identified by engaging, in the field, with practitioners who often think about ways to improve practices but lack incentives to share their ideas.[4] These ideas might emerge when our would-be reformer examines the procurement process in Malawi, especially if she does so alongside local practitioners and asks them if they have thought of ways to make the process work better. Whether the improvements turn out to be successful or not, they are often the quickest form of engagement that one can take in starting the process of addressing problems—and they are also the most immediate arena in which one can force action and learning in the process of building state capability. Existing practice is also the practice that agents in the change context know best, and "starting form where they are" is a potentially empowering way of ensuring these agents develop a properly constructed and deconstructed view of the problem (better understanding why existing practices are not working) and provide local ownership of the find-and-fit process.[5]

The next most accessible area in the design space is what we call "latent practice" (shown as B in Figure 8.1). This is the set of potential ideas and government capabilities that are possible in the context—given administrative and political realities—but require some focused attention to emerge. This attention could come in the form or Rapid Results type interventions, where groups of affected agents are given a challenge to solve the focal problem (or part thereof) in a defined period—with no new resources (Matta and Morgan 2011; Dillabaugh et al. 2012; Wilson 2013). In the example of Malawi's corruption and service delivery challenge, one might instruct relevant agents to act in a new way in areas where process gaps have been identified (like establishing a quick way of tracking procurement requests and responses to them). An example of this kind of activity comes from Burundi, where a rapid

---

[4] This is central to the work on appreciative inquiry, where authors and practitioners believe that local agents have positive ideas that need to be coaxed to the fore (Bushe 2013; Drew and Wallis 2014; Ridley-Duff and Duncan 2015).
[5] See also Chapter 8 of Andrews (2013).

results initiative focused on empowering officials to come up with creative latent ideas to deliver school textbooks that had been sitting in a warehouse for years (Campos et al. 2013). The officials went through various iterations in working around this challenge, ultimately engaging parliamentarians to deliver the books. The parliamentarians had always been available to do this work, but had never been asked.

These kinds of initiatives can be incredibly motivating and empowering for local agents, who get to see their own achievements in short periods. Ideas that emerge from these rapid initiatives can also become the basis of permanent solutions to existing problems (especially if learning processes are effectively in place, as will be discussed shortly). Latent potential can also be released when change agents construct a Hawthorne-type interaction where the hands-on practitioners are included into some kind of real-world experiment, and one hopes the awareness of being watched leads to behavior modifications and new ideas (Schwartz et al. 2013). These ideas focus on drawing ideas out of existing resources and agents, given the view that novelty is always latent in such agents but needs to be coaxed out (in the same way that juice is latent in an orange, and needs a good squeeze to be released).

The "positive deviance" domain (denoted by C at the top-right corner of Figure 8.1) is a third area in which change agents can look for policy and reform ideas. Positive deviance relates to ideas that are already being acted upon in the change context (they are thus possible), and that yield positive results (solving the problem, and thus being technically correct), but are not the norm (hence the idea of deviance) (Marsh et al. 2004).[6] For example, in every town with high levels of infant mortality, one can identify a household where no children die; they are the positive deviants, doing something that others are not doing but that is effective in addressing the problem in the context. As part of the search for policy and reform ideas, change agents need to find these positive deviants, celebrate them, examine their successful practices (i.e. determining why they are different), and diffuse the core principles of their success more broadly. The initial "finding" process offers a pragmatic and immediate option with which to initiate any change process, and could involve a search of evidence or practice (where change agents look for positive outliers in a large data set or go to the field and look for positive real-world experiences).

"External best practice" is the final idea domain we see as obvious in any design space. This domain (denoted by D in Figure 8.1) is full of ideas outside

---

[6] Marsh et al. (2004) define positive deviance as "an uncommon practice that confers advantage to the people who practice it compared with the rest of the community. Such behaviors are likely to be affordable, acceptable, and sustainable because they are already practiced by at risk people, they do not conflict with local culture, and they work." See other definitions and applications in Spreitzer and Sonenshein (2003, 2004) and Dumas and Maggi (2015).

of the change context that one has seen to address problems similar to those targeted for attention. These are often the first set of ideas reformers and policymakers look at and suggest. It is also typical for only one idea to emerge at any given time from this domain as well, given a prevalent desire to identify the "one best way" to do things. Many global indicators embed these ideas and encourage their replication across contexts. Actually, there are usually multiple external good or best practice ideas to learn from, and the find-and-fit process should start by identifying a few of these—rather than settling for one. In the case of Malawi's corruption concerns, for instance, one could identify ways in which Hong Kong's anticorruption commission has dealt with procurement and disbursement gaps, but one could also examine ideas emanating from Botswana and South Africa. Once identified, change agents need to translate the ideas to the change context—ensuring that the best practice ideas can be communicated from their external context into the new change context (explaining why the practice was done and how it was done). This is often much easier to do when the best practices come from similar contexts (and the "language" of government, society, and politics is similar) (Andrews 2012). Once the external best practice idea has been communicated in this translated detail, it becomes a candidate for experimentation in the change context.

We advocate trying more than one new idea at a time in any change context—much as 1804 adventurers would try two routes to get past a mountain they have not yet bypassed. In some situations, one of the ideas will work significantly better than the other(s) and stand out as the solution to be diffused more broadly into the context. Our research and experience shows that this is not commonly the case, however. In most cases of complex change the process yields positive and negative lessons from each idea—with no individual idea proving to be "the solution." These lessons lead to the emergence of new hybrids, or locally constructed solutions that blend elements and lessons from experiments with all of the ideas.[7] We see this in the example of Rwanda's municipal performance management system—one of the ISS "success" cases investigated in the study referred to in Chapter 6 (Andrews 2013). It blends external best practice block grants with new planning ideas and revived old positive deviance practices in the Imihigo contracting mechanism. The system could not have worked if only one idea was employed, and it would not have emerged if Rwanda had not experimented with many different ideas.

---

[7] See Andrews (2015c). This account is echoed in the panoramic historical narrative provided by Bayly (2004) of *how* particular states and sub-national institutions formed across the world in the nineteenth century. Kennedy (2013) provides a related account of how the superior "problem solvers" of the Allied forces "turned the tide" in World War II.

We saw similar mixed solutions emerging in the examples discussed in Chapter 7:

- Swedish budget and accounting reforms in the 1990s drew on many ideas. Accounting innovations were largely an extension of 1980s reforms and private sector practices that already existed, for instance. Important dimensions of the performance management system emerged from experiments at the local government level, which stimulated new latent ideas and unearthed positive deviants. International best practices were also influential, especially in bringing multi-year budgeting and fiscal rules to the fore. These various ideas were combined over a number of years, establishing a budgeting and accounting system that looks quite different to any other in Europe (or beyond), exhibiting all the hallmarks of a locally effective hybrid.

- Solutions also emerged from various parts of the design space in Nostria's efforts to better manage judicial demand and supply. The reform team found that most of the "missing" data was already generated by existing systems, for instance, but steps were needed to ensure this data was readily available (which led to practical steps to make the data available). They also found positive deviants in the sector, where some agencies and jurisdictions offered lessons to others in how to produce data and manage resources. They also learned lessons from a neighboring country about how to use standard software packages to analyze data and build budgets. Ultimately, their reform emerged as a blend of all these products, not a pure product in either category.

- As discussed in Chapter 7, Mantian officials faced forty-two challenges in their effort to promote economic activity in a poor performing sector. They found some solutions in existing policies, programs, and policies, given that a number of the challenges should actually have been resolved by past initiatives. For instance, companies noted that they needed financial help to innovate when in fact government had an active—but unused—innovation fund in place. They also created pressure to foster latent practice, requiring agencies to report monthly on how they had addressed challenges—and pushing relentlessly to ensure that solutions emerged and were then institutionalized. They also experimented with various best practice ideas promoted by international donors, as long as these ideas actually addressed one of the forty-two challenges. The reform team maintained a spreadsheet of all the "solutions" it was coordinating, and who was responsible for action in respect of each solution. The ideas in this spreadsheet varied considerably (in terms of where they came from, who they involved, what they involved, and how innovative they actually were). This variation showed how much bricolage goes into producing real state capability (to support private sector development, and beyond).

Table 8.1. A basic strategy to crawl your design space: looking for solution ideas

Sub-causal dimension of my problem	What substance do we need from any new idea? a. New policy or practice to fit into existing change space b. A way to expand authority c. A way to expand acceptance d. A way to expand ability	How can we work to find ideas in at least two of the following idea domains? a. Existing practice b. Latent practice c. Positive deviance d. External best practice
Sub-cause 1		
Sub-cause 2		
Sub-cause 3		

The message here is simple: finding and fitting solutions to complex problems requires first identifying multiple ideas and then trying these out, in an experimental manner, to allow the emergence of hybrids. The experimentation process needs to offer significant opportunity for learning and adaptation—and what some authors call bricolage (constructing a solution from a diverse range of things, given lessons about what works and does not work in each).[8] This demands an iterative process which we will discuss next. Before getting there, however, we recommend you use Table 8.1 to reflect on the various opportunities you have to source new ideas that can help you find-and-fit solutions to your challenge.

The table essentially asks you to first list the sub-causal dimensions of this challenge and then think about the kind of substance you are looking for in new ideas (e.g. Are you looking for a new policy idea or a way of expanding change space by expanding authority, acceptance, or ability?). Following this, there is a column in which you are encouraged to describe—briefly!—at least two ideas you could act upon in two of the design space domains. We encourage you to do the exercise on your own and then with a group, and to try and come up with at least two sets of activities you could quickly initiate to start actively finding and fitting real solutions to your problems.

---

[8] See, for instance, Christiansen and Lounsbury (2013) and Perkmann and Spicer (2014).

What Do Experimental Iterations Involve?

You should note that Table 8.1 does not provide a specific solution for your challenge. This will be frustrating for some, given that many popular policy or reform processes strive to yield such solutions from an early identification process. The solution then becomes the center of a project plan focused on implementation. Plans use mechanisms like logical frameworks to identify the steps required to turn the idea into a reality, locking one into a linear sequence of action designed to solve the problem. This approach is considered good practice for many in the development world, offering certainty about what will be done, in a designated timeframe, and with known content.

This approach is not well suited to complex challenges, however, where we do not really know what the solution is, or what surprises we will encounter in the context when we start any new initiative. It would be like the 1804 adventurers pre-identifying the exact route to take between St Louis and the West Coast in 1804, even though no one knew where the West Coast was or if any particular route made sense. Such an approach often encounters its own limits quickly, when reformers meet with unexpected constraints (like hostile politics or capacity deficiencies, which act like unexpected mountains or rivers that impede their progress). At this stage, reformers and policymakers are seldom equipped to respond to the realities they face, which certainly call for a change in their implementation strategy and probably also require a rethink of the solution they are attempting to introduce. Rigidities in the logical framework approach make such adjustments extremely difficult, however, and often lead to periods where reforms and new policy initiatives simply stagnate (given a lack of flexibility).[9]

A different approach is required when dealing with complex challenges—where policymakers and would-be reformers can try new ideas out, learn what works and why, adapt ideas, and repeat the process until a solution is found. We call this experimental iteration.

This kind of process is driven by the urgency of finding and fitting solutions to specific complex problems. Its aspirational end goal is thus defined by the state one hopes to reach when the problem has been solved (which you identified earlier, in Table 7.1). Given that chosen problems are complex, however, it does not pretend that there is only one starting point or idea to act upon, but rather that there are many entry points (as you would have shown in Box 7.4) and multiple ideas to engage at each entry point (as reflected in your thoughts in Table 8.1). It also does not assume that starting

---

[9] This kind of observation is emerging constantly in development studies. See, for instance, Duncan and Williams (2012), Faustino and Booth (2014), Fritz et al. (2014), and Manning and Watkins (2013).

ideas will hold intact as ultimate solutions, and therefore that the goal is simply to provide a linear chart to implement these ideas. Rather, this process provides a structured, step-by-step engagement in which one tests ideas, adjusts the ideas based on test results and lessons, and works progressively towards shaping a solution that actually works.

One should be able to see the characteristics that lead us to call the process experimental (where one is testing ideas that have not yet been finalized). The approach should not be confused with a randomized controlled trial, however, where one tests an idea in a scientific manner, randomizing who receives the "treatment" and attempting to control the messy influences of reality. The experimental approach here happens in a specific context and in the midst of reality, such that results are possible given the mess one is dealing with. The approach is also accelerated and done in real time, with those who will ultimately be the implementers. This gives some assurance that the process—and ultimate policy or reform product—will be locally owned and legitimate, and likely to lead to genuine improvements in state capability.

One should also be able to identify the characteristics that lead us to call this process iterative (where one tries an idea out again and again, learning each time, until the idea is properly specified as a functional solution to a nominated problem). Figure 8.2 shows what the iterative process looks like in its simplest form. The first iteration starts by identifying initial action steps (building on the already-completed problem analysis and idea identification activities). The initial steps should be highly specified, with precise determination of what will be done by whom in relation to all chosen ideas, and predetermined start and end points that create time boundaries for the first step. We propose working with tight time boundaries at the start of this kind of work, so as to establish the foundation of an action-oriented work culture, and to build momentum.[10] The boundaries help to define when action steps begin (stage 2 of each iteration), when the action stops and reflection begins (stage 3), and when the iteration-check will take place (stage 4 of each iteration).

The action step stage should be easily understood. This is where our Malawian reformers might take action to try some ideas out (initiating a field visit to examine existing practice, or starting a rapid results initiative to deliver text books, or trying out a new reporting mechanism that has been seen to work in South Africa). Stage 3 reflection involves stopping after taking this action and, in a group discussion, asking three questions: What was achieved? What was learned? What is next? Stage 4 is called an iteration check, where those involved in the work report to their authorizers on progress and lessons learned, and assess whether they have solved the problem (or

[10] See Andrews (2015a).

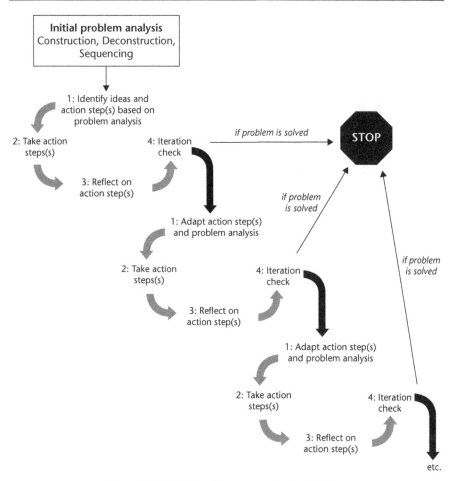

Figure 8.2. The iterative process in simple form

sub-causal dimension) they have been focused on. If the answer is yes (the problem is solved), then there is no need to iterate further and the challenge becomes one of stopping and diffusing the solution. If the answer is no, however, the group moves into a second iteration—adapting its ideas based on lessons learned and going through the same stages again. The group will move closer to a workable solution as it passes through more iterations, with more complex challenges requiring more iterations than other challenges.

Iterative experimentation like this mitigates the risk of making too many assumptions about proposed solutions, or about the context in which one is working. Every step provides an opportunity to test assumptions and tease out any lessons about what works with specific ideas in specific contexts. It is a process that many are using in other fields, and that development experts are increasingly considering for application in the face of complex challenges.

We see many successful reforms adopting such process as well, including the Swedish public budgeting reforms discussed earlier in this chapter (and Chapter 7). Accounting innovations in Sweden were particularly subject to an experimental process, starting in the 1980s when various local governments were encouraged to try using private sector accounting methods. Their efforts were labeled "pilots" but were more reflective of the experimental iterations described in this section: the local governments applied specific tools in defined periods, stopped and assessed lessons learned in these efforts, and then adapted the tools for another application. Observers note that this kind of iteration continued for most of the 1980s and yielded useful and usable accounting innovations that could be scaled up for implementation in the early 1990s.

Experimental iteration like this was also used to foster change in the other two examples of state capability building we have been referencing. One set of activities in Nostria focused on sourcing judicial demand and supply data from existing sources (remembering that their work began after a failed five-year project that intended to introduce a new electronic case management system). This is a stylized version of the first few iterations:

- The team identified potential opportunities in finding existing data and specified a first step, requiring all team members to identify existing data in their organizations and report on this at a team meeting the next afternoon.

- The next afternoon they all came with written descriptions of existing data. After listing the existing data, the team reflected on what had been learned. Lessons were simple but impressive: we have more data than we thought; it was quite easy to identify what we had; the real problem is that we do not share it. Reflecting on these lessons, the team agreed that the problem was not yet solved and more iteration was needed. It identified a next step: each member should bring her data to a team meeting, the next day. The list of available data and next step decision was shared with a senior official who was overseeing the group, to ensure continued support.

- The next day only half of the team members had data to show, and these data took the form of (generally) unusable reams of paper. The team reflected on this, given prompting questions: What was achieved? What was learned? What is next? Lessons centered on the political and bureaucratic walls team members encountered when trying to access data to share, in their relevant organizations (including the judiciary, prosecution, and ministry). Their superiors simply did not allow the sharing (even though these authorizers had committed their support to the initiative). The team members agreed that these walls had been up for a long time and were a key reason for the failure of prior efforts to establish case management systems. The next step, they argued, was to engage the political authorizers whom they had assumed were supportive of the work and ask for explicit permission to share. This required a new and more aggressive strategy to explain the grave—and shared—nature of the problem with the authorizers (which the team had assumed was already well communicated but now agreed could be presented more aggressively). Team members immediately proposed a strategy for this, and agreed to meet again two days later to compare results.

- Two days later the full team returned, with each member carrying an old clunky laptop. Their superiors had jointly agreed that all data could be shown to the full group but had to be kept in files in each laptop. This was not the best mode of sharing, of course, but was a step ahead of where the team had been two days previously. Team members thus opened their laptops and began looking for their files, all of which were in Excel. Only half of the group managed to find the files on their own, however, and it became very obvious that the others could not work in Excel (even though their official titles related to being in statistical or budget agencies). In reflecting on this step, the team noted that more effective sharing modalities were needed in the future (and decided a course of action to persuade authorizers of this). They also noted the need to strengthen their own analytical abilities, and started discussing options in the design space: they could approach the World Bank to host a workshop (as best practice, perhaps), or ask the civil service commission for help (existing practice), or they could see if their more capacitated team members could teach the others (building on their own positive deviants). They agreed that the latter option was quicker, cheaper, and more accessible. A workshop was planned for the next week, with one of the team members identified as the primary instructor.

- The workshop took place a few days after it had been intended (given common logistical and time management difficulties). It was a very inspiring event, where peers empowered peers with new knowledge (and were themselves empowered with new confidence). The team members' superiors all attended the closing of this workshop, and even invited the media to attend (and take photographs). This led to interesting lessons for the team, which agreed that it had more authority and ability to act and now knew more about what was needed. Half of the team members felt that they could share all their data more effectively now, and committed to do so before the next meeting. All team members agreed that meetings should be regular and at consistent times, and scheduled such for the beginning and end of each week, for the next six months.

- There were many more iterations, some of which led backwards instead of forwards and many of which generated difficult lessons. After seven months of these iterations the team produced an Excel spreadsheet with enough data to analyze national and provincial demand and supply and identify input gaps (where judges were needed, for instance). They could build a budget that showed why new inputs were needed, which led to a stronger request with the ministry of finance. The team was already thinking about the limitations of Excel, however, and had enrolled in a course on Access (a database software) with the goal of transferring their data to this platform in the coming year.

A similar process was adopted in Mantria. The core team met every few days for the first few weeks of their engagement, taking steps to identify ideas and responsible actors in all forty-two challenge areas on the fishbone diagram. They built significant momentum in so doing, and after a month they had developed an innovative spreadsheet detailing what was being done in all challenge areas and who was responsible. Every meeting would involve a full analysis of what was being done in each area, what was learned, and what was next. Given the many actors involved in addressing all these challenges, the team instituted a monthly schedule to ensure everyone was able to check in and report. The check-ins often led to vibrant discussion, sometimes involving the responsible actors in different areas (who were invited to engage). For instance, the coordinating team sometimes learned that responsible actors needed more authority (or pressure) to act, and sometimes needed support with new ideas, and sometimes tried ideas that did not work out—so the ideas had to be changed. After nine months of iterating, the team was able to show that all forty-two challenges had been effectively addressed. They could also point to evidence they had been collecting that showed the sector was growing and providing more employment. This pointed to real progress in getting to the "problem solved" goals set at the start, which led to a slowdown in the experimental iterations. Interestingly, however, other groups across government were starting to use adapted versions of the coordination spreadsheet that proved so useful in this work. This was itself an expression of expanded state capability.

These examples should show that experimental iterations are not necessarily slow or slow to produce results. We believe, actually, that the iterations need to be rapid and aggressive to build momentum and team spirit and to ensure continued and expanded authorization (which we discuss more in Chapter 9). The examples should also show that this work is not haphazard and informal. It actually requires a lot of structure and discipline, and needs formal sanction and support. The examples should also show that these approaches yield many results in the short, medium, and long run. The staggered nature of these results—which are often surprises—ensure that the process has continued claims to legitimacy (which is vital when trying to foster contested state build-ing initiatives that require bureaucratic and political support). Finally, the examples show that experimental iteration yields opportunities to learn that are crucial when pursuing wicked hard challenges. These lessons are often not forthcoming in more conventional linear project processes, which means that contextual difficulties commonly go unidentified and untreated and ultimately undermine project success. This was evident in both Nostria and Mantria, where past projects had failed because of a failure to learn and adapt to difficulties encountered in early iterations.

Although the benefits of experimental iteration seem very apparent, many development organizations make it difficult for staff to pursue such approaches, given the rigidity of Logframe and other linear planning methods. We often hear that funding organizations demand the structured, perceived certainty of a Logframe-type device and will not allow projects to be too adaptive. In response to this concern, we propose a new Logframe-type mechanism that embeds experimental iteration into a structured approach to make policy or reform decisions in the face of complex challenges. Called the Searchframe, it is shown in Figure 8.3.

The Searchframe facilitates a transition from the problem analysis into a structured process of finding and fitting solutions. An aspirational goal is included as the end point of the intervention, where one would record details of "what the problem looks like solved." In the Malawi example, we would include an aspirational target relating hoped-for decreases in corruption-related losses and improvements in service delivery in key sectors. Beyond this, key intervening focal points are also included, based on the deconstruction and sequencing analyses. These focal points reflect what the reform or policy intervention aims to achieve at different points along the path towards solving the overall problem. More detail will be provided for the early focal points, given that we know with some certainty what we need and how we expect to get there. For instance, the first focal points for Malawi might include "all disbursement loopholes are identified" and "weaknesses in disbursement are fully identified" and "we know what abilities are missing to address the diversion of resources by local officials." These are the focal points driving the action steps in early iterations, and they need to be set in a defined and meaningful manner (as they shape accountability for action). The other focal points (2 and 3 in the figure) will reflect what we assume or expect or hope will follow (perhaps reading something like "we will close disbursement loopholes" and "disbursements will reflect budgeted plans"). These focal points will not be rigid, given that there are many more underlying assumptions, but they will provide a directionality in the policymaking and reform process that gives funders and authorizers a clear view of the intentional direction of the work.

The Searchframe, unlike a Logframe, does not specify every action step that will be taken. Instead, it schedules a prospective number of iterations between focal points (which one could also relate to a certain period of time). Funders and authorizers are thus informed that the work will involve a minimum number of iterations in a specific period. Only the first iteration is detailed, with specific action steps and a specific check-in date. Funders and authorizers

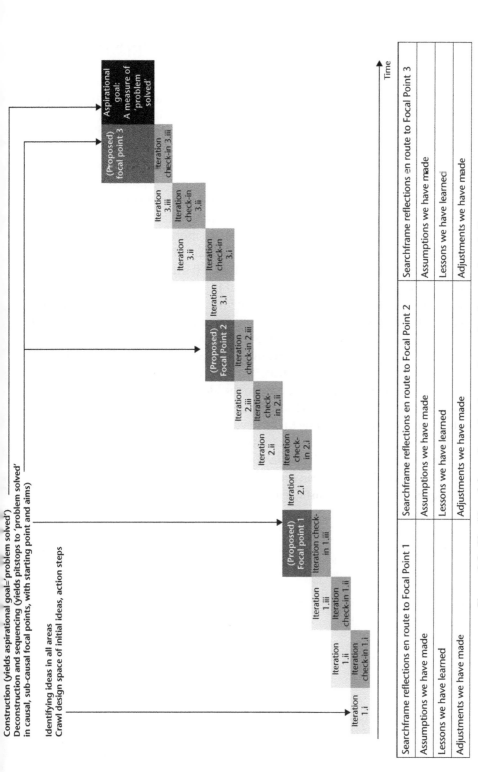

Figure 8.3. The "Searchframe" as a Logframe alternative for complex challenges

will be told to expect reports on all of these check-in dates, which will detail what was achieved and learned and what will be happening in the next iteration (given the Searchframe reflections shown in Figure 8.3). Part of the learning will be about the problem analysis and assumptions underpinning the nature of each focal point and the timing of the initiative. These lessons will feed into proposals to adjust the Searchframe, which will be provided to funders and authorizers after every iteration. This fosters joint learning about the realities of doing change, and constant adaptation of assumptions and expectations.

We believe this kind of iterative process is both well suited to addressing complex problems and meeting the structural needs of formal project processes. As presented, it is extremely information and learning intensive, requiring constant feedback as well as mechanisms to digest feedback and foster adaptation on the basis of such. This is partly because we believe that active discourse and engagement are vital in complex change processes, and must therefore be facilitated through the iterations.[11] We turn to some ideas about this learning very shortly. Before getting there, however, we propose that you stop and think about how experimental iteration might work in helping you find-and-fit solutions to your challenge. We have two exercises to help you in thinking about this. The first, centered on Table 8.2, requires you to detail action steps in response to the ideas you wrote down in Table 8.1, and provide time boundaries for a first iteration. The second, asks you to think about building a Searchframe to use in communicating the intended path you would propose to funders or other authorizers (showing them what the search framework looks like, as of now, in your head). Box 8.1 is provided to give you the chance to draw the Searchframe out (as is done in Figure 8.3), given the work you have done in past exercises.

Table 8.2. Structuring your first iteration

Sub-cause	Idea	Action step(s) (what, by whom, and when start)	Date to reflect (and who will be involved)	Date of Iteration check (and who will be involved)	How will we know if aim is reached?	When to start next iteration (if needed)?

[11] See Marshak et al. (2015) and Babineau and Lessard (2015) who found that organizational change in Canada's health sector depended on building acceptance among those undergoing change, which depended largely on creating active and agile dialogic processes. Other reading we found useful in describing the importance and process of iterative reform include Tsoukas and Chia (2002), Feldman and Pentland (2003), Abdollahi et al. (2015), and Dyba and Dingsoyr (2015).

Box 8.1. THE SEARCHFRAME FOR MY FIND-AND-FIT PROCESS

The Importance of Intense and Applied Learning

Complex challenges are commonly rife with unknowns, where information is deficient and knowledge is limited. This is the reality with many of the challenges in building state capability, especially in development: all we know in many situations is that capability is lacking; we do not know why it is lacking or what it will take to build the necessary capability. This poses real constraints on most management strategies used in capacity building initiatives, which typically require designers and implementers to know more than they do know (or could know). This is a sure-fire recipe for failure in policy, programs, and projects. What is worse, when projects fail, the designers and implementers of these policies, programs, and projects often do not know why their initiatives failed even after the fact, given the continued lack of information and knowledge.

We believe that capable states actually need information and knowledge, and that efforts to build state capability should thus center on ensuring an expansion of know-how. That is why every effort to build state capability needs to embed learning as a key element.

We saw this clearly in a research project that tried to explain why some health sector reforms build capacity whereas others did not.[12] One of the factors that set successful efforts apart was something we called "flexibility," a characteristic involving learning and being able to respond to lessons. This was high when policies, programs, and projects: (1) produced evidence of ongoing assessment of progress and results (not just periodic accountability-based monitoring and evaluation); (2) ensured constant feedback on how well key problems were being addressed, what lessons were being learned, and what issues were being encountered; (3) created opportunities to adjust project content, given lessons from ongoing assessments; and (4) showcased the ideas emerging from learning and incorporated these into project activities during implementation. We found that the average "flexibility" score for more successful projects was 2.72, compared with 1.06 in the less successful group (where 0 is the lowest and 4 the highest). This reflects the tendency of more successful projects to facilitate learning and ensure responses to lessons being learned—in real time.

Many readers might contend that this kind of learning is common in development, and point to randomized control trials (RCTs) and evaluations as ways in which learning is now institutionalized. The learning we are advocating differs with the learning generated by these tools, however. RCTs provide potential lessons about the theoretical validity of an idea in a controlled

---

[12] See Andrews (2013: Chapter 7).

setting, whereas ex post evaluations provide rear view lessons from already completed initiatives. Both cost significant amounts and (generally) yield lessons to specialists working outside of the implementation context (in a more theoretical domain). In contrast, we are talking about learning lessons about the usability of ideas and validity of assumptions in specific contexts, learned by agents engaged in doing the work in these contexts, and learned quickly with the aim of feeding back into the process as design and strategy adaptations.[13]

The prior discussion of experimental iteration provided examples of this learning in practice. In the Nostrian case, for instance, early lessons centered on the availability of data in the justice sector, capacity constraints of statistical experts, and limits to organizational authority. These lessons were gathered in sessions by the team involved in the reform, who were encouraged to reflect on experiences and observations they made while taking actions (given three questions: "what was achieved?" "what was learned?" "what is next?"). This reflective activity allowed what some call experiential learning, in groups, and led immediately into adjustments to reform ideas and strategies.

Experiential learning like this (which might also be called "action learning") is the process of learning through experience, or by doing. It involves the learner actively in a process of trying something and then reflecting on experience, where the learner is both source and user of emergent knowledge; as compared with many other approaches were the learner is a passive recipient of knowledge (and does not even have to use it). Such learning is not common in many organizations, and must thus be consciously encouraged and practically facilitated (Bamford et al. 2015; Senge 2014; Unertl et al. 2016). Facilitation involves routinizing moments of reflection for groups involved in the find-and-fit process (as is done in the experimental iterations) and providing reflective questions for these moments (to coax relevant lessons out of agents). The questions can be general (as in the Nostrian example above) or specific (where we would sometimes ask questions like "what did you learn about your level of authorization?" or "what did you learn about the usability of the idea you were experimenting with?"). The facilitation process should also ensure that lessons are visibly and practically used to adapt the next steps in any experimental iteration (such that those in the reform group can actually see the impact of their experience). In this respect, it is important to

---

[13] Readings reflecting on this kind of learning in different organizational contexts include (among others) Gertler (2003), Klein et al. (2015), Krause and O'Connell (2016), Kruger et al. (2015), Lam (2000), Le and Raven (2015), Li and Armstrong (2015), Liu and Maula (2015), and Yeniyurt et al. (2015). We particularly like Pulakos et al. (2015: 51) which addresses the importance of iteration and experiential learning in results management reforms in governments. In reflecting on successful reforms, the authors of this piece write, "Central to the intervention is that organizational members need to intentionally practice and solidify effective Performance Management behavior through a structured, on-the-job, experiential learning intervention that yields meaningful behavior change."

incorporate measures to ensure that lessons are appropriately reliable. Reflecting team discussions are useful in this respect (where one asks questions like, "Does anyone disagree with that lesson?" or "Is there any supporting or differing experience to share?"). This kind of reflection can help to triangulate and interpret experiences from individuals to the group, increasing both reliability of the lesson and buy-in to whatever implications the lesson has for group behavior.

Interestingly, we find that routinized and regular lessons are often seen as positive products of the PDIA process. Political authorizers in particular see the value of lessons that help them "see" more effectively in any policy or reform engagement. In a sense, this is like the value of a team of adventurers mapping out the territory from St Louis to the west coast in 1804. Taking time to stop, reflect, learn, and record the lessons about any new route allows others to follow the route immediately, with less hassle and uncertainty, which gives authorizers a greater scope of influence. Ultimately, the accumulated lessons lead to a situation where complex problems like going west in 1804 are tamed, becoming simple 2015 go west challenges.

Learning like this is not, however, common in many efforts to build state capability. Furthermore, many risk-averse politicians and career bureaucrats may resist this kind of learning—and the experimental process it involves— before you can even get it going. Resistance often reflects a view that this kind of learning lacks legitimacy, or that it will be undisciplined or ineffective (or is just too difficult to do in hierarchical rule based organizations).[14] This view needs to be countered by an explicit and disciplined strategy to foster such learning. This strategy helps to provide structure to the reflection activity shown as stage 3 in each the iteration cycle (see Figure 8.2). It should specify when the learning will happen in the iteration (creating the time boundary), what the key learning questions will be, who will be involved, and how lessons will be used. These questions are included in Table 8.3, which we have left otherwise blank to help you think of a learning strategy in your find-and-fit process. In filling the table out, reflect on the challenge you have been discussing and the experimental iteration process you described previously. What are the questions you think are most appropriate to ask? Who would need to be engaged? How regularly would you engage these agents? How would you use the lessons learned?

---

[14] We do not think that this kind or work is impossible in any context, although there is evidence showing that it may be more difficult to introduce in certain contexts. Bamford et al. (2015) find, for instance, that contextual pressures (like the appetite for change and cost of learning) can lead to only partial adoption of this kind of iterative learning. See also Lam (2000) and Gertler (2003).

Table 8.3. Fostering experiential learning in your find-and-fit process

Key questions	Your answers
What are the questions you think are most appropriate to ask?	
Who would need to be engaged?	
How regularly would you engage these agents?	
How would you use the lessons learned?	

Where Does This Leave You?

We have presented the thinking behind PDIA in many different countries, and in most contexts the ideas we share are well received. The find-and-fit straetgy here is considered common sense by many people we have presented to and worked with. Some actually tell us they found the approach useful and interesting but not new. At the same time, however, they will tell us that the approach is not possible in their organization. "It may be common sense," someone once said, "but common sense is the least common of the senses."

The most common reason why people tell us they cannot do PDIA is simple; "I will not get authorization for this kind of work." This reason is particularly common when talking with government officials in developing countries and officials working in development organziations (like bilateral agencies, the World Bank, regional development banks, or the OECD). We are told that managers and politicians in these contexts will not support an experimental process that will likely lead to failure before it geneates success. They do not believe that their supervisors will see "lessons" as results, and end up saying that they would love to work in this way but simply do not see it happening.

You may be in a similar situation as you finish the current chapter. You may think that the ideas presented here seem sensible but very different to what you normally do in your organization. They must, therefore, come acrosss as unlikely to be supported. We do not want to leave you here, however, and we do not want you to leave your thinking here either. The examples provided here—from Sweden to Nostria and Mantia—are real world situations in which learning and experimentation were central to reforms in hierarchical, politic-ally contested contexts where authorizers were also more adept to supporting easy pathways to solutions. The find-and-fit process we are describing here was possible in those contexts, however, and could be possible in your context too. It depends on how well you manage your authorizing environment, which is what we turn to next.

9

Managing your authorizing environment

A few years ago, one of us was working with an African government on health issues. The health minister was committed to building public sector capability to address women's health issues (given problems with maternal mortality). The minister assembled a team, and supported a problem analysis process (complete with construction, deconstruction, and sequencing exercises). She then supported the team in crawling the design space, which generated a number of potential solutions to explore through experimental iteration. When the team tried to initiate the first set of action steps, however, they ran into trouble. Most of the steps involved actions taken in provinces, where governors had significant power and where administrators were more accountable to their provincial authorizers than to the national minister of health. The minister tried to build support from provincial governors but they were generally resistant to the idea of working on the women's health issues in an experimental manner. Some of the governors asked why experiments were needed, and told the minister her job was to provide solutions rather than identify problems and propose experiments. Others noted that they had seen many pilots in the past and were tired of the failure associated with such. In short, therefore, they refused to authorize the work and the experimental iterations were stillborn.

There is a vital lesson from this story: one needs authority to undertake any initiative aimed at building state capability, and this authority is often difficult to attain. It is seldom located in one office or person, and is often harder to lock in with risky work. One runs into this problem regularly with 1804 challenges, given that they commonly involve significant risk and uncertainty and require engagement by many agents responding to different kinds of authority. A third PDIA principle recognizes this fact and notes, therefore, that every effort to address complex 1804 challenges must include an explicit strategy to establish an appropriate authorizing environment.

This strategy cannot simply be to garner the general support of one or other important authorizer, however. In the context of any effort to address a wicked hard 1804 challenge, establishing the "appropriate" authorizing environment poses several specific challenges to would-be reformers, policymakers and others engaged in building state capability for implementation. This chapter discusses these challenges, and offers practical ideas to meet them. It starts, however, by providing some background discussion on what the authorizing environment involves and why it matters.

Why the Authorizing Environment Matters

Authority is a key focal point in the literature on organizations. It has enjoyed prominence since (at least) the seminal work of Max Weber, which examined the ways in which social and political power were exerted in society (Weber

1978). Weber proffered a social–political view of authority, presenting it as the exercise of influence and control by some agents over others in social settings. This authority could be exerted through charismatic individuals (whose personal traits fostered influence), those holding traditional positions (where customs defined influence), or people enjoying stature because of formal rules (where influence was associated with a legally determined and conferred position of authority). Whereas there are obvious differences in where power comes from in these models (and how power is legitimized), they all essentially describe how some powerful agents influence and shape the behavior of other less powerful agents—constraining some activities while encouraging or supporting others.

Given the way authority constrains or supports certain behaviors, it must be said that authority structures have huge implications for what organizations do, how they do these things, when, where, and with whom.[1] In a prominent paper on the topic, Fama and Jensen (1983) identified these many manifestations, noting (for instance) that authorizers influence which projects are chosen, how obedience is exacted from subordinate employees, which actions are approved and ratified, who gets rewarded for what, and how. Similar manifestations are common in public organizations, where authority structures shape what is possible when trying to build state capability.[2] Powerful people (and processes that empower these people) determine what capability can be built, for instance, who will be involved in building this capability, how the process will work, how long it will continue, and what it will involve.

This means that would-be reformers need to pay attention to authority structures when they initiate any effort to build state capability. This is not news to those working at the coal face of development, in governments or in development organizations. It is indeed a central theme of the work by authors like David Booth and David Hulme (Faustino and Booth 2015; Routley and Hulme 2013). This work emphasizes the importance of navigating the local authorizing environment to ensure any initiative is locally led (or authorized) and politically smart (meaning, inter alia, that it has broad support and authorization). Authors like Mark Moore have been emphasizing the importance of navigating the authorizing environment for an even longer period, noting that any initiative to produce or improve public value needs to go beyond an individual with a good idea (Moore and Khagram 2004: 9): "It [is] not sufficient for a public manager to have his or her own view of public value; others ha[ve] to share it. In particular, the group of people in positions that could confer legitimacy and provide financial support to the manager

---

[1] See, among others, Aghion and Tirole (1997), Bolton and Dewatripont (2013), Etzioni (1959), Guillén (1994), Presthus (1960).
[2] See Dodlova (2013), Herbst (2014), Hughes (2013), Meyer (1968), Olsen (2015), and Wang and Ap (2013).

would have to agree with the conception of public value that was to be pursued."

It is not easy to build authorization to act, however. Authorizing environments are commonly fragmented, and difficult to navigate.[3] Policies, programs, and policies typically cross over multiple (or overlapping) jurisdictional domains in which many different agents and processes act to constrain or support behavior. Authorizing structures often vary vertically as well, with agents at different levels of an organization or intergovernmental structure enjoying control over different dimensions of the same process.[4] Consider, for instance, the example with which we started this chapter, where provincial governors were able to undermine a process that was supported at "higher" levels by the national minister. This fragmentation is likely greater with complex state building challenges that involve many agents and organizations.

Informality often reigns in these challenges as well, manifest in personality and relationship-driven authority structures. These structures are seldom well known, especially to outsiders, which makes it extremely difficult to know who really authorizes what in any context.[5] Whether formal or informal, authority structures are often also fickle and inconsistent. Authorizers will sanction new activities for many reasons, and may lose interest or energy or patience for many reasons as well. This means that one is never guaranteed continued support from any authorizer for any period of time, no matter what promises are made. Unfortunately, many project managers working for development organizations or in governments involved in reform learn this the hard way, when an initially supportive minister stops supporting a project soon after it begins.

The fickleness of authority is most evident when dealing with risky change initiatives that will almost certainly have unintended (or unanticipated) consequences. This should not be surprising, however. New institutional scholars remind us that authority is often given to those with power (or entrusted by the powerful).[6] These individuals are seldom appointed to their positions

---

[3] Distributed authority is common in many policy areas and countries. Frosch and Kaplan (1999) note that authority structures are shared in areas like clinical medicine, for instance, and Lieberthal and Lampton argue that fragmented authority structures are a main feature of Chinese bureaucracy. Janowitz (1998) even argues that complexity has led to fragmented and distributed authority in military settings, commonly assumed to have extremely centered authority mechanisms.

[4] See descriptions of varying authority structures, especially dependent on differences in culture and social and governmental structure in Cartwright and Cooper (1993) and Horling and Lesser (2004).

[5] See Chapter 3 in Andrews (2013) and the instances of legal pluralism and development conveyed in Tamanaha et al. (2012).

[6] This thinking is reflected in work on the paradox of embeddedness, which suggests that those most embedded in any context typically have power in such, and are simultaneously probably most averse to change. The paradox is that they are needed to effect change, given the authority they provide. See Greenwood and Suddaby (2006), Pache and Santos (2013), Seo and Creed (2002), and Waddock et al. (2015).

to foster dramatic change. They are, indeed, much more likely to support maintenance of the status quo, and hence resist dramatic change and the risk this involves. Furthermore, they are unlikely to entertain potential failure and uncertainty associated with complex challenges. As discussed in Chapter 5, this kind of authorizing environment is not conducive to novelty or supportive of the PDIA-type change process.

We do not believe that this should be the end of the story, however, or signal the death knell of PDIA-type initiatives (or any development initiatives dealing with complex change). As already discussed in this book, there are many examples where governments have adopted PDIA-type processes to foster deep change. These initiatives take the authorizing environment seriously, treating authority as variable rather than fixed, as an important influence on the change space that can be expanded with well-structured strategies (as discussed in Chapter 7). This is how we want you to think about authority and the authorizing environment, as we discuss dimensions of a dynamic authorizing environment strategy necessary to facilitate PDIA-type initiatives. These strategic dimensions require attention to three questions:

- What authority do we need?
- Where can we find what we need, given how authority is structured?
- How do we get the authority we need, and grow this authority over time?

What Authority Do We Need?

Questions about the authorizing environment always arise when we are teaching about PDIA. As mentioned, these questions tend to be infused with pessimism—participants question the likelihood of getting the authority needed for this kind of work. In response to this pessimism, we often ask participants to tell us their general experience with getting authority to support policies, programs, and projects, as well as their most positive and negative story about getting and keeping authority in a change process. Most answers are quite depressing, with participants noting how hard it is to ensure proper authorization of any change process (whether using PDIA or more linear project management mechanisms). The horror stories tend to tell of reform champions committing to a project and then withdrawing support shortly afterwards, or who were relieved of their position mid-way through the process and replaced by a less supportive non-champion authorizer. The most positive stories are about reform champions who actually hold interest and office for long enough to support initiatives to the end.

These answers reveal a lot about the strategy commonly adopted to attain authorization for policies, programs, and projects aimed at building state capability (Andrews 2013). First, the strategy is very narrowly focused—on getting authorization from high-level authorizers like government ministers. Second, the strategy is often general in nature—on "getting support"—with little definition of what is actually required from the authorizer(s). Third, the strategy is quite fatalistic—the high-level authorizer either pulls through and actually provides whatever support is needed or does not.

We believe that versions of this kind of narrow, general, fatalistic strategy are common in development. Such a strategy may even be appropriate for certain kinds of initiatives. Consider, for instance, the strategy to go west in 2015 (discussed in Chapter 6). This involved hiring a car and following a map, with minimal authorization required (by someone who could pay for the car). There was no need to authorize risky activities, or to support actions that could lead to failure. The authorizer simply needed to say "yes" at one point in time, allocate minimal resources at that time, and step back. Nothing more. This, arguably, is the kind of authorization one needs when undertaking simple logistical tasks, where one knows the solution, has full information about the challenge, does not require special skills or resources, and is not dealing with high stakes or risky business.

This is not the kind of authorization one needs to tackle more complex 1804 challenges, however. These challenges pose many more demands on those who provide authorization—and the processes through which they provide this authorization. Consider how much the 1804 Lewis and Clark expedition needed to make a full trek across the western half of the United States (as discussed in Chapter 6): a significant amount of money from Congress (with no promise that it would be used well or repaid); a number of specialized public officials and soldiers to be released from their other duties for an indeterminate period of time; permission for those mid-level officials to negotiate in the name of the government when encountering native tribes; the right to set up camps and bases along the route, and to pass through territories that were already inhabited; permission to hunt in already-settled areas; food and resources en route; horses, boats, and other vehicles to use to get past obstacles and cover long distances; assistance from guides and translators along the way; help from unknown and potentially hostile tribes; and more.

This list of needs is obviously not as long as the de facto list from the actual expedition. The expedition list was also probably not complete at any design or preparation or planning stage when Lewis and Clark were engaging with their champion, President Thomas Jefferson. The experimental nature of their journey meant that they would certainly encounter other needs along the way that they could not present before the president at the start. This meant that the president had to accept that there would be more needs that he would need to authorize, and also that he would have to be open to Lewis and Clark looking to others along the way for authorization (like local chiefs). This meant that Jefferson had to provide what we call "flexible authority" and "shareable authority" (where he would be willing to entertain emergent authorization requests and allow the engagement of other authorizers, giving up some of his own control and ownership in the process). He also needed to provide what might be called "grit authority," which is steadfast and patient, and ready to explain short-term failures to naysayers (given that these failures must be expected in such challenges).[7] These are additional needs for any group embarking on a complex and unpredictable journey to address 1804 challenges.

We believe that anyone attempting to launch an effort to build state capability should take stock of the kinds of authority needed, before starting and at regular intervals during the journey. This stands in stark contrast to the fatalistic approach where one assumes that the authorizer will work out what you need support for and simply provide it (or not). These needs often include decision rights over the reform agenda, specific people, time, money and resources, legal and regulatory matters, mechanisms to suspend or amend unhelpful processes and rules, and more. This is a demanding list, but it is perhaps not as demanding as the key elements one actually needs to tackle complex challenges, when experimenting to find and fit new solutions: "flexibility" and "shareability" and "grit" (or patience)—as noted above—from those providing authorization (where the last characteristic relates to the ability of an authorizer to manage waiting periods, failure, and changes in direction, given a passion for attaining the long-term goal). These are key attributes of supporters who create what adaptive leadership theorists call the holding environment (where support is provided for those working on the policy, program, or project "in spite of the divisive forces generated by adaptive work" which could include failure, the learning of uncomfortable lessons, or other disruption (Heifetz et al. 2009: 305)).

We believe that these needs can be met in change processes. We see examples in the Sweden budget reform example and in the Nostrian and Mantian cases (as discussed already, and built from Chapters 7 and 8):

- The Swedish reforms required significant authority from Parliament to cede some power to the executive. It required the minister of finance to allocate top people to change processes for a number of years. It also required a patient wait for nearly five years before new laws were introduced to institutionalize changes. These and other needs were not easy to satisfy, but were satisfied over time given specific strategies adopted by reformers.

- The Nostrian judicial reform team comprised experts from across the sector, in agencies that usually did not work together. The team needed authority

---

[7] We build on the idea of "grit" in the management literature. This concept has been headlined in research at the University of Pennsylvania, which finds that grit (defined as "perseverance and passion for long term goals") is a key ingredient to success in complex projects, such that "the achievement of difficult goals entails not only talent but also the sustained and focused application of talent over time" (Duckworth et al. 2007: 1087).

from all the heads of these agencies to meet regularly, work together, and share information. They needed these authorizers to accept that their reform process was experimental and did not offer immediate solutions as well, and that they would be working on a project with no clear solution or pay off. These needs were difficult to meet, but they were met over time.

• The Mantian reform involved agencies across government working with private companies. The coordinating agency needed to ensure the involvement of all these other players, keep them involved, and push them to allocate time and resources to a specific set of reform demands. The coordinating team did this under the auspices of a minister who had to be patient in waiting for results, spending political capital before knowing the return on such. These needs are commonly hard to meet but were met in the reform process.

The basis of any strategy to *get and keep* authority to do PDIA (and any other complex and contentious state building activity) is to maintain awareness of the authorization needs of the initiative. Table 9.1 is provided to help you think through the needs in respect of the challenge you have been working through (in Chapters 6–8). Take a few minutes to think about these needs now and generate a list in the table. Include some descriptions of the "flexibility," "shareabilty," and "grit" needs you might have—i.e. where you need an authorizer who is flexible in her support, open to sharing authorization, and patient with experiments.

We do not expect you to identify an exhaustive list of needs here, given that there will be emergent needs as you progress through your iterations. Furthermore, your list will always be based on many assumptions. We do anticipate, however, that in PDIA one will need to allow for regular opportunities to reflect on both the list content and its underlying assumptions. In particular, we propose that this list be part of the iterative check in every iteration cycle (discussed around Figure 8.2), where you can update your understanding of

Table 9.1. What are your authorization needs?

Potential categories	Your answers
Your own time and effort	
Other people's time and effort	
Resources	
Decision-making rights	
Other	
Flexible authorization	
Shareable authorization	
Grit authorization	

authorization needs (and assumptions) at regular intervals and engage authorizers about this. Chapter 8 recounts an example of this kind of update in
Nostria, where the reform team realized mid-stream in an activity that they
needed authorization to share data: they discussed this need with their
authorizer, and constructed a strategy to get the authorization. In the spirit
of this example, the content of Table 9.1 should be dynamic—but a good start
should help you think carefully about what you need right now, which
informs your steps to attain the relevant authorization to start your work.

Where and How Does One Find the Needed Authority?

Our guess is that you have a long list of needs in Table 9.1, given that you have
been addressing an 1804 challenge and not a 2015 challenge. Challenges in the
1804 category typically have a lot of needs, and are thus very demanding on the
authorizing environment. Therefore, an active strategy to manage one's authorizing environment cannot stop with listing authorizing needs; one also needs
to ask where the authorization will come from to meet these needs.

As already discussed, in our experience, many would-be reformers look for
authorization from the top officeholder of the organization proposing change.
An effort to build state capability through budget reforms, for instance, commonly looks to the minister of finance as the authorizer. In the example at the
start of this chapter, the health sector team looked to the minister of health for
authorization. The assumption is that this officeholder sits atop a hierarchical
bureaucracy in which decisions are made at the top, communicated downwards, and implemented as ordered.[8] This assumption draws on (what we see
as common) views that governmental bodies are bureaucratic hierarchies
characterized by effective downward authorization mechanisms. These
could be informal mechanisms (like the charisma or political persuasion of a
minister) or formal mechanisms (including line management and delegation
mechanisms that foster unity of direction and command). One expects that
authority does emanate from the top of the organization in these structures, as
in Figure 9.1 (a simple hierarchy with downward lines of command that pass
seamlessly through levels of management, until they reach the lowest levels).

---

[8] This thinking reflects the assumption of an "ideal type" bureaucracy (Weber 1978) or an
administration organized along the lines of classical theory (Gulick 1937). This kind of thinking
leads to management strategies that Nutt (1986) describes as "implementation by edict." A vast
literature shows that this approach has limits in most contexts, however, because there are no
"ideal type" bureaucracies, and authority seldom works this simply (Clegg 2012; Ezrow and Frantz
2013; Im 2014). In many senses the emergence of new public management, public choice, and
other reform types was because of failures in traditional bureaucracies, which signaled limits to this
kind of thought.

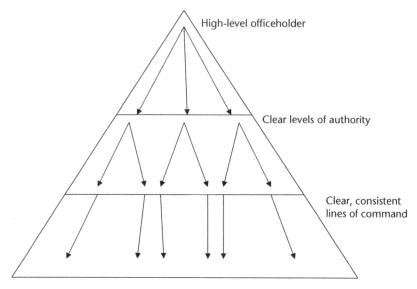

High-level officeholder

Clear levels of authority

Clear, consistent
lines of command

Figure 9.1. The common assumption of "ideal type" hierarchical bureaucracy

This expectation of effective downward authorization is often not met, however, and the authorization falls short of what one needs or hopes for (Horling and Lesser 2004; Nutt 1986). There are many reasons for this. Some are illustrated in Figure 9.2 (with examples from various countries and sectors evident in recent articles):[9]

- Most officeholders in public organizations actually have limited personal authority in their organizations, and find their efforts to impose such quite ineffective. Career bureaucrats who have been in the organization for long periods commonly stop the flow of these officeholders' commands down the organization (as shown by marker A in Figure 9.2). Personal charisma is not very effective in overcoming these kinds of structural gaps, especially in large organizations.

- Most bureaucratic organizations do not have the "ideal type" lines of command required for effective hierarchical authorization (shown by marker B in Figure 9.2). There are breaks in these lines (where mid-level managers simply fail to transmit commands) and deviations from such (where mid-level managers actually transmit different commands, exercising their own authority in mini-fiefdoms that are, de facto, not under the high officeholder's authority). Many bureaucracies lack feedback mechanisms flowing upwards to inform high-level officials of these gaps and deviations, which allows breaks in command to fester.

[9] See, for example, Campbell (2012), He (2012), Jones et al. (2013), and Poole (2016).

- Organizations not only have line authority systems (where commands flow downwards, typically, to ensure a goal-orientation exists); most organizations and governments also have staff and function authorizing mechanisms in place. Staff authority mechanisms shape the way resources are used, and functional authority mechanisms allocate authority for specific types of activities to specific groups. The different mechanisms commonly clash (as in marker C in Figure 9.2). For instance, an agent may be told to spend money on a particular project by a line supervisor (even the minister) but the budget department may not allow such spending given the rules they have for disbursement, and a functional team leader may lay claim to the funding for a special project. This kind of clash frustrates the flow of downward authority (often purposefully) and imposes limits on the authority of even the most influential high-level officeholder.

- Agents in organizations often have to deal with competing voices (or lines of authority) as well (illustrated through marker D in Figure 9.2). A local government official working in the health sector, for instance, may be taking orders from both the minister (through the ministry) and a local government official (the mayor or town clerk, for instance). Lines of command can exist outside of these competing bureaucratic structures as well, with commands also emanating from professional, political, religious, familial, and other domains (where agents are given directives on how to behave, who to serve, what to prioritize, and more by authorizing agents in the many domains they inhabit outside of their formal job). These competing voices can dilute influence of a communication line from any one source.

- Frequently, there are also tensions between those holding high-level office in different organizations or parts of the same organization (as reflected in E in Figure 9.2). Ministers and top managers are often political or professional competitors, or sit together in other settings (political parties, cabinets, boards) and can see each other as subordinates or superiors. This means that any one minister or manager may in fact be taking orders (formally or informally) from another minister or manager in a different organization. This obviously complicates authorization structures.

- Most organizations are part of broader sectors or networks in which many authorizing structures are at play (see F in Figure 9.3). This further complicates any views about authority. It is seldom possible for a hierarchy in a shared ecosystem to define its entire authorization structure or to contain the overlap of other authorizing mechanisms and influences. These influences can fragment internal authorizing mechanisms or introduce confusion about what is authorized and what is not authorized.

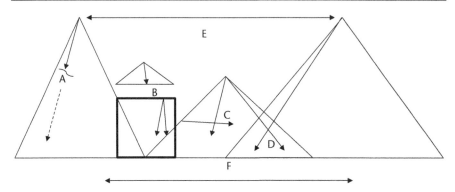

Figure 9.2. The reality: fragmented and dysfunctional authorization mechanisms

This discussion is not meant to frustrate or frighten you as a reader! It is simply intended as a reminder that authorizing structures are complex and we cannot assume that one authorizer will fulfil all our needs. There are many reasons why even the most well-meaning high-level office-holder will not be able to authorize all we need when doing active state building work, and we should acknowledge this upfront. Instead of only depending on individual champions for authorization, therefore, we should make a habit—and discipline—of actively navigating the authorizing environment in which we will work. In other words, we need to adopt a more expansive view of our authorizing environment when looking for support.

We see this in the examples discussed over the past few chapters. Sweden's budget reform was certainly championed by a group in the ministry of finance, but it was also authorized (crucially at points) by parliamentarians, local government leaders, ministers in line ministries, and other influential actors. This support cut across organizational boundaries and between the worlds of technical administration and politics. The Nostrian judicial reform was similar. Authority was initially provided by a supportive minister, but over time it was also provided by heads of the court system, prison service, and other central agencies, as well as local government officials, administrators in local courthouses, and more. The reform was complex, and required a complex authorizing arrangement.

It is not easy to navigate an authorizing environment, however, given the many unseen complexities in most contexts—which we have likened to icebergs in past work, where one can only see a small part of the rules and mechanisms driving behavior (Andrews 2013). The iterative nature of PDIA is helpful (and intentional) in this respect, as it fosters constant learning about the authorizing environment (in all reflections, at all times, one should be asking what one learned about the authorizing environment). Experiential lessons regarding the sources and nature of authority are much more useful than any theoretical or armchair pondering. This noted, however, we think it is very useful to start any initiative with some armchair pondering, asking where the needed authority will come from in one's authorizing environment.

We propose starting with identifying the primary authorizer(s) you plan to work with, given that we expect most reforms are initiated under the auspices of with authority of one or other high-level officeholder. (In the Nostrian example this was a supportive minister of justice, who opened the door to the work, agreed about the problem, and appointed a team to do experimental iterations.) Then, identify which needs you assume this authorizer will be able to meet. (In the Nostrian example, this included things like the following: access to officials in the ministry of justice, as well as data in the ministry, and—we hope—a holding environment in which to experiment, given that the minister promised to be flexible, to share authority, and to exercise patience and grit.) Similarly, you should then note which of your needs are obviously outside of the scope of your primary authorizer's supervision and influence. (This was a long list in Nostria, where the champion minister could obviously not authorize the participation of staff members from other justice sector agencies, or authorize access to information in those agencies, or ensure the flexibility and patience of other high-level officeholders.) The next step is to identify where or who you believe additional authorization will need to come from to fill the authorization gaps. (In Nostria this list included the chief justice, head of prosecutions, and more; given the influence they had on key resources, it also included mid-level bureaucrats responsible for budgeting and personal management.)

This exercise helps to promote awareness of the challenge involved with building true authority to foster change and build state capability. It is a more fleshed-out version of the conversations we promoted in Chapter 7, in the section on problem-driven sequencing. Such an exercise matters because it guides would-be reformers in recognizing where they have authority to act and where they do not (given that authority is a key ingredient in the change space discussed in Chapter 7). The exercise also ensures transparency about the assumptions one makes about the authorizing environment, which is a key element in the work on "theory of change" (where would-be reformers are encouraged to flesh out their theory as to why and how change will happen). These transparent assumptions can become a key part of the iteration and learning process (discussed in Chapter 8), guiding questions during reflection periods (shown in the iteration Figure 8.2 and in the Searchframe Figure 8.3). We find that reform groups learn a lot about their authorizing environment when iterating, but sometimes the lessons are hard to identify and capture because no one constructed a set of leading assumptions to reflect upon. Lessons are easier to capture when these assumptions exist a priori.

For this reason, we ask you to use Tables 9.2 and 9.3 to list the assumptions you currently have about your authorizing environment. Do the exercise on your own and then with group members, to see what you can already learn about different opinions and assumptions you all have about "the rules of the game." Please note that the table lists questions raised in the description we have just completed. It does not ask how you will ensure that you get the authority you need, simply that you flesh out what you think that authority is and where it might be found. We will move onto a discussion of gaining and growing authority once you are done.

Table 9.2. Where will you look for your authorization needs?

Who is your primary authorizer?		
Why do you assume her/his support?		
What are your needs (in the following categories, as determined in Table 9.1)	Do you think your primary authorizer will satisfy this need?	Who else needs to provide authorization to satisfy this need?
Your own time and effort		
Other people's time, effort		
Resources		
Decision-making rights		
Other		
Flexible authorization		
Shareable authorization		
Patient (grit) authorization		

Table 9.3. Assumptions about our authorizing environment complexity (see Figure 9.2)

Authorizing Environment Complexities	My assumptions
A. Limits to personal authority of high-level authorizers	
B. Breaks in formal command structures within organizations	
C. Conflicting authority structures within organizations (line, staff, and functional, etc.)	
D. Competing voices faced by mid-level employees and/or frontline bureaucrats	
E. Conflicts between high-level authorizers across an organization/sector	
F. Many horizontal authorizing structures overlap	

How Does One Gain and Grow the Needed Authority?

We expect that your completed Tables 9.2 and 9.3 are quite detailed. They probably also reveal quite a few gaps in authority needs and challenges you expect to face in addressing such needs. These are the areas where you will have to work hard to gain the authority required to make your policy, program, or project a success. The question, then, is how to gain the needed authority, and also to grow the authority in tandem with the growing scope and scale demands typical to complex challenges. These are the issues we will now address.

The first point to make is simply that you should treat all your assumptions about authority with the same degree of healthy skepticism. Even when you are sure that a champion will support certain needs, you should recognize that your certainty is actually just a strong assumption. And you should be open to the potential that your assumption is incorrect. This perspective will compel you to think strategically about all the authorization needs in Table 9.2 (not just those where you have gaps) and to reflect about all your assumptions (including those about your champion). This will mitigate any "authority blind spots" you might have.

The second point is that you need a concerted strategy in place to gain the authority you need from authorizers, and communication is at the heart of this process. Authorizers are often arm's-length removed from the details of change processes or of challenges with capacity building. They have many issues to deal with and need to determine how they allocate their time, energy, authority, and (often) political capital. This means that they are often unaware of the authorization needs in new initiatives, or unconvinced that they should cater to these needs. A communications strategy will inform them of both, persuading them to provide needed authority. As discussed in Chapter 7, we believe that a problem-driven approach is crucial in this regard. The goal is to construct the problem one is trying to solve (using data, focal events, and narrative) in a manner that makes the authorizer agree: "We have a problem . . . and must do something about it." This seems a simple and obvious element in any strategy, but we are amazed at how often it is ignored in development work. Policies, projects, and programs are introduced with very little effort at strategic framing, with the apparent assumption that authorizers will simply get behind any new initiative.

The communications and persuasion process is made more complex when one has multiple authorizers to engage. It is common for different authorizers to respond to different kinds of problem construction, and thus would-be reformers cannot settle once they have gained the ear of only one authorizer. In Nostria, for instance, the problem of case backlogs was enough to motivate the minister of justice to support a change initiative. She supported an experimental approach, given a narrative her team constructed about past failures in solution-driven reforms. Other authorizers were less convinced, however, and had become used to having case backlogs. They were also resistant to the idea of experimental reforms. The team needed to reconstruct the problem to convince them that it mattered (and hence was not just a condition to be lived with) and that there was no routine solution. This persuasion activity involved linking case backlogs to deficient data and ultimately to failed budget requests that most high-level officials were very concerned about. They were also made aware that their failed budget requests had persisted even after reforms that were designed to improve the situation. This led to them supporting the reform process and blessing the experimental approach the team chose to adopt.

When one is tackling complex reforms, it is important to ensure that authorizers do not just support action in a specific area. There needs to be an explicit authorization of the experimental approach one needs to adopt. The communication strategy can help in gaining this authorization, as it was in Nostria where the reform team used evidence of failed reforms in the past to motivate authorizers to do something new. The team "sold" the need for experimentation in this context, and communications strategies can be used to "sell" other aspects of a flexible reform process as well, including the need for learning from failure. Authorizers will be more supportive of such process if they are convinced that it is structured, that lessons and (potential) failure will result from forward-looking experimentation (rather than laziness of poor management), and that the process will be undertaken in a responsible and highly engaged manner—promoting accountability.[10] The strategy for experimental iteration outlined in Chapter 8 is designed to help you make this case to your authorizer. It is structured, focused on a goal ("problem solved") with multiple milestones and many regular reflection points where you and your team can report to the authorizer, enhancing accountability for all.

Table 9.4 poses some basic questions one could ask in designing a communications and persuasion strategy to gain authority to act in this manner. We recommend that you take a few minutes and fill your thoughts into the open spaces. These thoughts could become the basis of a first step to convince authorizers to support your initiative.

The third point is that you do not require full authority at the start of your initiative. It is common to find some authorizers offering more support at the start of a reform, and this authority often allows one to mobilize enough resources to initiate some action. We saw this in Mantia, where the reform team actually had very little authority over the forty-two point agenda to

---

[10] This is partly our own learning, but draws on various recent studies on the topic. Amy Edmondson's work on this topic has been particularly influential. She (and colleagues) tackle the problem of getting performance-driven organizations (and authorizers) to allow learning through failure. They find that the list of strategies discussed here matter a great deal in this process—see Edmondson and Singer (2012), Khana et al. (2016), Senge and Kim (2013), and Senge (2014).

Table 9.4. The basis of a communications and persuasion strategy

	Authorizer 1 (named in Table 9.2)	Authorizer 2 (named in Table 9.2)	Authorizer 3 (named in Table 9.2)	Authorizer 4 (named in Table 9.2)
Does the authorizer agree that you have a problem?				
What would make the authorizer care more about the problem?				
Does the authorizer support the experimental iteration you propose?				
What could convince the authorizer that you need an experimental iterative approach?				

Note: Do this for all the authorizers named in Table 9.2, identifying potential strategies you could use to gain their support.

address problems facing business. Many of the agenda items were under the authority of other ministries and local governments. The team was tempted to stop and wait until it gained the authority of these other agents before starting the work. However, they could identify five entry points for change that were directly under the control of their ministry and their supportive minister. They began work in these entry points, building momentum through real action. At the same time, they worked to gain authority from other ministers and ministries, so as to gradually expand both their authorization to act and reform impact. The momentum from early action steps was vital in convincing other authorizers to join, given that they could see the approach being taken and the results being achieved.

We see this happening quite regularly, and it raises an important point about tailoring iterations in the change process: *do not wait for full authority to start, and do not start with too many action steps or with overly demanding action steps.* More (and more demanding) action steps escalate the risk of failure, which one does not want to do in early iterations (given the potential to demotivate authorizers and implementers). Further, one does not want to over-ask from authorizers, especially at the start of an iterative process. This could cause the primary authorizer to over-commit early on (rendering her vulnerable to criticism and even to losing her authority) and it could cause other potential authorizers to shy away from supporting your initiative in future.

Beyond starting small (so as not to overwhelm your limited early authority) we also propose—as a third point—being strategic about growing your authorization as you progress through the experimental iterations. This requires acknowledging that authorizers are not just supporting an effort to enhance state capability because it yields new functionality (be this better services in

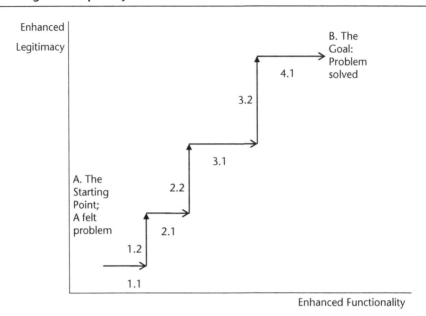

Figure 9.3. Iterating to progressively improve functionality and legitimacy

Malawi or higher employment in Mantia). Authorizers are also interested in the legitimacy they derive from the initiative—being seen as the ones who supported the work, and especially being associated with its successes. We show this in Figure 9.3, which reflects on the "success" of a state building initiative as involving both improvements to functionality (on the horizontal axis) and legitimacy (on the vertical axis). We argue that would-be reformers should strive to use each iteration to improve both of these success dimensions, enhancing functionality and ensuring authorizers get more legitimacy in the process. This involves taking a step to improve functionality (1.1) and then stopping to ensure legitimacy is also enhanced (1.2); then taking another step towards greater functionality (2.1) and stopping to consolidate support and ensure that authorizers are gaining in legitimacy.

This kind of thinking is built into the iterative processes discussed in Chapter 8, where action steps are taken, lessons are learned, and results are discussed with authorizers (in the iteration check; see Figure 8.2). It is useful to structure each of these discussions so that authorizers leave with news they can share to expand their legitimacy (about progress that has been made, or even lessons that have been learned). This will often lead to expanded authorization in the next step (given that the authorizer sees personal value in the exercise), which could facilitate bigger advances in functionality. Over time, the idea is to create a stairway to expanded state capability, with iterative improvements in both authority and functionality.

We saw an example of this in the work in Nostria. The initial work was done under the authority of a minister who was willing and eager to support an expansion in functionality in the justice sector. She was in a contentious relationship with other high-level officeholders in the sector (as is common), however, and could not authorize everything that was needed to achieve full success. Early iterations were thus necessarily cautious, involving work with only officials in the ministry. They were rapid, however, and targeted some quick wins—in terms of lessons learned about potential opportunities to improve the sector and in terms of expanded engagement across the sector. The minister was briefed on the lessons learned and the added members in the group, using this information to market the reform process with peers. She did so confidently, knowing that the process was yielding modest but real results (even in the first few iterations). As time went by, when iterations involved direct steps to enhance the skills of people in her ministry (through Excel courses, for instance), she ensured that other agencies had free and easy access to the same sessions. This enhanced her legitimacy and the legitimacy of the process, and led to other authorizers committing their support. They saw that the process yielded tangible results quickly and consistently, and that it was yielding change at a rate they—and their staff—could manage. Interestingly, authorizers were not deterred by the limited size of results in early iterations (as some observers in large development organizations advised they would be). Authorizers saw the process as legitimate because the results—no matter how small—were produced quickly and regularly. In a sense, these results gave authorizers "sound bite" legitimacy (something to mention in a cabinet meeting or weekly press report, as evidence of ongoing progress) instead of career-defining legitimacy (a big achievement). Politics is as much about sound bites as it is about career wins: PDIA allows many of the former en route to the latter. It is important to note that we are not talking about "quick wins" on their own here (which studies find matter but do not always open up into broader reforms).[11] We are emphasizing using quick wins to build space for reform, so the strategy in which these wins is pursued and communicated matters as much as (or more than) the wins themselves.

The final point we would like to make about gaining and growing authority centers on the use of coalitions in PDIA. As we have argued in this book, most state building challenges are complex. They involve many agents and impose many needs on would-be reformers. They also tend to be high stakes, rife with risk and uncertainty. Many authorizers will shy away from supporting action in these areas because of such characteristics. This is, we believe, a primary reason why low capability equilibria persist in many contexts (and why many

[11] See Bunse and Fritz (2012), Haggard (1997), Porter et al. (20112), and Teskey et al. (2012).

of the deficiencies associated with these low capabilities fester as conditions, never attracting the attention of a real problem). There are individual authorizers who do step out and support efforts targeting these challenges, however, and sometimes they make a big difference. However, we observe two realities that often limit the individual authorizers' potential to really support complex challenges. First, these authorizers often take on too much personal risk in the process and do not survive to actually follow through with the authorization they promise at the start. Second, these authorizers often lack the scope or breadth of influence required to address complex challenges, and end up supporting narrow interventions that cannot be scaled or diffused or sustained.

These limits to individual authority are commonly referenced in the growing literature on leadership in development (Andrews 2013). This literature routinely finds that deep and broad change is more commonly associated with work by groups of authorizers.[12] These groups typically engage in coalition-like structures, where they agree to combine efforts to address shared problems that they cannot solve on their own.[13] They provide the different kinds of authority needed to achieve a solution, and share risks involved in the process.

We believe that the authorizing needs of complex initiatives will always call for some kind of coalition arrangement. These initiatives may well start with an individual authorizer acting alone, but the authorization needs and risks will soon prove overwhelming. Would-be reformers should therefore strategize to build authorization coalitions from early on in any initiative, and constantly try to build the coalition. It is the key to managing risks associated with this kind of work and also to providing all of the authority needed in such circumstances.

Table 9.5 acts as a summary set of questions we believe any would-be reformer should ask when trying to gain and grow the authority to address a wicked hard, complex 1804-type challenge. You can use the table to reflect on addressing the authorization needs identified in Table 9.2. It asks you to go back to Table 8.2 and the ideas you proposed acting upon in early iterations of a find and fit process: Do you comfortably have enough authority to take these steps? What legitimacy will these steps yield for your authorizer? How will this legitimacy attract other authorizers to the initiative? Who might you be looking to include in a coalition, and what strategies do you have to create

---

[12] Haggard and Webb (1993), Krueger (2002), Leftwich (2010), and Lewis (1996).

[13] There are various interesting strands of such thought, as reflected in recent work. For instance, Oborn et al. (2011) note that the policy entrepreneurs referenced in work by people like Kingdon often have their biggest impact when drawing agents together in coalitions. Nowlin (2011) writes about the importance of coalitions in pushing policy processes forward, emphasizing the importance of balancing homogeneity and heterogeneity in the design of such. Faust (2010) discusses the way in which coalitions emerge to foster development agendas, changing as reform iterations demands.

Table 9.5. Questions to ask about gaining and growing authority

Your proposed first (or next) action step(s)	Do you comfortably have enough authority to take these steps?	What legitimacy will these steps yield for your authorizer?	How will this legitimacy attract other authorizers to the initiative?	Who might you be looking to include in a coalition, and how might this step help to create the coalition?

such coalition? We propose answering these questions at the start of any initiative and revisiting them in every reflection period, to ensure that you are constantly mindful of the challenge of gaining and growing authorization to do this work.

Where Does This Leave You?

We have covered a lot of ground in the last few chapters, and it is hoped that you have participated actively through the exercises. If so, you would have seen a challenge transformed into an attention-grabbing problem, and then into a deconstructed set of entry points for action. You would then have identified multiple options to address various entry point issues and crafted a strategy to conduct experimental iterations with these ideas, learning about what works and why. Finally, you would have considered the authorization needs of your initiative, as well as where those needs might be met and how to gain and grow necessary authority.

Our discussion has been very practical and applied, and we hope this is useful to you. The true test of all these ideas is when you apply them to your real challenge, however, and actually start the iteration process. This is when you get to see the way in which well-constructed problems mobilize attention, and how participatory problem analysis empowers colleagues to think in new ways. This is when you realize how much can be learned when one tries an action and then stops to reflect on what happened. Finally, when ideas turn to action one learns a huge amount about who really has power and authority, and who is really willing to use it to build state capability in areas where it has been lacking.

We hope that you have found the ideas and tools interesting enough to even consider taking the next step into action. We want to warn you not to do this on your own, however. Just as we believe there are limits to the influence of individual authorizers, we also believe that there are limits to the influence you can have—as development entrepreneur, would-be reformer, agitator, or whatever identity is appropriate. Many people are required to build state capability, playing many roles and sharing the risk involved. Broad engagement is also the key to building capability at scale. Chapter 10 explains why, and offers some practical ideas on how to engage broadly in your efforts to build state capability.

10

Building state capability at scale through groups

Matt uses comparative cases on public sector internal audit reform to teach about PDIA (Andrews and Seligmann 2013). A first case reflects on Malaysia's experience. In 1979, motivated by a small cadre of newly professionalized internal auditors in both the private sector and ministry of finance (and buoyed by the passage of international norms regarding internal audit), the country passed a law requiring government-wide adoption of internal audit, using international standards. A circular detailed how this should be done. Twenty-five years later, a research program found that only 35 of 202 state and local government bodies had internal audit units in place. Other entities either could not afford the practice or did not see a need for it (Ali et al. 2007). The government responded by producing a new circular demanding government-wide internal audit adoption. Progress has been better since then, but is still slow and selective.

In contrast, Burkina Faso introduced an internal audit reform in 2007 that was not actually called an "internal audit reform." It emerged when a new prime minister appointed a respected academic, Henri Bessin, to address the high levels of corruption in the country (which was the focus of regular citizen rallies and growing political tension). Three existing inspection and oversight bodies were merged for this purpose, and the World Bank was asked to provide advice on reform options. Mr Bessin's team adopted a step-by-step approach, starting with a combined report from all three entities (outlining what they did to address corruption and what they intended to do in the future). The report was presented publicly, and gave the prime minister a quick and visible early product on which to build legitimacy for the broader reform.

This led to a next step, where Mr Bessin gathered cabinet ministers (under the auspices of the prime minister) to explore areas in which his unit might start applied investigations. At a workshop, the ministers were asked about the biggest problems in their ministries. A few ministers were forthcoming with examples, which Mr Bessin and World Bank colleagues explained were a manifestation of "risks" that could be mapped and addressed. In response, a small group of ministers agreed to host five pilot "risk-mapping" exercises. These built on basic internal audit methods translated into a Burkina-compatible approach, and were implemented by local officials and consultants in a matter of months. They proved a success, and generated enthusiasm among ministers who reaped greater functionality and legitimacy from the exercise. As a result, the work was scaled from five to eleven ministries, and the teams who undertook the risk maps were sent for international training in more formal internal audit methods. They then undertook performance audits in an expanded set of ministries, and adopted a formal corruption investigations focus. By 2012, they had completed over 600 investigations.[1]

[1] See a 2014 United States State Department Briefing (http://www.state.gov/documents/organization/227134.pdf).

The role has grown since that time, even after Mr Bessin retired and the government was ousted in a coup d'état.

We start our final chapter with these stories because they speak to questions we often hear when discussing PDIA and efforts to build state capability: "Can these efforts scale up?" and "Are these efforts sustainable?" The stories reveal different answers to these questions—and help us to explain what we think scaling and sustainability goals should entail in complex state building processes, and how these should be pursued:

- Malaysia's case tells a strangely positive story in respect of both concepts, using standard interpretations of each. It involved rapid scaling—what some call "explosions"—and affected large numbers of agencies covered by audit laws (that were also meant to adopt the practices, in what Uvin and Miller (1996) would call a significant "quantitative" scaling initiative).[2] The change was sustained as well, with laws maintained for twenty-five years—and the low level of implementation also holding firm—suggesting that the government reached a new static equilibrium in which systems and practices were "enduring" (even if they were not performing).

- In contrast, the Burkina case shows slower, less expansive, and more muddled scaling—through what Uvin and Miller (1996) calls "expansion" (where one builds on pilots) or "association" (where one builds on and through relationships). The numbers were less impressive, with one unit providing internal audit services to a small, incrementally growing set of entities. There were other kinds of scaling, however, with the new unit performing more activities over time, expanding its mandate, and enhancing its resources. Uvin and Miller (1996) calls these the functional, political, and organizational expressions of scaling up,[3] which combine with common quantitative manifestations to foster multi-dimensional scaling (which we call 4-D scaling, given the four dimensions). Interestingly, the continuous change suggests that it would be a misnomer to describe Burkina reforms as "sustained." Instead, they contributed to what Chambers et al. (2013) call "dynamic sustainability" (involving ongoing improvement to systems and capabilities, not an end goal or resting point where one system or capability is simply maintained).

We are not fans of rapid but false scaling, as was experienced in Malaysia, or the static sustainability one sees in the same case. Rather, we believe that the

---

[2] Where "quantitative" scaling involves producing "more" units of something—arguably the most common understanding of "scaling up" or "taking things to scale."

[3] Put simply, "functional" scaling involves learning how to do more actions and activities; "political" scaling implies expanding a mandate and political support; "organizational" scaling refers to the growth in an organization itself, typically through additions to resources.

Burkina Faso case is a good example of scaling and sustainability in state building exercises, especially when these exercises pertain to complex challenges. One needs gradual 4-D scaling in such situations—where capability expands in all four ways; *quantitative* ("more" entities are affected), *functional* ("more" activities are performed), *political* ("more" support is attracted, and mandates are broadened), and *organizational* ("more" resources are allocated to areas of growing capability)—with organizations learning more things and achieving more political space to move and use new capability. One also needs dynamic sustainability, where improvements are made, consolidated, and improved upon, reflecting a progressive and adaptive expansion in capability rather than the achievement of some apparent premature medium-term end point. Think of the 1804 challenge we encountered in Chapter 6: Where would the Lewis and Clark explorers have been if they managed to scale by "numbers" only, making ground from St Louis to the west coast but with no codified knowledge of how they got there, and no added political authorization from indigenous leaders along the way, or extra resources to survive and make it back to St Louis? Imagine, further, if individuals in the United States stopped after the Lewis and Clark journey and "sustained" their achievements, instead of building on them: We would not have the easy 2015 journey from St Louis to Los Angeles if adventurers did not follow with their own dynamic additions to knowledge and practice. We would not, in fact, have Los Angeles.

We believe further that the goals of 4-D scaling and dynamic sustainability are attained through a blend of "expansion" and "association" (where small steps or pilots allow learning and then action at scale, and where many agents are engaged to diffuse the new action), rather than "explosion" (where an intervention is devised and scaled with haste). In keeping with the 1804 metaphor, we believe that one builds big journeys out of many small action steps, and through relational links that allow learning along the way, diffusion of lessons, and creative progress in groups. You cannot have a big bang scaling up initiative when you don't know what you are scaling, or how it will fit the many contexts you are scaling to, or when you lack trust and acceptance from those who have to adopt and then live with the new thing you are scaling.

We have embedded various strategies that promote 4-D scaling and dynamic sustainability in the PDIA process. Think, for instance, of the way problem deconstruction draws attention to the areas in which scaling is actually required (where the "causes" of a problem typically overlap with areas in which one needs quantitative, functional, political, or organizational change—often at scale). Think, also, how iterative processes promote dynamic learning and adaptation, and how action and reflection opportunities foster improved functional and organizational scaling (where organizations are trying new things, learning how to do them, and building resources to do them again).

Think, further, about the PDIA focus on building authorization (which promotes quantitative and political scaling over time).

People are at the center of all these PDIA elements. We have discussed this in some length regarding the need to get authority for PDIA initiatives, and have alluded to it in mentioning the work of "teams" at various points in prior chapters. These discussions do not, however, do justice to the breadth and depth of "agency" required to make PDIA happen—especially if the change process aims to achieve broad and deep scaling and dynamic sustainability. We focus on this topic here, in the final chapter. We start by presenting a stylized discussion of the Burkina Faso case to show what we mean by building broad and deep agency for PDIA, drawing on theory about embedded agency and change. Following this, we discuss "who" we believe one needs in a PDIA change process—focusing on a selection of key functions that need to be played at different points in the change process. We then discuss "how" one mobilizes agents to play the roles and provide the functions required, emphasizing strategies to leverage, convene, and connect. We conclude the chapter (and book) by asking, as usual, what this means for you: What role will you play in PDIA, given where you sit or stand in any given challenge situation?

Why Broad Engagement Matters

Gaps in state capability tend to fester. People in governments accept these gaps and learn to live with them, all the while going to work, collecting paychecks and climbing organizational ladders to positions of prominence. This was arguably the case in Burkina Faso in the early 2000s. Corruption was considered high and growing at this time, with the country performing poorly on most corruption indicators (reflected, for instance, in a decline in its Transparency International Corruption Index score, from thirty-four in 2005 to twenty-nine in 2007). This was becoming a problem for the government, with social and political tensions increasingly focused on the issue—asking why the country no longer lived up to its name (with "Burkina Faso" meaning "land of the upright or honest people"). In this atmosphere, long-time President Blaise Campoaré appointed a new Prime Minister, Tertius Zongo, to head the government. He became the head of government—denoted by the central position "A" in the large circle in Figure 10.1, which represents a defined social or policy network or field—let us say "the Burkina Faso government."

Zongo was part of the elite in his country, having spent over twenty years in and around government and holding high-level portfolios prior to his final appointment (like minister of finance). As discussed in Chapter 9, centrally located agents (or elites) like Zongo are commonly considered the most embedded in their contexts. They are empowered by pre-existing rules of the

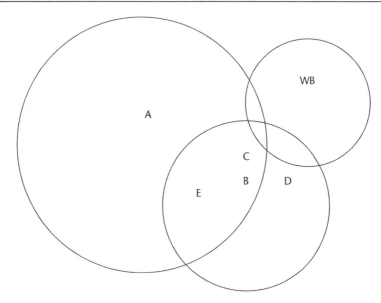

Figure 10.1. Broad agency even at the start of a change process
Source: Authors' analysis, based on the approach in Andrews (2013: ch 9)

game and social and political structures, and are the greatest beneficiaries of such—having the most power, biggest office, and largest paycheck. Because of this, a theory called the paradox of embedded agency suggests that we should not expect them to regularly perceive the need for change, have access to change ideas, or risk their interests in pressing for change.[4] This, theorists would argue, is a major reason why capability gaps persist in most places (given that one cannot get the authority needed to address pressing problems).[5]

In contrast, agents at the periphery of the network (like agent B in Figure 10.1) are more weakly embedded in the established network and coexist in other social spheres (like the mid-sized circles, which signifies the network of agents and entities working on anticorruption in Burkina Faso at the time). These agents can often see the problems in the status quo, and even have ideas to address them, and have less to lose in promoting change. They lack the authority to actually promote the change, however, and need a connection to authorizers for this.

Change in such situations requires a connection between the authorizer and the problem identifier. Mr Zongo found such an agent in the form of Henri

---

[4] See Andrews (2013), Battilana and D'aunno (2009), and Seo and Creed (2002).
[5] Adaptive leadership theorists (Heifetz et al. 2009) suggest that authorizers actually find themselves at huge risk when supporting change, arguing that they are often removed or pushed aside when they do step out and try to promote adjustments to the status quo (as other elites de-authorize their change efforts, and them).

Bessin, a respected academic who Mr Zongo knew from his own days teaching accounting and finance. Bessin had enough overlap and respect in the Burkina government to warrant an appointment by Mr Zongo (as the head of a new entity to address corruption). Bessin was also independent enough to have new ideas, given past work in France and elsewhere. Importantly, however, he did not have the implementation experience in Burkina Faso that existed in extant organizations also working on anticorruption (including inspections, audit, and investigation bodies). As a result, he reached out to these entities (C, D, and E in Figure 10.1), and started his work with a joint report on what they all had done previously and planned to do in the future. He also lacked direct experience working on the kinds of financial and service delivery corruption that concerned many Burkinabe citizens, but found the World Bank did have this experience and enlisted their help (even though they occupied a different, and only partially overlapping, social circle).

This is a simplistic, stylized way of showing how the Burkina Faso reform began. Note, however, how clearly we already see the multiple agents needed for reform, playing different roles in different parts of the reform network. This was not the work of one person, but of a broad set of agents—from the start. Broad engagement like this helps to overcome the constraints of embedded agency—such that authorizers can support reforms even if they do not know what the core problems or solutions are, and with less risk than when they act alone (with broad engagement and support helping shore up legitimacy of the reform or policy intervention).

As alluded to in the introduction, the reform grew (or scaled up) at this point. The report produced by Mr Bessin and his colleagues (with help from the World Bank) was well received and "championed" by the prime minister in a motivational public meeting. It became a tool the prime minister could use in mobilizing other cabinet ministers to meet with Mr Bessin and his team, at a workshop focused on identifying new activities and engagement opportunities for the anticorruption authorities. Figure 10.2 shows these cabinet ministers as F, G, H, I, and J; all close to the center of power and surrounding Prime Minister A. They were asked to identify the major problems they faced, and Mr Bessin explained that his team would help them uncover the causes of risk associated with these problems (much as a problem deconstruction exercise would do). Not all of these ministers agreed to participate in this activity, but the handful that did gave Mr Bessin and his team authority to work with people in their ministries (F*, G*, H*, I,* and J*). These people were vital to the work, because they knew their sectors and ministries and departments better than anyone in Mr Bessin's team. Mr Bessin's team also included some local consultants at this time (shown as "K" in the figure) and World Bank advisers (L), who offered new skills and money to do the "risk-mapping" pilots.

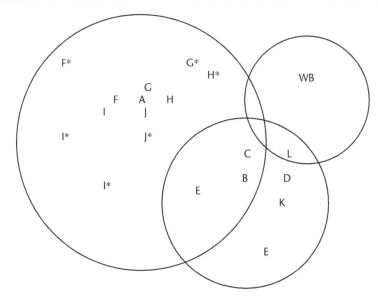

Figure 10.2. Even broader agency as change processes scale and progress
Source: Authors' analysis, based on the approach in Andrews (2013: ch 9)

The risk-mapping pilots demonstrated what proper internal audit and control could offer government, and showed how these tools could resolve the problems worrying individual cabinet ministers. This led to additional cabinet members signing up for an expanded set of risk-mapping exercises a few months later. At the same time, funding for training started to grow (from additional sources) and Mr Bessin's team were offered training opportunities in France. Each of these advances (and many others alluded to in the introduction) involved the addition of people into the reform process, helping to consolidate gains and then build upon them (in the spirit of dynamic sustainability). Cumulatively, they helped to foster 4-D scaling: more entities were being covered by the intervention (quantitative scaling), Mr Bessin's organization was learning new activities (functional scaling), their mandate was growing (political scaling), and resource allocations were expanding (organizational scaling).

The importance of broad and deep engagement should be obvious, even from these overly simplistic and stylized figures. It should be equally obvious that efforts to build state capability demand more breadth and depth as one looks to implement real actions and then to scale these up (in any of the four scaling manifestations discussed). Broad engagement means expanded authority, a better sense of the problems, an improved stock of ideas to solve problems, a more accurate view of implementation challenges, and more. All of these contributions help to take the opacity out of complex challenges, improve understanding of these challenges, and create agreement on what to do in the face of such challenges.

When we talk about broad engagement, we are not just referring to the idea of having many people involved in efforts to build state capability, however. As in the example presented above (in Figures 10.1 and 10.2), a broad engagement is one in which many people provide *real and different leadership roles* from many *different places* in the social or state structure. In the example, this includes the leadership of the Prime Minister, Mr Bessin, the World Bank, individual cabinet ministers, and all others who took risks to engage in this change process. The different roles played by these agents are all vital to ensure the find and fit process benefits from diverse views and ideas. Additionally, having people at different positions in the system allows for expanded coverage and diffusion of new ideas and capabilities—all vital if one wants to ensure 4-D scaling and dynamic sustainability (given that there are many people to advance the reform, not one or two champions).

We see this breadth and diversity of engagement in other cases as well, including in the reform cases discussed in prior chapters. Swedish budget reforms emerged from blended contributions (of ideas and authority, resources and time) emanating from specialists in think tanks, politicians and experts in Parliament, career bureaucrats in the ministry of finance, the newly appointed minister of finance, officials in other parts of the national government, local government members, and more.[6] The diversity of ideas led to creative reforms, and the breadth of engagement meant that the reforms could be diffused across government—accepted by highly different groups of agents and implemented at scale and in a sustained fashion. The private sector reforms in Mantia tell a similar story. A team in the ministry of industry had the mandate to lead these reforms, but only managed to achieve the reach required for results through the links it forged with other government agencies (addressing over forty challenges in very different organizational settings). These included the customs bureau, ministries of infrastructure and land, social services agencies, Prime Minister's Office, and various local governments. Connections to all of these entities were made with real people, who needed to be motivated and empowered and authorized to engage. Once engaged, however, they spread the ideas and urgency of reform to their own organizations, bringing impact at scale through an organic process of diffusion.

These examples illustrate that broad engagement matters, but they do not help to explain exactly "who" is needed in a broad engagement or how these people can be mobilized and organized to foster change at scale. We move to that now.

---

[6] We provide a list of references in Chapter 7 to illustrate the sources referred to in the Swedish case. These sources are themselves diverse and make the point of diversity quite apparent.

The People You Need

The idea that broad sets of agents are required to make successful change happen raises many questions: Who needs to provide such agency? When? How? In 2008 a multi-donor group called the Global Leadership Initiative (GLI) commissioned work to answer such questions (Andrews et al. 2010). The research started by selecting reforms in which change seemed to be progressing successfully in some of the toughest contexts one could imagine—post-war Afghanistan, and Rwanda, and the Central African Republic. To better understand the change experienced in these initiatives, participants and close observers of the reforms were identified and interviewed, using a structured protocol. Questions were asked about who led reforms at the start of reform and years afterwards, and why these agents were considered leaders.

When asked about leaders at the start of reform, 148 respondents pointed to 103 agents, across 12 reforms. This reinforced the idea that multiple agents were needed in reforms—not just as participants but as providers of "leadership." Interviewees were asked why they identified these agents as "leaders." All responses were transcribed, summarized, and classified according to emerging themes. This helped to identify functions played by people identified as "leaders":

- some provided formal authority for change;
- others inspired and motivated change;
- some recognized the problems needing change;
- others supplied ideas for solutions;
- some provided financial resources needed to start change;
- others empowered other agents, offering continuous and practical support and encouragement;
- some contributed implementation advice to ensure reform designs were realistic;
- others assisted the interaction of small groups of agents directly, by "convening" their engagements; and
- still others were classified as "connectors" because they reached out beyond core groups and teams, facilitating indirect links to distributed agents.

In follow-up work (Andrews 2015a) we find these functions are commonly present in major reform initiatives. Interestingly, we also find that the person commonly called "the champion" or identified as "the leader" usually plays three of these functional roles (and very seldom plays others): authorizer, motivator, and convener. This is what we see the prime minister doing in the Burkina Faso case as well (authorizing and re-authorizing the reform at various points, motivating all parties at the time of the report and beyond, and convening cabinet ministers to discuss next steps). Our stylized presentation of the Burkina Faso case also resonates with the GLI finding that agency and leadership broadened as implementation advanced and interventions scaled (Andrews et al. 2010). The GLI researchers identified 146 agents as leaders in the implementation of the 12 reforms. This was forty-three more than were identified at the start of the initiatives (about a 30 percent broadening of agency).

When asked why they identified such agents as implementation leaders, interviewees once again reflected predominantly on what the agents did to facilitate change. Interestingly, a larger proportion of "leaders" provided formal authority in this stage than at the start (19 percent as compared with 16 percent). The expansion of this "authorizer" group reflects the increased formalization of state-building reforms over time (which required greater formal authority), as well as the fact that most reforms become more distributed during implementation (and more diffused authority is required when more organizations are involved, as we see in the Burkina Faso example). Other functions proving more prominent in the implementation stage included:

- the provision of implementation advice (increasing from 6 to 17 percent, indicating the greater focus on applied action in diverse contexts);
- the empowerment of other groups to participate (increasing from 9 to 12 percent);
- problem identification and communication (which rose from 4 to 7 percent); and
- facilitating connections to distributed groups (which grew from 10 to 14 percent, showing that connectivity matters a great deal when scaling reform).

The evidence from these interventions suggests that efforts to build state capability require leadership contributions from multiple agents during initiation and even more during implementation and scaling. It also helps to point to the kinds of people required in these processes, given the roles they play. Table 10.1 summarizes the key functions these people need to provide in three categories commonly used (by functional theorists) to define the roles people play in fostering change (Hackman and Walton 1986): substantive contributions relate to those providing ideas to make change happen; procedural contributions refer to those navigating organizational rules and systems; maintenance contributions are the relational roles vital to mobilizing others to participate in the change process.

You should ensure that your initiative involves people playing these roles, with champions potentially occupying three of the slots (authorizer, motivator, and convener) but others on hand to ensure the others are also in place. To help in this respect, Table 10.2 give you a chance to reflect on the people you believe

Table 10.1. The roles you need from people involved in your state building initiative

Function set	Roles
Substantive contributions	1. Construct, communicate problems 2. Come up with ideas for reform 3. Provide implementation view
Procedural contributions	4. Provide formal authority 5. Motivate and inspire reform 6. Empower other agents 7. Provide financial support
Maintenance contributions	8. Conveners of small groups 9. Connectors to distributed agents

Source: Andrews (2013)

Table 10.2. Who will play the roles needed in your initiative?

Function set	Roles	Who you think will play the role?
Substantive contributions	1. Construct, communicate problems 2. Come up with ideas for reform 3. Provide implementation view	
Procedural contributions	4. Provide formal authority 5. Motivate and inspire reform 6. Empower other agents Provide financial support	
Maintenance contributions	7. Conveners of small groups 8. Connectors to distributed agents	

Source: Andrews (2013)

will play different roles in the strategy you have been developing to address the complex challenge you identified in Chapter 6. Take a minute filling the table in, with real people's names. Note where you have gaps, as well as where you have multiple names to include; these give you a sense of where your "agency strategy" needs to provide more focus (or could perhaps be more relaxed).

Mobilizing People to Build Capability at Scale

It is useful to identify the different role players needed for effective state building. It can also be frustrating, however, because the list is probably long and the people identified come from many different domains. You may be wondering how you will mobilize them all into a PDIA process. This section offers some ideas. The ideas derive from the work of Silvia Dorado (and more recent application by Westley et al. (2013)). Dorado calls functions like those in Table 10.2 "resources" that agents provide and are "integral to change" (Dorado 2005: 390).

She identifies three approaches to mobilize these "resources": leveraging, convening, and accumulating. We often employ these approaches when mobilizing agents for PDIA processes, with a fourth we call connecting.

"Leveraging" describes a process in which politically skilled agents initiate change by identifying projects, and then build internal support and external acceptance for such. This process depends on having agents that can influence change from a central position and simultaneously identify people to provide alternative ideas and package these as viable solutions. This calls for an authorizer who is loosely embedded in the context or is connected (directly or indirectly) to idea providers and translators. Prime Minister Zongo arguably played this role at the start of the Burkina Faso case. He was embedded in local politics but also enjoyed connections beyond such sphere, which he used to identify and appoint Mr Bessin (who was less embedded and could bring a legitimate voice of change to augment Zongo's vision).

The leveraging approach usually involves strategies discussed in Chapter 7— where those working with the authorizer build urgency and acceptance around established problems. This is what Mr Bessin did (with the help of the World Bank) in getting cabinet ministers to reflect on the problems they were facing (as an entry point for change). It is also the approach that Mantian authorities used to obtain support from other ministries and agencies—showing these agencies that firms faced problems related to their area of expertise leveraged their support.

Going beyond leveraging, the "convening" approach entails creating inter-organizational arrangements that bring different people and their resources and functional strengths together to "jumpstart a process of change" (Dorado 2005: 391). Events can be used to foster this convening (like the inter-ministerial workshop in Burkina Faso) as can mechanisms like coalitions and teams (as in the PDIA cases of Mantia and Nostria, discussed in prior chapters). Teams are essentially convening mechanisms that bring select agents together, in repeated engagements, to combine efforts in search of solutions around shared problems. A convener is often required to bring teams or coalitions together, because opportunities for engagement and coordination are not organic. This key player is a "catalytic agent" who bridges "unaware, unsure or skeptical actors to explore the possibilities of cooperation" (Kalegaonkar and Brown 2000: 9). Both Prime Minister Zongo and Mr Bessin played this role in Burkina Faso, especially assembling the cabinet members for discussion—but also the teams to work on actual risk maps.

It is important to note that convening mechanisms like teams take a lot of energy and effort to actually work effectively. One needs to have the right process for this as well. A few key process elements are embedded into PDIA to help in this respect. The emphasis on repeated action engagements is an example. Studies show that teams work better when they work together, and the repeated activities help to ensure this happens. The emphasis on identifying a clear problem to solve, and a goal (problem solved) is also crucial for any team: studies show that focused and goal-directed teams tend to be more effective than others.

Connectors play a similar role to conveners, though they make links between agents without necessarily bringing these agents together. The connector thus gives reforms and other interventions "reach," ensuring that distributed groups can engage even over distances and differences. Consider the way Mr Bessin connected the prime minister and other ministers to capacities in local consulting firms, indirectly, to ensure that the former groups benefited from the talents of the latter agents.

In their study on reforms, Andrews et al. (2010) find that the most important leadership functions across all twelve reform cases related to convening and connecting. Conveners brought smaller groups of key agents together, with direct ties, to initiate and guide reform. They did this mostly by hosting formal and informal meetings and gatherings and establishing diverse teams. These teams became the nerve center of reforms. In contrast, connecting agents created indirect ties between other actors to facilitate broad interaction, ensuring that ideas were shared between core groups devising reforms and distributed agents experimenting with new proposals. These connectors were particularly important in implementation, where the role of distributed agents was also greater—fostering diffusion of the changes and allowing new capabilities to reach scale.

These kinds of convening and connecting roles are vital in the mobilization process in many successful reforms. The work in Mantia and Nostria involved regular meetings, for instance, organized and facilitated by specific people who exhibit the classic traits of a convener: being liked and trusted by many, organized and persuasive, and open to others' ideas. It is important to note that these people were often the quietest in meetings, and when they did engage it was to move meetings along or to facilitate reflection. In both of these examples the convener worked with relatively small teams (of five to seven people) who met face to face regularly. These people all connected to other groups and people outside of the core team, however, which ensured breadth of reach.

The convening and connection arrangements described here are perhaps best illustrated in a snowflake metaphor (as shown in the figure at the start of this chapter, and used in other work on organizing (McKenna and Han 2014)). A core team is convened at the center of the snowflake, with all members connecting outwards to other people who convene their own teams. This structure can expand outwards and still stay stable given the strong convening at its core. It balances the competing need to have smaller teams (capable of actually getting things done) while also achieving broad reach.

It is important and interesting to note that convening and connecting agents accounted for more than 25 percent of named "leaders" in the GLI study (Andrews et al. 2010). There was also a key role for those motivating and inspiring reform, however, especially in early periods. This indicates some "leveraging" in the mobilization process (where a high-level office holder mobilized people by inspiring them), although the coexistence of these agents with conveners and connectors suggests that motivation was an insufficient mobilizer. Conveners and connectors were still required, particularly in the implementation period where the role of motivators was smaller and the role of connectors grew. This speaks, potentially, to the importance of third party ties between powerful high-level agents at the center of a network (like a minister), and implementers at the periphery. Direct ties between such agents are not common and are certainly not conducive to equal engagement or mutual empowerment (especially in hierarchical contexts). Peripheral implementers may view centrally located motivators like ministers of even mayors as powerful authoritarians trying to control them—as subordinates—which could foster resistance to change. Less prominent conveners and connectors, in contrast, can build connections to distributed implementers and more effectively mobilize their engagement.

The final strategy for mobilizing broad agency is "Accumulating." This involves a long and probabilistic process whereby new designs emerge and are implemented and diffused through the unorganized interaction of multiple agents. There is no central agent facilitating this interaction, which happens largely because of luck and/or the natural coordinating characteristics of open social systems, both of which are argued to emerge as a change process takes shape (and as the intervention becomes dynamic). This is the emergent leadership one finds referenced in complexity theory, and is exemplified in an effective free market system (where all agents have freedom of information, movement, and interaction, and ideas and engagement patterns emerge to foster continuous and dynamic change).

What Is Your Role in Building State Capability?

It is likely that mobilization always involves a blend of leveraging, convening, connecting and accumulating. We certainly embed ideas of the first three into the PDIA work we support: building authority and a problem narrative to facilitate leverage, creating teams for convening, fostering broad connections, and hoping for emergence and accumulating forces.

The salient observation is that mobilization matters, however, to ensure that broad agency is in place to foster change. We believe that you could benefit from thinking about the viability of using all of these strategies in your context.

Table 10.3. Which mobilization mechanism/strategy best fits your situation?

Mechanism/strategy	Key role players	Contextual considerations
Leveraging	Who are the motivators?	Are there trust and power issues that might undermine the motivation? How much reach do the motivators have?
Convening and Connecting	Who are the conveners?	Are mechanisms like teams commonly used? Are the mobilizers trusted and neutral?
	Who are the connectors?	How organized are the mobilizers?
Accumulating	None	How open and emergent is your context? Can agents engage freely with each other?

Table 10.3 allows such thought, asking you to reflect upon who you might see playing key roles in either mobilization strategy (motivators in leveraging and conveners and connectors in convening). It also invites you to think about the contextual viability of both strategies. As with prior exercises, your thoughts at this stage (when we assume you are still preparing for an initiative) will not be final or complete. These thoughts allow some structure to your "agency" or "people" strategy, however, and also give you a foundation to use in structuring learning throughout the reform process. We imagine you returning to reflect on these thoughts when you are considering lessons from your various experimental iterations, constantly identifying new people to include and noting opportunities and constraints to using different mobilization mechanisms.

The challenge of mobilizing agents to build state capability is not easy, regardless of the mechanism one employs, especially in places where gaps have festered for long periods (or where no capability ever existed). We like to think of these challenges as adventures or expeditions into the unknown—much like the 1804 Lewis and Clark expedition discussed in Chapter 6. Anyone signing up to such an expedition needs to be aware of the demands and risks of the journey; this is not the same as building a road or following a map in a car down that road. The journey is dangerous, and potentially costly, and must therefore be embarked upon with thoughtful care and consideration. It will involve failure, and days where it is difficult to see such failure as learning (which we obviously encourage). It is also a potentially exciting and rewarding journey, however, that will energize and empower those who are open to trying new things out, learning, and adapting.

Onward

We are grateful that you have managed to read your way all the way to the end of this book and can only imagine it is because you are in fact open to exactly this kind of experience. We have been working with people all over the world

Table 10.4. What role will you play in your chosen effort to build state capability?

Function set	Roles	What role will you play, and why?
Substantive contributions	1. Construct, communicate problems 2. Come up with ideas for reform 3. Provide implementation view	
Procedural contributions	4. Provide formal authority 5. Motivate and inspire reform 6. Empower other agents Provide financial support	
Maintenance contributions	7. Conveners of small groups 8. Connectors to distributed agents	

Source: Andrews (2013)

who are thirsty for a new way of doing development, and especially of working with governments in developing countries. You may want to join that community, at www.doingdevelopmentdiffernetly.com. You will meet people there who are trying new things out, working iteratively, and pushing boundaries. Not everyone is using the PDIA approach as we present it here, and that is appropriate and important: the more variation in methods, the more opportunity we all have to learn.

As you consider your next steps after reading this book, we want to make one last suggestion: try and reflect on what your roles are in addressing the challenge you have been working with since Chapter 6. Use Table 10.4 to do this. Make sure that you do not identify yourself as playing more than three roles, please—this is our rule-of-thumb limit to the number of roles any one person should play in any given effort to build state capability. Every role involves risk, and we think that people playing more than three roles are likely taking on too much risk and putting their survival in jeopardy. Furthermore, we believe that groups are needed to make change happen and build state capability; and you limit the size of your group if you occupy too many roles. Good luck in your efforts to build state capability, and please make sure to check in with us on your progress![7]

---

[7] Further updates to the building state capability program can be found at: http://bsc.cid.harvard.edu.

References

Abdollahi, M., Arvan, M., and Razmi, J. 2015. An integrated approach for supplier portfolio selection: Lean or agile? *Expert Systems with Applications, 42*(1), pp. 679–90.

Adams, W. and Brock, J.W. 1993. *Adam Smith Goes to Moscow: A Dialogue on Radical Reform.* Princeton, NJ: Princeton University Press.

Adler, D., Sage, C., and Woolcock, M. 2009. Interim institutions and the development process: opening spaces for reform in Cambodia and Indonesia. University of Manchester: Brooks World Poverty Institute Working Paper 86.

Aghion, P. and Tirole, J. 1997. Formal and real authority in organizations. *Journal of Political Economy 105*(1), pp. 1–29.

Ali, A. Gloeck, J., Ahmi, A., and Sahdan, M. 2007. Internal audit in the state and local governments of Malaysia. *Southern African Journal of Accountability and Auditing 7*, pp. 32–41.

Allen, M. and Dinnen, S. 2010. The North down under: Antinomies of conflict and intervention in Solomon Islands. *Conflict, Security and Development 10*(3), pp. 299–327.

Anders, G. 2002. Like chameleons: Civil servants and corruption in Malawi. *Bulletin de l'APAD*, 23–4, pp. 2–19.

Andrews, M. 2006. Beyond "best practice" and "basics first" in adopting performance budgeting reform. *Public Administration and Development 26*(2), pp. 147–61.

Andrews, M. 2008. The good governance agenda: Beyond indicators without theory. *Oxford Development Studies 36*(4), pp. 379–407.

Andrews, M. 2011. Which organizational attributes are amenable to external reform? An empirical study of African public financial management. *International Public Management Journal 14*(2), pp. 131–56.

Andrews, M. 2012. The logical limits of best practice administrative solutions in developing countries. *Public Administration and Development 32*(2), pp. 137–53.

Andrews, M. 2013. *The Limits of Institutional Reform in Development.* New York: Cambridge University Press.

Andrews, M. 2015a. Explaining positive deviance in public sector reform. *World Development 74*(10), pp. 197–208.

Andrews, M. 2015b. Doing complex reform through PDIA: Judicial sector change in Mozambique. *Public Administration and Development 35*(4), pp. 288–300.

Andrews, M. 2015c. Has Sweden injected realism into public financial reforms in partner countries? Expert Group for Aid Studies (EBA) Report 05. Stockholm: EBA.

Andrews, M. and Bategeka, L. 2013. Overcoming the limits of institutional reform in Uganda. WIDER Working Paper 2013/111.

References

Andrews, M., Grinstead, A., Nucifora, A., and Saligmann, R. 2010. Mozambique's PFM reform lessons. Mimeo, World Bank Africa Region, PREM.

Andrews, M., McConnell, J., and Wescott, A. 2010. *Development as Leadership Led Change*. Washington, DC: World Bank.

Andrews, M., Pritchett, L., and Woolcock, M. 2013. Escaping capability traps through problem driven iterative adaptation (PDIA). *World Development 51*(11), pp. 234–44.

Andrews, M., Pritchett, L., and Woolcock, M. 2015. The challenge of building real state capability. Harvard University: Center for International Development Working Paper 306.

Andrews, M. and Seligmann, R. 2013. A tale of two internal audit reforms. Unpublished case study used in teaching Harvard Kennedy School course on Public Financial Management in a Changing World.

Atherton, P. and Kingdon, G. 2010. The relative effectiveness and costs of contract and regular teachers in India. CSAE WPS/2010–15.

Babineau, L. and Lessard, L. 2015. Organizational agility, project management and healthcare reorganization: A case study in organizational change. *Journal of Modern Project Management, 3*(1).

Bacharach, S. and Mundell, B. 1993. Organizational politics in school: Micro, macro, and logics of action. *Educational Administration Quarterly 29*(9), pp. 423–52.

Bamford, D., Forrester, P., Dehe, B., and Leese, R.G. 2015. Partial and iterative lean implementation: Two case studies. *International Journal of Operations & Production Management 35*(5), pp. 702–27.

Banerjee, A., Chattopadhyay, R., Duflo, E., Keniston, D., and Singh, N. 2012. Can institutions be reformed from within? Evidence from a randomized experiment with the Rajasthan police. MIT Department of Economics, Working Paper 12–04.

Banerjee, A., Deaton, A., and Duflo, E. 2004. Wealth, health, and health services in rural Rajasthan. *American Economic Review 94*(2), pp. 326–30.

Banerjee, A., Duflo, E., and Glennerster, R. 2008. Putting a band-aid on a corpse: Incentives for nurses in the Indian public health care system. *Journal of European Economic Association 6*(2–3), pp. 487–500.

Barber, M. 2015. *How to Run a Government*. London: Allen Lane.

Barnett, W. and Carroll, G. 1995. Modeling internal organizational change. *Annual Review of Sociology 21*, pp. 217–36.

Bartunek, J.M. and Moch, M.K. 1987. First-order, second-order, and third-order change and organization development interventions: A cognitive approach. *Journal of Applied Behavioral Science 23*(4), pp. 483–500.

Barzelay, M. and Gallego, R. 2006. From "new institutionalism" to "institutional processualism": Advancing knowledge about public management policy change. *Governance 19*(4), pp. 531–57.

Bates, R. 2008. *When Things Fell Apart: State Failure in Late-century Africa*. Cambridge: Cambridge University Press.

Battilana, J. and D'aunno, T. 2009. Institutional work and the paradox of embedded agency. In T.B. Lawrence, R. Suddaby, and B. Leca (eds), *Institutional Work: Actors and Agency in Institutional Studies of Organizations*. New York: Cambridge University Press, pp. 31–58.

Bayly, C.A. 2004. *The Making of the Modern World, 1780–1914: Global Connections and Comparisons*. Maiden, MA/Oxford: Blackwell.

Bertrand, M., Djankov, S., Hanna, R., and Mullainathan, S. 2007. Obtaining a driver's license in India: An experimental approach to studying corruption. *Quarterly Journal of Economics 122*(4), pp. 1639–76.

Besley, T. and Ghatak, M. 2005. Competition and incentives with motivated agents. *American Economic Review 95*(3), pp. 616–36.

Besley, T. and McLaren, J. 1993. Taxes and bribery: The role of wage incentives. *Economic Journal 103*(416), pp. 119–41.

Bold, T., Kimenyi, M., Mwabu, G., Ng'ang'a, A., and Sandefur, J. 2013. Scaling up what works: Experimental evidence on external validity in Kenyan education. Center for Global Development Working Paper.

Bolongaita, E. 2010. An exception to the rule? Why Indonesia's Anti-Corruption Commission succeeds where others don't—A comparison with the Philippines' Ombudsman. *U4 Issue*, August, 4. Norway: U4 Anti-Corruption Resource Center, Chr. Michelsen Institute.

Bolton, P. and Dewatripont, M. 2013. Authority in organizations. In R. Gibbons and J. Roberts (eds), *The Handbook of Organizational Economics*. Princeton, NJ: Princeton University Press, pp. 342–72.

Booth, D. 2011. Aid effectiveness: Bringing country ownership (and politics) back in. *Overseas Development Institute Working Paper 336*. London: ODI.

Bourdieu, P. 1993. *The Field of Cultural Production*. New York: Columbia University Press.

Brafman, O. and Beckstrom, R. 2006. *The Starfish and the Spider: The Unstoppable Power of Leaderless Organizations*. London: Penguin.

Brixi, H., Lust, E., and Woolcock, M. 2015. *Trust, Voice and Incentives: Learning from Local Success Stories in Service Delivery in the Middle East and North Africa*. Washington, DC: World Bank.

Brunsson, K. 1995. Puzzle pictures: Swedish budgetary processes in principle and practice. *Financial Accountability & Management 11*(2), pp. 111–25.

Buehler, M. 2009. Of geckos and crocodiles: Evaluating Indonesia's corruption eradication efforts. Presentation at CSIS/USINDO, Washington, DC, November 23.

Bunse, S. and Fritz, V. 2012. Making public sector reforms work: Political and economic contexts, incentives, and strategies. Policy Research Working Paper 6174. Washington, DC: World Bank.

Burkitt, B. and Whyman, P. 1994. Public sector reform in Sweden: competition or participation? *Political Quarterly 65*(3), pp. 275–84.

Bushe, G.R. 2013. Generative process, generative outcome: The transformational potential of appreciative inquiry, in D.L. Cooperrider, D.P. Zandee, L.N. Godwin, M. Avital, and B. Boland (eds), *Organizational Generativity: The Appreciative Inquiry Summit and a Scholarship of Transformation* (Advances in Appreciative Inquiry, vol 4). Bingley, UK: Emerald Group, pp. 89–113.

Cameron, K.S. 1986. Effectiveness as paradox: Consensus and conflict in conceptions of organizational effectiveness. *Management Science 32*(5), pp. 539–53.

Campbell, D. 2012. Public managers in integrated services collaboratives: What works is workarounds. *Public Administration Review 72*(5), pp. 721–30.

Campos, J.E., Randrianarivelo, B., and Winning, K. 2013. Escaping the capability trap: Turning "small" development into "big" development. World Bank Policy Research Working Paper 6717. Washington, DC: World Bank.

Carlile, P.R. and Lakhani, K. 2011. Innovation and the challenge of novelty: The novelty–confirmation–transformation cycle in software and science. Harvard Business School Technology & Operations Mgt. Unit Working Paper 11–096.

Carpenter, D. 2001. *The Forging of Bureaucratic Autonomy: Reputations, Networks, and Policy Innovation in Executive Agencies, 1862–1928*. Princeton, NJ: Princeton University Press.

Carter, D., Seely, P., Dagosta, J., DeChurch, L., and Zaccaro, S. 2015. Leadership for global virtual teams: Facilitating teamwork processes. In J.L Wildman and R.L. Griffith (eds), *Leading Global Teams*. New York: Springer, pp. 225–52.

Cartwright, S. and Cooper, C.L. 1993. The role of culture compatibility in successful organizational marriage. *Academy of Management Executive 7*(2), pp. 57–70.

Chambers, D.A., Glasgow, R.E., and Stange, K.C. 2013. The dynamic sustainability framework: addressing the paradox of sustainment amid ongoing change. *Implementation Science 8*(1), p 1.

Chan, N. 2010. Narrative change and its microfoundations: Problem management, strategic manipulation, and information processing. Paper presented at in Political Theory and Policy Analysis workshop, Indiana University-Bloomington, April 3.

Chand, V. 2006. *Reinventing Public Service Delivery in India: Selected Case Studies*. New Delhi: Sage.

Chang, H.J. 2003. Kicking away the ladder: Infant industry promotion in historical perspective 1. *Oxford Development Studies 31*(1), pp. 21–32.

Chetty, R., Friedman, J.F., and Rockoff, J.E. 2011. The long-term impact of teachers: teacher value-added and student outcomes in adulthood. Cambridge: NBER Working Paper 17699.

Chirambo, R. 2009. Corruption, tribalism and democracy: Coded messages in Wambali Mkandawire's popular songs in Malawi. *Critical Arts: A Journal of North–South Cultural Studies 23*(1), pp. 42–63.

Chong, A., La Porta, R., Lopez-de-Silanes, F., and Shleifer, A. 2014. Letter grading government efficiency. *Journal of the European Economic Association 12*(2), pp. 277–99.

Christensen, C. 1997. *The Innovator's Dilemma*: The *Revolutionary Book That Will Change the Way You Do Business*. Boston, MA: Harvard Business School Press.

Christensen, T. and Lægreid, P. 2003. *Administrative reform policy: The challenge of turning symbols into practice. Public Organization Review 3*(1), pp. 3–27.

Christiansen, L.H. and Lounsbury, M. 2013. Strange brew: Bridging logics via institutional bricolage and the reconstitution of organizational identity. *Research in the Sociology of Organizations, 39*, pp. 199–232.

Clegg, S. 2012. The end of bureaucracy. *Research in the Sociology of Organizations 35*, pp. 59–84.

Dacin, M.T., Goodstein, J., and Scott, W.R. 2002. Institutional theory and institutional change: Introduction to the Special Research Forum. *Academy of Management Journal 45*(1), pp. 45–57.

Dambrin, C., Lambert, C., and Sponem, S. 2007. Control and change: Analysing the process of institutionalization. *Management Accounting Research 18*(2), pp. 172–208.

Das, J. and Hammer, J. 2007. Money for nothing: The dire straits of medical practice in Delhi, India. *Journal of Development Economics 83*(1), pp. 1–36.

de Búrca, G., Keohane, R.O., and Sabel, C. 2014. Global experimentalist governance. *British Journal of Political Science 44*(3), pp. 477–86.

De Souza Briggs, X.N. 2008. *Democracy as Problem Solving*. Cambridge, MA: MIT Press.

Deaton, A. 2013. *The Great Escape: Health, Wealth and the Origins of Inequality*. Princeton, NJ: Princeton University Press.

Desai, D., Isser, D., and Woolcock, M. 2012. Rethinking justice reform in fragile and conflict-affected states: Lessons for enhancing the capacity of development agencies. *Hague Journal on the Rule of Law 4*(1), pp. 54–75.

Dhaliwal, I. and Hanna, R. 2014. Deal with the devil: The successes and limitations of bureaucratic reform in India. National Bureau of Economic Research Working Paper w20482.

Dillabaugh, L.L., Lewis Kulzer, J., Owuor, K., Ndege, V., Oyanga, A., Ngugi, E., Shade, S.B., Bukusi, E., and Cohen, C.R. 2012. Towards elimination of mother-to-child transmission of HIV: the impact of a rapid results initiative in Nyanza Province, Kenya. *AIDS Research and Treatment*.

DiMaggio, P. and Powell, W. 1983. The iron cage revisited: institutional isomorphism and collective rationality in organizational fields. *American Sociological Review 48*(2), pp. 147–60.

DiMaggio, P. and Powell, W. (eds) 1991. *The New Institutionalism in Organizational Analysis*. Chicago, IL: University of Chicago Press.

Dodlova, M. 2013. Political accountability and real authority of government bureaucracy. CESifo Working Paper Series 4443.

Doig, A., Watt, D., and Williams, R. 2005. *Measuring "Success" in Five African Anti-Corruption Commissions*. March. Norway: U4 Anti-Corruption Resource Center, Chr. Michelsen Institute.

Dorado, S. 2005. Institutional entrepreneurship, partaking, and convening. *Organization Studies 26*(3), pp. 385–414.

Drew, S.A. and Wallis, J.L. 2014. The use of appreciative inquiry in the practices of large-scale organisational change. *Journal of General Management, 39*(4), pp. 3–26.

Drumm, B.R. 2015. Distinguishing earth, water, fire, and air: Factor analysis to determine the four fundamental elements of state capability. BA senior thesis, Harvard University.

Dubash, N.K. 2008. Institutional transplant as political opportunity: The practice and politics of Indian electricity regulation. CLPE Research Paper 31/2008. New Delhi: Centre for Policy Research.

Dubnick, M. 2003. Accountability through thick and thin: Preliminary explorations. Queen's University Belfast, Institute of Governance, Public Policy, and Social Research, Working Paper QU/GOV/4/2003.

Duckworth, A.L., Peterson, C., Matthews, M.D., and Kelly, D.R. 2007. Grit: Perseverance and passion for long-term goals. *Journal of Personality and Social Psychology 92*(6), pp. 1087–101.

Duflo, E., Dupas, P., and Kremer, M. 2007. Peer effects, pupil–teacher ratios, and teacher incentives: Evidence from a randomized evaluation in Kenya. Poverty Action Lab, mimeo.

Duflo, E., Greenstone, M., Pande, R., and Ryan, N. 2013. Truth-telling by third-party auditors and the response of polluting firms: Experimental evidence from India. *Quarterly Journal of Economics 128*(4), pp. 1499–545.

Duflo, E., Hanna, R., and Ryan, S. 2012. Incentives work: Getting teachers to come to school. *American Economic Review 102*(4), pp. 1241–78.

Dumas, M. and Maggi, F.M. 2015. Enabling process innovation via deviance mining and predictive monitoring. In *BPM-Driving Innovation in a Digital World*. New York: Springer, pp. 145–54.

Duncan, A. and Williams, G. 2012. Making development assistance more effective through using political–economy analysis: What has been done and what have we learned? *Development Policy Review 30*(2), pp. 133–48.

Dyba, T. and Dingsoyr, T. 2015. Agile project management: from self-managing teams to large-scale development. In *International Conference on Software Engineering (ICSE), 2015 IEEE/ACM 37th IEEE*. New York: Springer/IEEE, vol 2, pp. 945–6.

Easterly, W. 2002. The cartel of good intentions: The problem of bureaucracy in foreign aid. *Journal of Policy Reform 5*(4), pp. 223–50.

Edmondson, A.C. and Singer, S.J. 2012. Confronting the tension between learning and performance. *Reflections 11*(4), pp. 34–43.

Ensminger, J. [nd]. Inside corruption networks: Following the money in community driven development. Mimeo, California Institute of Technology.

Etzioni, A. 1959. Authority structure and organizational effectiveness. *Administrative Science Quarterly 4*(1), pp. 43–67.

Evans, P. 2004. Development as institutional change: The pitfalls of monocropping and the potentials of deliberation. *Studies in Comparative International Development 38*(4), pp. 30–52.

Ezrow, N. and Frantz, E. 2013. Revisiting the concept of the failed state: Bringing the state back in. *Third World Quarterly 34*(8), pp. 1323–38.

Fama, E.F. and Jensen, M.C. 1983. Separation of ownership and control. *Journal of Law and Economics 26*(2), pp. 301–25.

Faust, J. 2010. Policy experiments, democratic ownership and development assistance. *Development Policy Review 28*(5), pp. 515–34.

Faustino, J. and Booth, D. 2014. *Development Entrepreneurship: How Donors and Leaders Can Foster Institutional Change*. London: Overseas Development Institute.

Faustino, J. and Booth, D. 2015. Development entrepreneurship: How donors and leaders can foster institutional change. Working Politically in Practice, Case Study 2. San Francisco, CA/London: Asia Foundation and Overseas Development Institute.

Feldman, M.S. and Pentland, B.T. 2003. Reconceptualizing organizational routines as a source of flexibility and change. *Administrative Science Quarterly 48*(1), pp. 94–118.

Ferguson, J. 1994. *The Anti-Politics Machine: Development, Depoliticization, and Bureaucratic Power in Lesotho*. Minnesota, MN: University of Minnesota Press.

Freedman, L. 2013. *Strategy: A History*. New York: Oxford University Press.

Fritz, V., Kaiser, K., and Levy, B. 2009. *Problem-Driven Governance and Political Economy Analysis*. Washington, DC: World Bank.

Fritz, V., Levy, B., and Ort, R. (eds) 2014. *Problem-Driven Political Economy Analysis: The World Bank's Experience*. Washington, DC: World Bank.

Frosch, D.L. and Kaplan, R.M. 1999. Shared decision making in clinical medicine: past research and future directions. *American Journal of Preventive Medicine 17*(4), pp. 285–294.

Fudge, C. and Gustafsson, L. 1989. Administrative reform and public management in Sweden and the United Kingdom. *Public Money & Management 9*(2), pp. 29–34.

Galvin, T. 2002. Examining institutional change: Evidence from the founding dynamics of US health care interest associations. *Academy of Management Journal 45*(4), pp. 673–96.

Geertz, C. 1973. *The Interpretation of Cultures*. New York: Basic Books.

Gersick, C. and Hackman, J. 1990. Habitual routines in task performing groups. *Organizational Behavior and Human Decision Processes 47*(1), pp. 65–97.

Gertler, M.S. 2003. Tacit knowledge and the economic geography of context, or the undefinable tacitness of being (there). *Journal of Economic Geography 3*(1), pp. 75–99.

Glouberman, S. and Zimmerman, B. 2004. Complicated and complex systems: What would successful reform of Medicare look like?, in P.G. Forest, G.P. Marchildon, and T. McIntosh (eds), *Romanow Papers: Changing Healthcare in Canada*. Toronto: University of Toronto Press, vol 2, 31.

Goldstein, H. 1990. *Problem-Oriented Policing*. New York: McGraw-Hill.

Greenwood, R. and Hinnings, C.R. 1996. Understanding radical organisational change: Bringing together the old and new institutionalism. *Academy of Management Review 21*(4), pp. 1022–54.

Greenwood, R. and Suddaby, R. 2006. Institutional entrepreneurship in mature fields: The big five accounting firms. *Academy of Management Journal 49*(1), pp. 27–48.

Greenwood, R., Suddaby, R., and Hinings, C.R. 2002. Theorising change: The role of professional associations in the transformation of institutional fields. *Academy of Management Journal 45*(1), pp. 58–80.

Grindle, M. 2004. Good enough governance: Poverty reduction and reform in developing countries. *Governance 17*(4), pp. 525–48.

Gruber, M., De Leon, N., George, G., and Thompson, P. 2015. Managing by design. *Academy of Management Journal 58*(1), pp. 1–7.

Guillén, M.F. 1994. *Models of Management: Work, Authority, and Organization in a Comparative Perspective*. Chicago, IL: University of Chicago Press.

Guldbrandsson, K. and Fossum, B. 2009. An exploration of the theoretical concepts policy windows and policy entrepreneurs at the Swedish public health arena. *Health Promotion International 24*(4), pp. 434–44.

Gulick, L. 1937. Notes on the theory of organization. *Classics of Organization Theory 3*, pp. 87–95.

Gupta, A. 2012. *Red Tape: Bureaucracy, Structural Violence, and Poverty in India*. Durham, NC: Duke University Press.

Hackman, J. 2002. *Leading Teams: Setting the Stage for Great Performances*. Boston, MA: Harvard Business School Press.

Hackman, J.R., Walton, R.E., and Goodman, P.S. 1986. Leading groups in organizations. In P.S. Goodman (ed.), *Designing Effective Work Groups*. San Francisco, CA: Jossey-Bass.

Haggard, S. 1997. Reform of the state in Latin America. In S. Burki and G. Perry. (eds), *Development in Latin America and the Caribbean*. Washington, DC: World Bank.

Haggard, S. and Webb, S.B. 1993. What do we know about the political economy of economic policy reform? *World Bank Research Observer 8*(2), pp. 143–68.

Hall, P. and Suskice, D. 2001. *Varieties of Capitalism: The Institutional Foundations of Comparative Advantage*. Oxford: Oxford University Press.

Hallward-Driemeier, M. and Pritchett, L. 2011. How business is done and the "Doing Business" Indicators: The investment climate when firms have climate control. Policy Research Working Paper 5563. Washington, DC: World Bank.

Hallward-Driemeier, M. and Pritchett, L. 2015. How business is done in the developing world: Deals versus rules. *Journal of Economic Perspectives 29*(3), pp. 121–40.

Harper, T. 2011. The tools of transition: Education and development in modern southeast Asian history, in C. A. Bayly, V. Rao, S. Szreter, and M. Woolcock (eds), *History, Historians and Development Policy: A Necessary Dialogue*. Manchester: Manchester University Press.

Hart, O. and Holmstrom, B. 2010. A theory of firm scope. *Quarterly Journal of Economics 125*(2), pp. 483–513.

Hart, O., Shleifer, A., and Vishny, R.W. 1997. The proper scope of government: Theory and an application to prisons. *Quarterly Journal of Economics 112*(4), pp. 1127–61.

Hays, S.P. 1959. *Conservation and the Gospel of Efficiency: The Progressive Conservation Movement, 1890–1920*. Cambridge, MA: Harvard University Press.

He, A.J. 2012. Is the Chinese health bureaucracy incapable of leading healthcare reforms? The case of Fujian province. *China: An International Journal 10*(1), pp. 93–112.

Heifetz, R.A. 1994. *Leadership without Easy Answers*. Cambridge, MA: Harvard University Press.

Heifetz, R.A., Grashow, A., and Linsky, M. 2009. *The Practice of Adaptive Leadership: Tools and Tactics for Changing Your Organization and the World*. Boston, MA: Harvard Business School Press.

Herbst, J. 2014. *States and Power in Africa: Comparative Lessons in Authority and Control*. Princeton, NJ: Princeton University Press.

Hirschmann, A. 1967. *Development Projects Observed*. Washington, DC: Brookings Institution.

Holmstrom, B. and Milgrom, P. 1991. Multitask principal–agent analyses: Incentive contracts, asset ownership, and job design. *Journal of Law, Economics, & Organization 7*, pp. 24–52.

Hong, K.K. and Kim, Y.G. 2002. The critical success factors for ERP implementation: An organizational fit perspective. *Information and Management 40*, pp. 25–40.

Horling, B. and Lesser, V. 2004. A survey of multi-agent organizational paradigms. *Knowledge Engineering Review 19*(4), pp. 281–316.

Hughes, S. 2013. Authority structures and service reform in multilevel urban governance: The case of wastewater recycling in California and Australia. *Urban Affairs Review 49*(3), pp. 381–407.

Im, T. 2014. Bureaucracy in three different worlds: The assumptions of failed public sector reforms in Korea. *Public Organization Review 14*(4), pp. 577–96.

Innovations for Successful Societies (ISS). 2012. *Instilling Order and Accountability: Standard Operating Procedures at Indonesia's Ministry of Finance, 2006–2007*. Princeton University: Innovations for Successful Societies.

Institute for Development Studies (IDS). 2010. *An Upside-Down View of Governance.* Brighton: Centre for the Future State, Institute for Development Studies.

Janowitz, M. 1998. Changing patterns of organizational authority: The military establishment. *The Military and Society: The Training and Socializing of Military Personnel,* pp. 237–58.

Johnson, C. 1982. *MITI and the Japanese Miracle: The Growth of Industrial Policy, 1925–1975.* Stanford, CA: Stanford University Press.

Jones, L., Exworthy, M., and Frosini, F. 2013. Implementing market-based reforms in the English NHS: Bureaucratic coping strategies and social embeddedness. *Health Policy 111*(1), pp. 52–9.

Kalegaonkar, A. and Brown, L.D. 2000. *Intersectoral Cooperation: Lessons for Practice.* Boston, MA: Institute for Development Research.

Kapur, D. 2007. *Public Institutions in India: Performance and Designa.* New York: Oxford University Press.

Kaufmann, D. and Kraay, A. 2002. Governance without Growth. Policy Research Working Paper 2928. Washington, DC: World Bank.

Kaufmann, D., Kraay, A., and Mastruzzi, M. 2009. Governance Matters VIII: Aggregate and Individual Governance Indicators, 1996–2008. Policy Research Working Paper 4978. Washington, DC: World Bank.

Kaufmann, D., Kraay, A., and Mastruzzi, M. 2010. The Worldwide Governance Indicators: A Summary of Methodology, Data and Analytical Issues. Policy Research Working Paper 5430. Washington, DC: World Bank.

Kaufmann, D., Mehrez, G., and Gurgur, T. 2002. *Voice or Public Sector Management? An Empirical Investigation of Determinants of Public Sector Performance Based on a Survey of Public Officials.* World Bank Research Working Paper.

Kennedy, P. 2013. *Engineers of Victory: The Problem Solvers Who Turned the Tide in the Second World War.* New York: Random House.

Kenny, C. 2010. *Getting Better: Why Global Development Is Working—And How We Can Improve the World Even More.* New York: Basic Books.

Khanna, R., Guler, I., and Nerkar, A. 2016. Fail often, fail big, and fail fast? Learning from small failures and R&D performance in the pharmaceutical industry. *Academy of Management Journal 59*(2), pp. 436–59.

Kingdon, J.W. 1995. *Agendas, Alternatives, and Public Policies.* 2nd edn. New York: HarperCollins.

Klein, L., Biesenthal, C., and Dehlin, E. 2015. Improvisation in project management: A praxeology. *International Journal of Project Management 33*(2), pp. 267–77.

Klitgaard, R. 1997. Cleaning up and invigorating the civil service. *Public Administration and Development 17*(5), pp. 487–509.

Knaus, G. 2011. The rise and fall of liberal imperialism. In R. Stewart and G. Knaus, *Can Intervention Work?* New York: Norton.

Knight, J. 1997. Social institutions and human cognition: Thinking about old questions in new ways. *Journal of Institutional and Theoretical Economics 153*(4), pp. 693–9.

Korten, D.C. 1980. Community organization and rural development: a learning process approach. *Public Administration Review 40*(5), pp. 480–511.

Kotter, J. 1990. *Leading Change.* Boston: Harvard Business School Publishing.

Krause, G.A. and O'Connell, A.J. 2016. Experiential learning and presidential management of the US federal bureaucracy: Logic and evidence from agency leadership appointments. *American Journal of Political Science* 60 (4), pp. 914–931.

Krueger, A.O. 2002. *Political Economy of Policy Reform in Developing Countries*. Cambridge, MA: MIT Press, vol 4.

Kruger, J.S., Kruger, D.J., and Suzuki, R. 2015. Assessing the effectiveness of experiential learning in a student-run free clinic. *Pedagogy in Health Promotion 1* (2), pp. 91–94.

Laffont, J.J. and Tirole, J. 1993. *Theory of Incentives in Procurement and Regulation*. Cambridge, MA: MIT Press.

Lagneau-Ymonet, P. and Quack, S. 2012. *What's the Problem? Competing Diagnoses and Shifting Coalitions in the Reform of International Accounting Standards*. New York: Campus Verlag, pp. 213–46.

Lam, A. 2000. Tacit knowledge, organizational learning and societal institutions: An integrated framework. *Organization Studies 21*(3), pp. 487–513.

Lancaster, C. 1999. *Aid to Africa: So Much to Do, So Little Done*. Chicago, IL: University of Chicago Press.

Larson, G., Ajak, P.B., and Pritchett, L. 2013. South Sudan's capability trap: Building a state with disruptive innovation. Helsinki: UNU-WIDER Working Paper 2013/120.

Lazear, E.P. 1995. *Personnel Economics*. Cambridge, MA: MIT Press.

Le, Q.V. and Raven, P.V. 2015. An assessment of experiential learning of global poverty issues through international service projects. *Journal of Teaching in International Business, 26*(2) pp. 136–58.

Leeson, P. 2007. Better off stateless: Somalia before and after government collapse. *Journal of Comparative Economics 35*(4), pp. 689–710.

Leftwich, A. 2010. Beyond institutions: Rethinking the role of leaders, elites and coalitions in the institutional formation of developmental states and strategies. *Forum for Development Studies 37*(1), pp. 93–111.

Leonard, H.B. 2002. A short note on public sector strategy-building. Mimeo, Kennedy School of Government, Harvard University. Available at: http://www.atlas101.ca/pm/wp-content/uploads/2015/12/Leonard-Note-on-Strategy-2002.pdf (accessed August 12, 2016).

Levy, B. 2014. *Working with the Grain: Integrating Governance and Growth in Development Strategies*. New York: Oxford University Press.

Levy, B. and Fukuyama, F. 2010. *Development Strategies: Integrating Governance and Growth*. Policy Research Working Paper 5196. Washington, DC: World Bank.

Lewis, P.M. 1996. Economic reform and political transition in Africa: The quest for a politics of development. *World Politics 49*(1), pp. 92–129.

Li, M. and Armstrong, S.J. 2015. The relationship between Kolb's experiential learning styles and Big Five personality traits in international managers. *Personality and Individual Differences 86*, pp. 422–6.

Liker, J.K. 2004. *The Toyota Way: Fourteen Management Principles from the World's Greatest Manufacturer*. New York: McGraw-Hill.

Lindblom, C. 1958. Policy analysis. *American Economic Review 48*(June), pp. 298–312.

Lindblom, C. 1959. The science of "muddling through." *Public Administration Review 19*(2), pp. 79–88.

Lindblom, C. 1979. Still muddling, not yet through. *Public Administration Review 39*(6), pp. 517–26.

Lister, S. 2006. Moving forward? Assessing public administration reform in Afghanistan. Afghanistan Research and Evaluation Unit Briefing Paper (September).

Liu, Y. and Maula, M. 2015. Local partnering in foreign ventures: Uncertainty, experiential learning, and syndication in cross-border venture capital investments. *Academy of Management Journal*, pp.amj-2013.

Lundquist, K. 2001. *Accrual Accounting in Swedish Central Government*. Stockholm, Sweden: Ekonomistyrningsverket.

McCay, B.J. 2002. Emergence of institutions for the commons: Contexts, situations, and events. In E. Ostrom (ed), *The Drama of the Commons*. Washington, DC: National Research Council, pp. 361–99.

Macintyre, A. 2007. *After Virtue*. Notre Dame, IN: University of Notre Dame Press.

McKenna, E. and Han, H. 2014. *Groundbreakers: How Obama's 2.2 Million Volunteers Transformed Campaigning in America*. New York: Oxford University Press.

Manning, N. and Watkins, J. 2013. Targeting results, diagnosing the means: innovative approaches for improving public sector delivery. World Bank, unpublished draft.

Marsh, D.R., Schroeder, D.G., Dearden, K.A., Sternin, J., and Sternin, M. 2004. The power of positive deviance. *British Medical Journal 329*(7475), p. 1177.

Marshak, R.J., Grant, D.S., and Floris, M. 2015. Discourse and dialogic organization development. *Dialogic Organization Development: The Theory and Practice of Transformational Change*, p. 77.

Matta, N. and Morgan, P. 2011. Local empowerment through Rapid Results. *Stanford Social Innovation Review* (summer), pp. 51–5.

Mattisson, O., Nasi, S., and Tagesson, T. 2004. Accounting Innovations in the Public Sector: A Comparative Analysis of the Accrual Accounting Reform Process in the Swedish and Finnish Local Governments, Paper presented at the 27th Annual Congress of the European Accounting Association, Prague.

Meyer, J.W., Boli, J., Thomas, G.M., and Ramirez, F.O. 1997. World society and the nation state. *American Journal of Sociology 103*(1), pp. 144–81.

Meyer, M.W. 1968. The two authority structures of bureaucratic organization. *Administrative Science Quarterly 13*, pp. 211–28.

Milgrom, P. and Roberts, J. 1992. *Economics, Organization and Management*. New York: Prentice Hall.

Mintzberg, H. 1979. The structuring of organizations: A synthesis of the research. University of Illinois at Urbana-Champaign's Academy for Entrepreneurial Leadership Historical Research Reference in Entrepreneurship.

Miyazaki, T. 2014. Fiscal reform and fiscal sustainability: Evidence from Australia and Sweden. *International Review of Economics & Finance 33*, pp. 141–51.

Molander, P. 2000. Reforming budgetary institutions: Swedish experiences. *Institutions, Politics and Fiscal Policy*. New York: Springer, pp. 191–214.

Molander, P. and Holmquist, J. 2013. Reforming Sweden's budgetary institutions—Background, design and experiences. Rapport till Finanspolitiska rådet.

Moore, M. 1995. *Creating Public Value: Strategic Management in Government*. Cambridge, MA: Harvard University Press.

Moore, M. 2015. Creating efficient, effective, and just educational systems through multi-sector strategies of reform. Harvard Kennedy School, mimeo.

Moore, M. and Khagram, S. 2004. On creating public value: What business might learn from government about strategic management. Corporate Social Responsibility Initiative Working Paper 3. Cambridge, MA: Kennedy School of Government, Harvard University.

Mosse, D. 2005. *Cultivating Development: An Ethnography of Aid Policy and Practice.* London: Pluto Press.

Mowl, A.J. and Boudot, C. 2014. Barriers to basic banking: Results from an audit study in South India. NSE Working Paper Series WP-2014-1.

Mukand, S. and Rodrik, D. 2005. In search of the holy grail: Policy convergence, experimentation, and economic performance. *American Economic Review 95*(1), pp. 374–83.

Nowlin, M.C. 2011. Theories of the policy process: State of the research and emerging trends. *Policy Studies Journal 39*(s1), pp. 41–60.

Nunberg, B. 1995. *Managing Civil Service Reform: Lessons from Advanced Industrial Countries.* Washington, DC: World Bank.

Nutt, P.C. 1986. Tactics of implementation. *Academy of Management Journal 29*(2), pp. 230–61.

Oborn, E., Barrett, M., and Exworthy, M. 2011. Policy entrepreneurship in the development of public sector strategy: the case of London health reform. *Public Administration 89*(2), pp. 325–44.

Ohno, T. 1988. *Toyota Production System: Beyond Large-scale Production.* Portland, OR: Productivity Press.

Oliver, C. 1992. The antecedents of deinstitutionalization. *Organization Studies 13*(4), pp. 563–88.

Olsen, J.P. 2015. Democratic order, autonomy, and accountability. *Governance 28*(4), pp. 425–40.

Olson, O. and Sahlin-Andersson, K. 1998. Accounting transformation in an advanced welfare state: The case of Sweden. In O. Olson, J. Guthrie, and C. Humphrey (eds), *Global Warning! Debating International Developments in New Public Financial Management.* Oslo: Cappelen Akademisk forlag, pp. 241–75.

Ostrom, E. 1990. *Governing the Commons.* Cambridge: Cambridge University Press.

Ostrom, E. 1995. *Incentives, Rules of the Game, and Development.* Washington, DC: World Bank.

Ostrom, E. 2008. Design principles of robust property-rights institutions: What have we learned? In K.G. Ingram and Y.H. Hong (eds), *Property Rights and Land Policies.* Cambridge, MA: Lincoln Institute of Land Policy, pp. 25–51.

Pache, A.C. and Santos, F. 2013. Embedded in hybrid contexts: How individuals in organizations respond to competing institutional logics. *Research in the Sociology of Organizations 39*, pp. 3–35.

Pascale, R., Sternin, J., and Sternin, M. 2010. *The Power of Positive Deviance.* Cambridge, MA: Harvard Business School Press.

Paulsson, G. 2006. Accrual accounting in the public sector: experiences from the central government in Sweden. *Financial Accountability & Management 22*(1), pp. 47–62.

PEFA 2006. Public Expenditure and Financial Accountability performance measurement framework. PEFA Secretariat. Washington, DC: World Bank.

Perkmann, M. and Spicer, A. 2014. How emerging organizations take form: The role of imprinting and values in organizational bricolage. *Organization Science 25*(6), pp. 1785–806.

Peters, T.J. and Waterman, R.M. 1982. *In Search of Excellence: Lessons from America's Best Run Companies*. New York: Warner Books.

Pinker, S. 2011. *The Better Angels of our Nature: Why Violence Has Declined*. New York: Viking.

Pires, R.R.C. 2011. Beyond the fear of discretion: Flexibility, performance, and accountability in the management of regulatory bureaucracies. *Regulation & Governance 5*(1), 43–69.

Pollittt, C. and Bouckaert, G. 2004. *Public Management Reform*. Oxford: Oxford University Press.

Poole, G.S. 2016. Administrative practices as institutional identity: bureaucratic impediments to HE "internationalization" policy in Japan. *Comparative Education*, pp. 1–16.

Porter, D., Andrews, M., Turkewitz, J.A., and Wescott, C.G. 2011. Managing public finance and procurement in fragile and conflicted settings. *International Public Management Journal 14*(4), pp. 369–94.

Premfors, R. 1991. The "Swedish model" and public sector reform. *West European Politics 14*(3), pp. 83–95.

Presthus, R.V. 1960. Authority in organizations. *Public Administration Review 20* (spring), pp. 86–91.

Pritchett, L. 2002. It pays to be ignorant: A simple political economy of rigorous program evaluation. *Journal of Policy Reform 5*(4), pp. 251–69.

Pritchett, L. 2009. Is India a flailing state? Detours on the four-lane highway to modernization. HKS Faculty Research Working Paper Series RWP09-013.

Pritchett, L. 2013. *The Rebirth of Education: Schooling Ain't Learning*. Washington, DC: Center for Global Development.

Pritchett, L. 2014. The risks to education systems from design mismatch and global isomorphism: Concepts, with examples from India. UNU-WIDER WP/2014/039.

Pritchett, L. and Aiyar, Y. 2015. Taxes: Price of civilization or tribute to Leviathan? Center for Global Development Working Paper 412.

Pritchett, L. and de Weijer, F. 2010. Fragile states: Stuck in a capability trap? Background paper for the *World Development Report 2011*. Washington, DC: World Bank.

Pritchett, L., Samji, S., and Hammer, J. 2012. It's all about MeE: Learning in development projects through monitoring ("M"), experiential learning ("e") and impact evaluation ("E"). Washington, DC: Center for Global Development Working Paper 322.

Pritchett, L. and Sandefur, J. 2013. Context matters for size: why external validity claims and development practice do not mix. *Journal of Globalization and Development 4*(2), pp. 161–97.

Pritchett, L. and Sethi, G. 1994. Tariff rates, tariff revenue, and tariff reform: some new facts. *World Bank Economic Review 8*(1): pp. 1–16.

Pritchett, L. and Viarengo, M.G. 2009. The illusion of equality: The educational consequences of blinding weak states. Center for Global Development Working Paper 78.

Pritchett, L. and Viarengo, M. 2015. The state, socialization and private schooling: When will governments support alternative producers? *Journal of Development Studies 51*(7), pp. 784–807.

Pritchett, L. and Woolcock, M. 2004. Solutions when the solution is the problem: Arraying the disarray in development. *World Development 32*(2), pp. 191–212.

Pritchett, L., Woolcock, M., and Andrews, M. 2010. Capability Traps? The Mechanisms of Persistent Implementation Failure—Working Paper 234. Washington, DC: Center for Global Development Working Paper 234.

Pritchett, L., Woolcock, M., and Andrews, M. 2013. Looking like a state: Techniques of persistent failure in state capability for implementation. *Journal of Development Studies 49*(1), pp. 1–18.

Pulakos, E.D., Hanson, R.M., Arad, S., and Moye, N. 2015. Performance management can be fixed: An on-the-job experiential learning approach for complex behavior change. *Industrial and Organizational Psychology 8*(01), pp. 51–76.

Putnam, R. 1993. *Making Democracy Work: Civic Traditions in Modern Italy.* Princeton, NJ: Princeton University Press.

Radelet, S. 2015. *The Surge: The Ascent of the Developing World.* New York: Simon & Schuster.

Radnor, Z. and Walley, P. 2008. Learning to walk before we try to run: adapting lean for the public sector. *Public Money and Management 28*(1), pp. 13–20.

Ramalingam, B. 2013. *Aid on the Edge of Chaos: International Cooperation in a Complex World.* New York: Oxford University Press.

Riddle, V. 2009. Policy implementation in an African state: An extension of Kingdon's multiple-streams approach. *Public Administration 87*(4), pp. 938–54.

Ridley-Duff, R.J. and Duncan, G. 2015. What is critical appreciation? Insights from studying the critical turn in an appreciative inquiry. *Human Relations 68*(10), pp. 1579–99.

Rivkin, S.G., Hanushek, E.A., and Kain, J.F. 2005. Teachers, schools, and academic achievement. *Econometrica 73*(2), pp. 417–58.

Rodrik, D. 2007. *One Economics, Many Recipes: Globalization, Institutions, and Economic Growth.* Princeton, NJ: Princeton University Press.

Rodrik, D. 2008. The new development economics: We shall experiment, but how shall we learn? Harvard Kennedy School Faculty Working Paper Series.

Roemer, J. 1998. *Equality of Opportunity.* Cambridge, MA: Harvard University Press.

Romer, P. 1993. Object gaps and idea gaps in economic development. *Journal of Monetary Economics 32*(3), pp. 543–73.

Rondinelli, D. 1993. *Development Projects as Policy Experiments: An Adaptive Approach to Development Administration.* 2nd edn. London: Routledge.

Rose, R. 2003. *What's wrong with best practice policies—and why relevant practices are better On Target? Government by Measurement.* London: House of Commons Public Administration Select Committee, HC 62-II, pp. 307–17.

Routley, L. and Hulme, D. 2013. Donors, development agencies and the use of political economic analysis: getting to grips with the politics of development? ESID Working Paper 019–13. Manchester: University of Manchester.

Sabel, C. and Jordan, L. 2015. *Doing, Learning, Being: Some Lessons Learned from Malaysia's National Transformation Program.* Washington, DC: World Bank.

Schwartz, D., Fischhoff, B., Krishnamurti, T., and Sowell, F. 2013. The Hawthorne effect and energy awareness. *Proceedings of the National Academy of Sciences 110*(38), pp. 15242–6.

Scott, J.C. 1998. *Seeing Like a State: How Certain Schemes to Improve the Human Condition Have Failed*. New Haven, CT: Yale University Press.

Scott, J.C. 2009. *The Art of Not Being Governed: An Anarchist History of Upland Southeast Asia*. New Haven, CT: Yale University Press.

Senge, P.M. 1996. Leading learning organizations. *Training and Development 50*(12): pp. 36–7.

Senge, P.M. 2014. *The Dance of Change: The Challenges to Sustaining Momentum in a Learning Organization*. New York: Crown Business.

Senge, P. and Kim, D.H. 2013. From fragmentation to integration: Building learning communities. *Reflections 12*(4), pp. 3–11.

Seo, M.G. and Creed, W.E.D. 2002. Institutional contradictions, praxis and institutional change: A dialectical perspective. *Academy of Management Review 27*(2), pp. 222–7.

Serrat, O. 2009. *The Five Whys Technique*. Manila: Asian Development Bank.

Shannon, C. 1948. A mathematical theory of communication. *Bell System Technical Journal 27*, pp. 379–423, 623–56.

Singerman, D. 1995. *Avenues of Participation: Family, Politics, and Networks in Urban Quarters of Cairo*. Princeton, NJ: Princeton University Press.

Slack, T. and Hinings, C. 1994. Institutional pressures and isomorphic change: An empirical test. *Organization Studies 15*(6), pp. 803–27.

Snow, D.A. and Benford, R.D. 1992. Master frames and cycles of protest. In A.D. Morris and C. McClurg Mueller (eds), *Frontiers in Social Movement Theory*. New Haven, CT: Yale University Press, pp. 133–55.

Snyder, S. 2013. The simple, the complicated, and the complex: Educational reform through the lens of complexity theory. OECD Education Working Papers, 96.

Sparrow, M. 2008. *The Character of Harms: Operational Challenges in Control*. New York: Cambridge University Press.

Spreitzer, G.M. and Sonenshein, S. 2003. Positive deviance and extraordinary organizing. In K. Cameron and J. Dutton (eds), *Positive Organizational Scholarship: Foundations of a New Discipline*. San Francisco, CA: Berrett-Koehler, pp. 207–24.

Spreitzer, G.M. and Sonenshein, S. 2004. Toward the construct definition of positive deviance. *American Behavioral Scientist 47*(6), pp. 828–47.

Steinhilber, S. 2013. *Strategic Alliances: Three Ways to Make Them Work*. Boston, MA: Harvard Business School Press.

Stewart, R. 2010. Afghanistan: What could work? *New York Review of Books*, January 14.

Sunstein, C. and Ullmann-Margalit, E. 1999. Second-order decisions. *Ethics 110*(1), pp. 5–31.

Tamanaha, B., Sage, C., and Woolcock, M. (eds) 2012. *Legal Pluralism and Development: Scholars and Practitioners in Dialogue*. New York: Cambridge University Press.

Teskey, G., Schnell, S., and Poole, A. 2012. Getting beyond capacity: Addressing authority and legitimacy in fragile states. IRSPM 16th Annual Conference, Rome.

References

Thomas, M.A. 2015. *Govern Like Us: US Expectations of Poor Countries*. New York: Columbia University Press.

Tsoukas, H. and Chia, R. 2002. On organizational becoming: Rethinking organizational change. *Organization Science 13*(5), pp. 567–82.

Unertl, K.M., Holden, R.J., and Lorenzi, N.M. 2016. Usability: Making it real from concepts to implementation and end-user adoption. In *Healthcare Information Management Systems*. Cham, Switzerland: Springer, pp. 165–75.

United States Marine Corps. 1997. *Warfighting*. Washington, DC: United States Marine Corps.

Uphoff, N. 1992. *Learning from Gal Oya: Possibilities for Participatory Development and Post-Newtonian Social Science*. Ithaca, NY: Cornell University Press.

Uvin, P. and Miller, D. 1996. Paths to scaling-up: alternative strategies for local nongovernmental organizations. *Human Organization 55*(3), pp. 344–54.

van de Waal, N. 2001. *African Economies and the Politics of Permanent Crisis, 1979–1999*. New York: Cambridge University Press.

van Manen, S., Avard, G., and Martínez-Cruz, M. 2015. Co-ideation of disaster preparedness strategies through a participatory design approach: Challenges and opportunities experienced at Turrialba volcano, Costa Rica. *Design Studies 40*, pp. 218–45.

Von Hagen, J. 1992. Budgeting Procedures and Fiscal Performance in the European Communities. Unpublished manuscript, University of Mannheim and Indiana University School of Business.

Waddock, S., Meszoely, G.M., Waddell, S., and Dentoni, D. 2015. The complexity of wicked problems in large scale change. *Journal of Organizational Change Management 28*(6), pp. 993–1012.

Wade, R. 1982. The system of administraitve and political corruption: Canal irrigation in South India. *Journal of Development Studies 18*(3), pp. 287–328.

Wang, D. and Ap, J. 2013. Factors affecting tourism policy implementation: A conceptual framework and a case study in China. *Tourism Management 36*, pp. 221–33.

Watkins, S. and Swidler, A. 2013. Working misunderstandings: Donors, brokers, and villagers in Africa's AIDS industry. *Population and Development Review 38*(s1), pp. 198–218.

Watkins, S. and Swidler, A. 2017. *AIDS Altruism in Africa: A Romance*. Princeton, NJ: Princeton University Press [forthcoming].

Weber, M. 1919 [1965]. Politics as a vocation. In H.H. Gerth and C.W. Mills (translated and edited) *From Max Weber: Essays in Sociology*. New York: Oxford University Press.

Weber, M. 1978. *Economy and Society: An Outline of Interpretive Sociology*. Berkeley, CA: University of California Press.

Wehner, J. 2007. Budget reform and legislative control in Sweden. *Journal of European Public Policy 14*(2), pp. 313–32.

Westley, F.R., Tjornbo, O., Schultz, L., Olsson, P., Folke, C., Crona, B., and Bodin, Ö. 2013. A theory of transformative agency in linked social–ecological systems. *Ecology and Society 18*(3), p. 27.

Williamson, O. 1975. *Markets and Hierarchies*. New York: Free Press.

Wilson, D.S. 2013. Toward a science of organizational change: Rapid results, polycentric governance, and evolution. Available at: https://www.prosocialgroups.org/sites/default/files/Rapid%20Results%20October%208%202013.pdf (accessed August 12, 2016).

Wilson, J.Q. 1989. *Bureaucracy: What Government Agencies Do and Why They Do It.* New York: Basic Books.

Womack, J.P. and Jones, D.T. 2010. *Lean Thinking: Banish Waste and Create Wealth* in *Your Corporation.* New York: Simon & Schuster.

Wong, K.C. 2011. Using an Ishikawa Diagram as a tool to assist memory and retrieval of relevant medical cases from the medical literature. *Journal of Medical Case Reports 5*, 120–3.

Woolcock, M. 2013. Using case studies to explore the external validity of 'complex' development interventions. *Evaluation 19*(3), pp. 229–48.

Woolcock, M. 2014. Defining and engaging with fragile states: An alternative approach to theory, measurement and practice. Helsinki: UNU-WIDER Working Paper 2014/097.

World Bank. 2004. *World Development Report 2004: Making Services Work for the Poor.* Washington, DC: Oxford University Press for the World Bank.

World Bank. 2011. *Forensic Audit Report: Arid Lands Resource Management Project—Phase 2.* Washington, DC: World Bank Integrity Vice Presidency.

Yeniyurt, S., Townsend, J.D., Cavusgil, S.T., and Ghauri, P.N. 2015. Mimetic and experiential effects in international marketing alliance formations of US pharmaceuticals firms. *International Business Strategy: Theory and Practice*, p. 323.

Zakocs, R.C. 2006. What explains community coalition effectiveness? *American Journal of Preventive Medicine 30*(4), pp. 351–61.

Index

Printed and bound by CPI Group (UK) Ltd, Croydon, CR0 4YY